Major General S. F. Mott, C.B.
From a portrait presented by the 53rd (Welsh) Division (T.F.)

THE 53rd (WELSH) DIVISION

HISTORY OF THE 53rd (WELSH) DIVISION

(T.F.)

1914—1918

By Major C. H. DUDLEY WARD, D.S.O., M.C.

(*Late Welsh Guards*)

The Divisional Sign.

CARDIFF
WESTERN MAIL LIMITED
1927

CONTENTS

	Page
FOREWORD: By Field-Marshal The Right Honourable Viscount Allenby, G.C.B., G.C.M.G.	
THE 53RD (WELSH) DIVISION	9
GALLIPOLI	17
EGYPT	53
PALESTINE: First Battle of Gaza	69
Second Battle of Gaza	99
Third Battle of Gaza (Khuweilfeh)	113
JERUSALEM	141
THE TURKISH COUNTER-ATTACK	167
JERICHO	183
TELL ASUR	189
THE VALLEY OF THE JORDAN	103
REORGANISATION	211
THE BATTLES OF MEGIDDO	219
COMMANDING OFFICERS	247
APPENDICES	250

   EMBARKATION AT DEVONPORT.
   POSTINGS OF BATTALIONS TAKEN FROM THE DIVISION.
   CORPS ORDER FOR THE CAPTURE OF JERUSALEM.
   CORPS ORDER FOR ADVANCE FROM JERUSALEM.
   DIVISION ORDER FOR ADVANCE ON JERICHO.
   DIVISION ORDER FOR TELL ASUR.
   INSTRUCTIONS FOR APRIL OFFENSIVE OF XXIST CORPS.
   ORDERS FOR THE BATTLES OF MEGIDDO.
   THE FIVE BATTALIONS IN FRANCE.

PAGE MAPS

	Page
THE BATTLE OF ROMANI	62
FIRST BATTLE OF GAZA	96
SECOND BATTLE OF GAZA	108
TELL ASUR	200
THE BATTLE OF THE SOISSONNAIS AND OF THE OURCQ	278

FOLDING MAPS

SUVLA BAY.
THIRD BATTLE OF GAZA.
THE CAPTURE OF JERUSALEM.
MEGIDDO.

FOREWORD.

IT was in July, 1917, that I first made the acquaintance of the 53rd Division which, under the command of my old friend General Mott, lay facing the Turkish lines—in the torrid heat of summer—on the southern borders of Palestine.

Earlier the Division had fought valiantly, in the First and Second Battles of Gaza. Now it was preparing for the next effort, which was to crash through the enemy's defence and drive his armies—in defeat—to and beyond Jerusalem.

When time was ripe, the Welsh Division brilliantly consummated the victory, storming the rocky slopes of Khuweilfeh, and stubbornly maintaining that position against repeated counter-strokes, fiercely pressed, all through the first week of November.

This enabled the troops destined for the turning of the Turkish left to mount their attack unmolested.

Then the 53rd Division went on, in direct pursuit, following the retreating foe on the high road to Hebron and Jerusalem, along the crest of the Judean range of mountains, and making secure the right flank of our main advance.

Hebron was occupied; and on the 9th December, 1917, the 53rd and 60th Divisions joined hands to the south and west of Jerusalem.

In co-operation, these two Divisions swept the enemy from Jerusalem's precincts, and they share the honour and the joy of having been the immediate agents in setting free the Holy City after continuous bondage.

The occupation of Jerusalem brought no repose. Fighting, fierce fighting, kept everyone hard at work until the end of the year; and early in 1918 the 53rd Division was still fully occupied. Positions were being consolidated, and preparations had to be made for further progress. During February and March, consolidation proceeded until serious danger from counter-attack was no longer to be apprehended.

Comparative quiet ensued; but between June and August pressure in the Western Theatre of War drew away many battalions to France. The blanks caused by their departure were filled by units from India, and by a Battalion of the Cape Corps from South Africa.

Changed as was now the personnel, yet the soul of the Welsh Division was living, and still animated all ranks.

When the great attack of September, 1918, was launched, the reorganised Division was ready.

In the Battles which scattered her armies and drove out of the War the Turkish Empire, the achievements of the young and inexperienced troops—who formed the majority in the 53rd Division—rivalled the exploits of those veterans who had already set an example which won and will for ever retain our Empire's admiration.

ALLENBY, F.M.

24, Weatherby Gardens,
London, S.W.

21.III.27.

SHORT CHRONOLOGICAL LIST OF EVENTS GIVING THE GENERAL WAR SITUATION from 28th June, 1914, to 22nd April, 1915.

The Archduke Franz Ferdinand of Austria was assassinated at Sarajevo on the 28th June.
Austro-Hungarian ultimatum to Serbia, 23rd July.
Austria-Hungary declares war on Serbia, 28th July.
Germany declares war on France, 3rd August.
Germany declares war on Belgium, 4th August.
Great Britain declares war on Germany at 11 p.m., 4th August.
Montenegro declares war on Austria-Hungary, 5th August.
Austria-Hungary declares war on Russia, 6th August.
Serbia declares war on Germany, 6th August.
Great Britain and France declare war on Austria-Hungary, 12th August.
Landing of British Expeditionary Force of four Divisions and one Cavalry Division completed, 16th August.
Austria-Hungary declares war on Belgium, 22nd August.
Japan declares war on Germany, 23rd August.
British retreat from Mons, 24th August.
The British retreat behind the Marne ended 5th September.
The German retreat from the Marne commenced, 9th September.
The German retreat ends (Battle of the Aisne), 15th September.
Turkey commenced hostilities against Russia, 29th October.
Russia declared war on Turkey, 2nd November.
Great Britain and France declare war against Turkey, 5th November.
Advanced troops of the Indian Expeditionary Force effected a landing in Mesopotamia at Fao, 6th November.
Battles of Ypres end, 22nd November.
Turkey commences an offensive against Russia in the Caucasus, 17th December.
The Grand Duke Nicholas (Commander-in-Chief) suggested a British expedition against Turkey to ease the Russian situation in the Caucasus, 30th December.

1915

The British War Council decide that the Admiralty shall prepare a Naval Expedition against the Dardanelles, 13th January.
Turkey commences an advance on Egypt through Sinai, 26th January.
The British Government definitely decide to attack the Dardanelles, 28th January.
Action on the Suez Canal, 3rd February.
The British Government decides to send 29th Division to the Dardanelles, 16th February.
Allied Naval attack on the Dardanelles commences, 19th February.
Lemnos occupied by British submarines, 23rd February.
The French Government decide to send an Expeditionary Force to the Dardanelles, 4th March.
Sir Ian Hamilton appointed Commander-in-Chief of the Mediterrauean Expeditionary Force, 12th March.
Allied Naval attack on the Dardanelles repulsed, 18th March.
General Liman von Sanders appointed to command the Turco-German forces at the Dar danelles, 25th March.
The Battles of Ypres, with the first German gas attack, commenced 22nd April.

THE 53rd (WELSH) DIVISION
1914—1918

OUT of the various commissions that were appointed after the South African War to enquire into the military state of Great Britain came three important creations: The Committee of Imperial Defence, the General Staff, and the Territorial Force.

The Territorial Force was a Home Defence Force of 14 divisions, but at the back of those minds responsible for its being there was present the possibility of its use abroad should a national emergency arise. The old Volunteers had come forward in a crisis, and the Territorial Force would, undoubtedly, do the same. When the time came, in August, 1914, they did.

The Territorial Associations, however, were never used to full advantage during the Great War, indeed, they were rather badly treated; all the big contractors were put on a War Office list which excluded any other contracts whatever, and the County Associations had to seek out small firms and individuals with no experience to fulfil their requirements. They were allowed to raise 2nd, 3rd, and Reserve Battalions, but the great mass of the nation that volunteered was swept into the New Armies, or Kitchener Armies as they were popularly called. The Territorial Force, however, justified its existence; it has a proud record, and its claims now cannot be ignored.

The 53rd was the original Welsh Territorial Division. During the War the contribution of man power by Wales was exceedingly high, and is not shown by the number of divisions called Welsh. The New Army division, the 38th, was well-known; the 68th was a Territorial division for home defence; and Welsh battalions abounded throughout the army. Welshmen are stout fighters, courageous, tenacious, and possessing great physical endurance. The record of the 53rd Division reveals these qualities in full.

THE ORIGINAL WELSH DIVISION

When the order for mobilization was issued on the 5th August, 1914, the Welsh Division, Territorial Force, was constituted as follows:—

INFANTRY

THE CHESHIRE INFANTRY BRIGADE. (Col. E. A. COWANS.)
    4th Battalion Cheshire Regiment.
    5th   „   „   „
    6th   „   „   „
    7th   „   „   „

THE NORTH WALES INFANTRY BRIGADE. (Col. F. C. LLOYD.)
    4th Battalion Royal Welch Fusiliers.
    5th   „   „   „   „
    6th   „   „   „   „
    7th   „   „   „   „

THE WELSH BORDER INFANTRY BRIGADE. (Col. J. J. F. HUME.)
    1st Battalion Monmouthshire Regiment.
    2nd   „   „   „
    3rd   „   „   „
    1st Battalion Herefordshire Regiment.

The 7th Battalion Welch Regiment (a Cyclist Battalion) was also within the Command, and there were five infantry battalions marked as Army Troops attached to the Division:

THE SOUTH WALES INFANTRY BRIGADE.
    Brecknock Battalion South Wales Borderers.
    4th Battalion Welch Regiment.
    5th   „   „   „
    6th   „   „   „

and the 4th Battalion Shropshire Light Infantry, which was attached to the Welsh Border Infantry Brigade.

ARTILLERY

1ST WELSH (HOWR.) BRIGADE R.F.A.
    1st Glamorgan Battery.
    2nd   „   „
    1st Welsh Ammunition Column.

2ND WELSH BRIGADE R.F.A.
    3rd Glamorgan Battery.
    4th   „   „
    Cardigan Battery.
    2nd Welsh Ammunition Column.

CHESHIRE BRIGADE R.F.A.
   1st Cheshire Battery.
   2nd   ,,   ,,
   3rd   ,,   ,,
   3rd Welsh Ammunition Column.

4TH WELSH BRIGADE R.F.A.
   1st Monmouthshire Battery.
   2nd   ,,   ,,
   3rd   ,,   ,,
   4th Welsh Ammunition Column.
   The Welsh Royal Garrison Artillery.

ROYAL ENGINEERS

The Cheshire Field Company.
The Welsh Field Company.
The Welsh Division Telegraph Company.

THE ROYAL ARMY SERVICE CORPS

The Divisional Headquarters Company.
The Cheshire Brigade Company.
The North Wales Brigade Company.
The Welsh Border Brigade Company.

THE ROYAL ARMY MEDICAL CORPS

The 1st, 2nd, and 3rd Welsh Field Ambulances.

. . . . .

On the 3rd August, 1914, the Infantry Brigades, less the Herefords who were to go on Army manœuvres, were in camp, when all training was cancelled and they were ordered back to their Headquarters. The next day came the general order for mobilization (issued to them on the 5th), and the Territorial Force was embodied for war.

At the end of August, 1914, the Division concentrated in the neighbourhood of Northampton, and during the succeeding months battalion training was constantly interrupted by trench digging operations on the East coast.

HOME COUNTY BATTALIONS

From the Territorial point of view the unsympathetic treatment referred to commenced with a deliberate breaking up of formations.

At the outbreak of war the Welsh Division was ready, and was promptly raided by the War Office as though it had been a casual pool of battalions for re-inforcement.

This is not the place to follow the fortunes of individual battalions thus removed from the Division. The first to go was the Brecknock Battalion South Wales Borderers, in October; then the 6th Cheshires, the 2nd Monmouthshires, the 4th R.W.F., the 6th Welch, the 4th Shropshire Light Infantry, the 5th Cheshires, the 1st Monmouthshires, the 3rd Monmouthshires, all followed in quick succession.*

Nine battalions were taken away, but, as noted above, there were five infantry battalions marked as Army troops within the command, so that it meant the importation of four battalions to make up the Division. But Brigadier-General J. Hume had eleven battalions posted to The Welsh Border Brigade before it settled down, in April, 1915, to its final form—it had then assumed a non-Welsh complexion.

In a report made at the end of 1915, Brigadier-General Hume said:

" In order to set forth the situation fully it will be necessary to go back to the order for mobilization issued on August 5th, 1914. On that date the brigade which I had the honour to command was designated the Welsh Border Brigade, consisting of the 1st, 2nd, and 3rd Battalions Monmouthshire Regiment, and the 1st Battalion Hereford Regiment. These battalions mobilised at Pembroke Dock, where the brigade remained, occupied in defensive work, until the 10th August. On this date it was moved by rail to Oswestry, and went into billets, and the organisation and war training commenced. On August 31st, it was moved to Northampton, joining the H.Q. and the remainder of the Welsh Division. There the training was continued until November the 1st. On that date the brigade was moved to Suffolk, and put upon the work of entrenching the East coast. After arrival there on November 1st, the same evening telegraphic orders were received for the 2nd Monmouthshires to be sent back by rail to Northampton, forthwith to equip and prepare to proceed to Flanders. This it did on November 2nd, leaving some two days later for the front. After remaining in the neighbourhood of Ipswich and Grandesbrugh, occupied in digging trenches, orders were received on November 4th for the remainder of the brigade to return to Northampton with a view to being clothed and equipped for service in India. On returning to Northampton, the 2/2nd Monmouthshires were brought up from Pontypool and posted to the Brigade.

* See Appendix.

"The order to proceed to India was cancelled 30th November, and the 1st and 3rd Monmouths, and 1st Herefords were sent to Bury St. Edmunds to continue entrenching. On the 10th January, the Brigade, less 2/2nd Monmouths, rejoined the Division at Cambridge. On the 4th February, orders were received for the 1st and 3rd Monmouths to proceed to France. On the 20th February, 2/1st and 2/3rd Monmouths joined the Brigade. On the 19th April, the Welsh Division was reorganised; the 1st Herefords were transferred to the North Wales Brigade, and the three second line Monmouths were sent to Northampton to join the 2/1st Welsh Division. On the 24th April, the following battalions were posted to the Brigade :—

(1) A composite battalion of the Queens Royal West Surrey Regiment one company each of four second line battalions;
(2) 4th Royal Sussex Regiment;
(3) A composite battalion of the Buffs, made up from East and West Kent second line units.
(4) A composite battalion of the Middlesex Regiment, made up from two second line battalions (8th and 9th)."

On paper it looks worse than it was. Although one regrets the breaking up of one of the original brigades of the Division, the new units were stout Home County battalions.

Brigadier-General Hume makes the point that he was given no opportunity to train his brigade, that he had no machine guns, no transport, and that the three composite battalions were unarmed. But it would seem that these battalions had more training than the report leads one to suppose—generally speaking, over six months.

On the 3rd July, 1915, General Lindley, commanding the 53rd (Welsh) Division received the order to prepare his Division (less Artillery) for service in the Mediterranean. The first battalions to move were the 5th and 6th Royal Welch Fusiliers, who entrained at Irchester during the night of the 13th for Devonport. Embarkation was completed on the 19th July, when the fleet of eight transport ships sailed.

ORDER OF BATTLE

158TH INFANTRY BRIGADE
    5th Royal Welch Fusiliers.
    6th Royal Welch Regiment.
    7th Royal Welch Regiment.
    1st Herefordshire Regiment.

159TH INFANTRY BRIGADE.
    4th Cheshire Regiment.
    7th Cheshire Regiment.
    4th Welch Regiment.
    5th Welsh Regiment.

160th Infantry Brigade

4th Sussex Regiment.
2/4th Royal West Surrey Regiment (Queens).
2/4th Royal West Kent Regiment.
2/10th Middlesex Regiment.

Divisional Troops

53rd Welsh Divn. Cyclist Coy.
53rd Welsh Divn. S.A.A. Column and Park.
H.Q. Divn. R.E.
1st Welsh Field Coy., R.E.
21st Cheshire Field Coy. R.E.E
53rd Welsh Divn. Signal Co
1st Welsh Field Ambulance.
2nd Welsh Field Ambulance.
3rd Welsh Field Ambulance.

GALLIPOLI

GENERAL WAR SITUATION
During the Months April—December, 1915.

The first landing at the Dardanelles is effected, 25th April.
The Battle of Krithia commences, 28th April.
Second Battle of Krithia commences, 6th May.
In France the Allied Spring Offensive commences, 9th May.
Italian Government declares war against Austria, 23rd May.
Third Battle of Krithia, 4th June.
British advance up the Euphrates begins, 27th June.
First Battle of the Isonzo begins 29th June.
Great Austro-German offensive on the Eastern front begins, 13th July.
Second Battle of the Isonzo begins 18th July.
Operations for the landing at Suvla Bay commence, 6th August.
Italy declares war on Turkey, 21st August.
In France, Allied Autumn offensive begins (Loos), 25th September.
French and British forces land at Salonika, 5th October.
General Sir Charles Munro was appointed to succeed Sir Ian Hamilton, 15th October.
General Sir William Birdwood takes over temporary command at Gallipoli, 17th October.
Third Battle of the Isonzo begins 18th October.
Lord Kitchener left England for the Dardanelles, 4th November.
Sir Charles Munro to command Salonika Force; Sir William Birdwood to command Mediterranean Expeditionary Force, 4th November.
Fourth Battle of the Isonzo begins 10th November.
Lord Kitchener arrives at Dardanelles, 10th November.
The Battle of Ctesiphon (Mesopotamia) commences, 22nd November.
Sir Charles Munro appointed Commander-in-Chief of the reconstituted Mediterranean Expeditionary Force, with Sir William Birdwood as General Officer Commanding Dardanelles Army, 25th November.
Field-Marshal Von der Goltz takes command of Turkish forces in Mesopotamia, 24th November.
Monastir captured by Bulgarians, 2nd December.
The Siege of Kut begins, 7th December.
Field-Marshal Sir John French resigns, 15th December.
Sir A. J. Murray, Chief of Imperial General Staff resigns, 22nd December.

GALLIPOLI

"NAC OFNA OND GWARTH"
THE FIRST LANDING AT HELLES

ON the night of the 21/22nd July, the fleet of transports passed Gibraltar, and entered the Mediterranean. Although the destination of the Division was "unknown," there was little doubt as to what it was. The Dardanelles had been the storm centre in that part of the world for months. The course of the fleet was Malta, Alexandria, and then Imbros.

Prior to the landing of the 53rd Division, the situation can be stated briefly. When Sir Ian Hamilton received his orders, he proceeded to the Dardanelles, and watched the battle between the Allied fleets and the Turkish land forces on the 18th March. He then made a reconnaissance, from the sea, of the North Western shore of the peninsula, from its Isthmus to Cape Helles.

The precipitous nature of the northern half of the coast precluded any landing at all, and the southern half presented difficulties which Sir Ian says had no parallel in military history, "except possibly in the sinister legends of Xerxes."

There are three dominating features on the peninsula. At the extreme south (Helles) there is a hill, 600 feet in height, Achi Baba "dominating, at long field gun range, what I have described as being the toe of the peninsula"; then up the Straits, defending the Narrows from any attack across the peninsula from the west, is the Kalid Bahr plateau, "a natural fortification artificially fortified," rising to a height of 700 feet; finally, there is, towards Suvla Bay, the Sari Bair mountain, "running up in a succession of almost perpendicular escarpments to 970 feet. The whole mountain seemed to be a network of ravines, and covered with thick jungle."

None of the hills are very high; once landed the difficulty of the country is its roughness. And this roughness limited the number of possible landing places. Here and there, at the mouths of narrow gullies that broke through the cliffs, were small, sandy beaches. Sir Ian Hamilton was under no illusion. "The beaches were either so well defended by works and guns, or else so restricted by nature that it did not seem possible, even by two or three simultaneous landings, to pass the

B

troops ashore quickly enough to enable them to maintain themselves against a rapid concentration and counter attack, which the enemy was bound, in such case, to attempt. It became necessary, therefore, not only to land simultaneously at as many points as possible, but to threaten to land at other points as well." The first of these necessities involved another unavoidable if awkward contingency, the separation by considerable intervals of the landing forces.

On the 25th April troops were launched to storm five separate beaches round the toe of the peninsula, and one other beach up the western coast, towards Suvla Bay, known as Anzac Cove. A foothold was gained at each of these two points of attack—the one towards Achi Baba, the other towards Sari Bair—and, with a few minor modifications, this was the situation when the 53rd Division sailed from Devonport.

A further effort was now to be made. From the first, Sir Ian Hamilton had hoped that by landing a force under the heights of Sari Bair, he would be able to strangle the Turkish communications to the south, and so clear the Narrows for the fleet. Although these hopes had not materialised, he still considered they were well founded. "The Australians and New Zealanders had rooted themselves very near to the vitals of the enemy. By their tenacity and courage they still held open the doorway from which one strong thrust forward might give us command of the Narrows "—so he determined to reinforce the Australian and New Zealand Army Corps, at Anzac Cove and, in combination with a landing at Sulva Bay, storm Koja Chemen Tepe (Hill 305) and, working from that dominating point " grip the waist of the peninsula " by the further capture of Maidos and Gaba Tepe. The plan was to launch a big containing attack at Helles, while Anzac, aided by Suvla Bay, was to deliver the knock down blow !

The battle opened at Helles on the 6th August, with an assault on some 1,200 yards of Turkish trench. It met with unexpected resistance, but as the aim of this southern operation was to contain the enemy, Sir Ian persevered, in spite of the obvious increase of strength and morale of the Turks, and the battle did not die down until the 9th, when the troops engaged were relieved. There was no great gain of terrain, but inasmuch as Turkish reinforcements had been drawn into the fight the main purpose had been achieved.

On the same day, the 6th, the 1st Australian Brigade (Brig.-Gen. N. M. Smythe, V.C.) attacked the extreme of the Turkish left at Anzac, *i.e.*, as far as possible from the main attack which was to be directed against the enemy's right.

The main ridge of Sari Bair runs parallel to the coast, but throws a number of spurs, separated by deep and steep-sided gullies, towards the sea. The water courses in the ravines were dry, at that time of year, but they were choked by dense jungle so that progress was not easy and direction might be lost. The three main ravines on the Anzac front were Chailak Dere, Sazli Beit Dere, and Aghyl Dere, and up their tortuous length the main attack, in two columns, was to work its way during the night of the 6th, to storm the main ridge. But this movement depended first on the right covering force, which was to seize Table Top, and other enemy positions covering the foot hills between the Chailak Dere and the Sazli Beit ravines; and second, on a left covering force, which was to march northwards, along the beach, and capture a hill called Damakjelik Bair with the double object of protecting the left flank of the left assaulting column up the Aghyl Dere ravine, and helping the landing of the IXth Corps at Suvla Bay.

The plateau of Table Top was carried by midnight, and the right assaulting column had entered Sazli Beit Dere and Chailak Dere. The left covering force had captured Damakjelik Bair by 1.30 a.m., and so secured the flank of the assaulting column up the Aghyl Dere.

On the right, the crest of Chunuk Bair was won and lost; on the left the Australians assaulted the slopes of Koja Chemen Tepe—but the grand coup did not come off. The Australian and New Zealand Division, and the 13th Division fought on desperately until the 10th August, with victory within, but ever eluding, their grasp. The Sari Bair ridge, which gave observation across the Narrows, was the key of the whole tactical plan, and the Anzac attack was the vital and all important one, but it had been conceived with the idea of support from Suvla Bay. The responsibility for this surprise landing rested with Sir Francis Stopford, commanding the IXth Corps. The landing was to be made by the 10th Division (less the 29th Brigade) and the 11th Division, and it is the situation in Suvla Bay with which we are most concerned.

The IXth Corps order is as follows (we omit para. 5 which deals with embarkation, landings, etc.):—

IXTH CORPS OPERATION ORDER, NO. 1. Aug. 3rd, 1915.

1. The main object of the G.O.C. Mediterranean Force is to seize a position across the Gallipoli Peninsula, from Gaba Tepe to Maidos, with a protected line of supply from Suvla Bay.

2. The general objective assigned by the G.O.C. in C. British Mediterranean Expeditionary Force to the Australian and New Zealand

Army Corps is to throw back the right wing of the Turkish Army opposed to it, and drive them south, towards Kilid Bahr and thus secure a position commanding the narrow part of the peninsula from Gaba Tepe to Maidos.

For this purpose the Australian and New Zealand Army Corps has been temporarily reinforced by units of the IXth Corps, consisting of the 13th Division, the 29th Infantry Brigade of the 10th Division, as well as the 29th Indian Infantry Brigade. In order to attract the enemy's reserves to the south an attack will be delivered on the afternoon of August 6th from within the Ansac position against the front and left centre of the Turkish line, being specially directed against the enemy's position about Pt. 152 (sq. 68b).

At 10 p.m. the same evening (August 6th) the enemy's outposts opposite the Australian and New Zealand Army Corps left, near the Fisherman's Hut, are to be rushed.

A main attack, timed to start about the hour the first troops of the IXth Corps are landing, will be directed against Chunuk Bair, which it is hoped will reach the summit of the main ridge about 2.30 a.m. (soon after moonrise).

The capture and retention of Sari Bair (Pt. 305) is essential for the success of the whole undertaking.

3. Troops as per margin (11th Division, 10th Division—less 29th Infantry Brigade—two Highland Mountain Batteries, one Squadron Motor Cyclists R.N.A.S., six Machine guns), under the orders of G.O.C. IXth Corps, will secure Suvla Bay as a base of supply. Having accomplished this primary object, the G.O.C. IXth Corps will endeavour to give direct assistance to the G.O.C. Australian and New Zealand Corps in his attack on Hill 305, by an advance on Biyuk Anafarta, with the object of moving up the eastern spur of that hill.

The Corps Commander considers that the security of Suvla Bay will not be assured until he is in a position to deny to the enemy the heights which connect Anafarta Sagir and Ejelmer Bay.

4. According to information, dated 22nd July, the strength of the enemy north of Kilid Bahr was estimated at 30,000 men. Of these, 12,000 were reported permanently maintained in the trenches facing the Anzac position. Whilst the majority of the remaining 18,000 were then known to be in reserve, about Boghali, Koja Dere, and Eski Keui (*i.e.*, mainly south and south-east of Hill 305).

There were, however, about three battalions located in, or about, the Anafarta Villages, also one battalion at Ismail Oglu Tepe, and another at Yilghin Burnu with outposts at Lala Baba and Ghazi Baba.

A few mounted troops and gendarmerie were also reported in the country north of Anzac, and it was considered possible that the hills due east of Suvla Bay were held by a party of gendarmerie.

The enemy, on the same date, had artillery at Yilghin Burnu and Ismail Oglu Tepe, consisting of one 9.2-in. one 4.2-in., and three field guns. These guns were in emplacements and protected by infantry trenches and wire entanglements. The guns appeared to be sited so as to direct fire towards the south. Trenches and wire were observed on the southern side of the position ; no wire had been located on the northern side. The enemy may now have more guns in position, as three guns, each drawn by six oxen, were recently seen entering Anafarta Sagir.

Some trenches have also been located about Lala Baba.

6. Troops, as per margin, under the command of Major-General F. Hammersley, C.B., will be the first to land. . . . (11th Division— two Highland Mountain Batteries, one Squadron Motor Cycles R.N.A.S., six Machine Guns. Also one Brigade R.F.A., 11th Division, and 10 Heavy Battery will be landed at Anzac beforehand. Horses will disembark at Anzac, morning of the 7th, when it is hoped that this artillery will move along the beach to join the 11th Division).

With a view to the successful accomplishment of the task allotted to the IXth Corps, the force under the orders of General Hammersley having taken steps to safeguard the landing places referred to in para. 5, will :—

(*a*) Secure the enemy posts at Lala Baba and Ghazi Baba, and establish a footing on the ridge running north-eastward along the coast through Karakol Dagh and Kiretch Tepe Sirt, thence as far, if possible, as Pt. 156, Sq. 136j.

(*b*) Occupy the positions Yilghin Burnu-Ismail Oglu Tepe.

(*c*) Seize the road junction at Baka Baba, and establish connection northwards between this point and such troops as have been detailed under (*a*) to advance on Pt. 156.

Subsequent action of the whole force will be governed by a correct appreciation of the situation which is dependent on accurate information of the strength and dispositions of the enemy. This can only be obtained by bold reconnaissance pushed forward by all leading bodies of troops.

The information regarding the strength of the enemy was fairly accurate—actually there were two battalions of gendarmerie, and one of infantry, in all, 2,000 rifles. They were led by a Bavarian Officer, Major Willmer, and they accomplished a magnificent feat of arms. But it did not seem an over-sanguine hope that the first British Division to land would be able to picquet and hold all the important heights within artillery range of the bay, and that the remainder of General Stopford's Force would be able to push forward, through the Anafartas, to the east of Sari Bair, and give the coup-de-grace to the Turks opposing the Anzac advance.

On the evening of the 6th August, the 11th Division sailed from Imbros and, during the night, the 32nd and 33rd Brigades were landed on B and C Beaches. At the request of General Stopford, the 34th Brigade was landed on A beach. The latter modification of plan was afterwards regretted, as the lighters grounded a good way from the shore and the men had to drop into 4ft. 6in. of water, and also because the Turkish sentries and picquets were roused and the Brigade came under a flanking fire from Lala Baba and Ghazi Baba.

The 32nd Brigade sent two battalions to take Lala Baba, and eventually the whole Brigade was pushed forward to help the 34th Brigade, which was being held up by a post on Hill 10.

There was confusion—it was dark, the country was unknown and, most fatal of all, no one seems to have had a clear idea of what was wanted or what it was that units were expected to do !

When it was light enough to see, the enemy commenced to shell, and set fire to the scrub on Hill 10.

About daybreak six battalions of the 10th Division sailed into the Bay and commenced to land, not on A beach, as had been intended, but on C beach; so, in order to reach the position they had been given, on the left, they had to march by Lala Baba and Hill 10 under both artillery and rifle fire, which caused delay and more confusion. But the naval authorities who had been unwilling to use A beach after their experience with the 34th Brigade, found an alternative landing place near Ghazi Baba, where one battalion of the 31st Brigade, which had not yet been sent to C beach, was landed and was followed by the remainder of the 10th Division, by this time arriving in the Bay.

The enemy about Hill 10 retreated in an easterly direction, towards Sulajik and Kuchuk Anafarta Ova, followed by the 34th and 32nd Brigades of the 11th Division, and by the 31st Brigade of the 10th Division which thus found itself on the right of the battle, between Hill 10 and the Salt Lake, instead of on the left working along the Kiretch Tepe Sirt.

When night fell there was no great victory to report. General

Hammersley could announce no further progress towards the important Ismail Oglu Tepe than Chocolate Hill; and General Mahon, commanding the 10th Division, could only say that he was opposed by a strongly entrenched enemy on the Kiretch Tepe Sirt ridge. But Division Commanders further reported that their men were exhausted and could not move.

The heat and lack of water have been given as important factors in this collapse. Ample provision had been made for water, but the measures taken for its distribution at Suvla Bay were totally inadequate. Water existed in fair quantities throughout the area, and no doubt much of it had been polluted by the Turks, but no attempt seems to have been made to organise or supervise its use.

What was the condition of troops? Colonel Neil Malcome, G.S.O.1 of the 11th Division, sent one of his officers round the line to make a report; about a year later the officer wrote his impressions.

"On the morning of the 8th August, I was sent by you to: (1) make a general reconnaissance; (2) ascertain position of troops; (3) impress on commanders the importance of gaining the high ground W. Hill (Oglu), and north-eastwards without delay. I was to suggest that if we didn't get the high ground quickly the Turks probably would, and that an offence was contemplated on the night of 8/9th.

"I left D.H.Q. about 8 a.m. and walked towards Chocolate Hill. En route I passed the line of trenches dug from the Salt Lake to the sea, and found the 6th Lincolns and 6th Borders coming into them, having been relieved north of Chocolate Hill by the 7th South Staffords. The men were quite cheerful, and I was told that the Brigadier (Maxwell) had gone to Chocolate Hill. On arriving there I found the place *crammed* with men, both 31st and 33rd Brigades. The men were tired and thirsty, but not depressed, and there was plenty of bully and biscuits to eat. I met Generals Maxwell and Hill, and we went to Hill 50 together. The enemy was very quiet, just a casual bullet now and then. The Brigadiers both agreed that there were very few Turks on W. Hill, and that the men, given a few hours rest and some water, could well go on and attack W. Hill. I warned them to expect orders.

"I then went northward, and saw the South Staffords. The troops were in good order. They had, I think, got a little water from Ali Bey Cheshme. I believe, but will not swear to it, that the South Stafford were already on Hill 70 (Scimitar Hill), anyhow they were good fighting value.

"I then turned rather more westwards, and crossed the scene of the previous day's fighting. There were a few corpses and some equipment lying about (not in excess), but most of the dead had been buried. I then came to the 6th Yorks. The battalion only had five officers with it (the senior with a few months' service only), and the men were distinctly demoralised. In my opinion, the battalion wanted relief.

"I then visited the West Ridings, York and Lancaster (practically untouched) and the West Yorks. I stayed with them some time and watched the Dorsets have a set-to with some Turks and progress slightly. I did not see the Manchesters.

"I then went to Hill 10, and saw Colonel Minogue and Shuttleworth. They were both confident they could get on when ordered, provided they were not asked to cover too wide a front, and that the troops from Chocolate Hill moved forward simultaneously. They agreed with me that the 6th Yorks were of no fighting value.

"I then went towards the Beach, and saw the two Fusilier battalions, both somewhat shaken, especially the Lancashire Fusiliers. I did not see the Brigadier (Sitwell).

"I then went towards Lala Baba, along the beach. Just north of the Cut a water lighter was aground some 100 yards from the shore. (It was the hose pipe of this lighter the men cut to fill their water bottles quicker, if you will remember, and the water thus lost to the troops). I reached Lala Baba about 3.30. Unfortunately you and General Hammersley were out, but I told Duncan what I had seen, and aired my views as to the chance of any attack succeeding.

"About 4 p.m. General Stopford arrived at D.H.Q. I was called to him, and I gave him the same account as I have given you, marking the positions of the various battalions on his map, and telling him that the various commanders I had seen were confident that an attack was feasible. He seemed very pleased and said that we must attack at once, lest the Turks forestalled us. The words he finished up with I remember; he said, 'It may cause us casualties, but not one tenth of those we shall suffer if we delay.' He seemed perfectly confident, and said General Hammersley was to go and see him on the Jonquil directly he returned to camp.

"About 4.30 you and General Hammersley returned to camp. As there was hurry getting off the boat to go to the Jonquil I did not have much time to speak to you, but I gave you my impressions, which I think agreed with the plan you and the G.O.C. had settled upon.

"I don't know exactly what happened at the conference on the Jonquil, but about 5.30 you and the G.O.C. returned, and orders were drawn up for an attack that night on the high ground W. Hill—Anafarta

Sagir. Now I can't find that order, though I have searched high and low for it, but I remember that the 6th East Yorks. were to replace the 6th Yorks. in the 32nd Brigade ; that one battalion of the 32nd Brigade was to form a defensive flank about Anafarta Sagir ; that the 31st Brigade, plus the 6th Lincolns and 6th Borders were to attack W. Hill ; that the Division reserve was to consist of the 9th Lancs. Fusiliers, and the 6th Yorks. (the Dorsets and the Manchesters were at the time under the command of the G.O.C. 10th Division). Troops to be on the move at midnight.

"This order had not been out an hour when a message came from the G.O.C. (who was apparently at Suvla at the time) that he wished the high ground north of Anafarta Sagir occupied as well as the ridge to the south. This necessitated an alteration of the orders. The West Ridings and East Yorks were detached from the 32nd Brigade and directed on Tekke Tepe ; this caused delay, and the troops did not get on the move until 4 a.m. instead of midnight. Johnstone's detachment was isolated and overwhelmed, and this laid bare the left flank of the 32nd Brigade (West Yorks) and things went from bad to worse, as you well know.

"That is the end of my narrative.

"To take General Hammersley's points : Duncan went off to 32nd Brigade when the alteration was decided on. He may have given verbal orders, but he most certainly handed in the written amendment as well, if my memory serves me right.

J. D. Coleridge. 20/8/16."

From this officer's report the troops do not seem to have been in a bad way on the morning of the 8th. But nothing was done on the 8th. It seems that Sir Ian Hamilton had excuse for his bitter reflection that " The one fatal error was inertia. And inertia prevailed ! " With 2,000 rifles, three field batteries, and two mountain batteries opposing General Stopford's two divisions !

Although the battle at Anzac was desperate, and he incurred great risk by cutting himself adrift from direct communication with Anzac and Helles, Sir Ian had set out for Suvla, arriving there about 5 p.m. He knew that Turkish reinforcements were already moving on Suvla, and being informed, on his arrival, that only the 32nd Brigade was in a position to move, he gave a direct order that this one brigade should attempt to make good the heights before the Turkish reinforcements got on to them. This was the change of orders referred to in the letter to Colonel Malcolme : the 33rd Brigade were to attack the ridge running southwest from Anafarta Sagir, the original objective, at dawn, and the 32nd Brigade were to occupy the heights north of Anafarta Sagir at once.

"At 19.30, Major Duncan, G.S.O.2, 11th Division, came to Brigade H.Q. on Hill 10, and gave verbal orders for the operation next day. These were to the effect that an attack was to be made at 05.00 next morning on the ridge running southwest from Anafarta Sagir; the 32nd Infantry Brigade, less the 6th Yorkshires, and plus the 6th East Yorkshire Regiment and 67th Field Company were to make a night march, and seize and make good by daylight the following heights north of Anafarta Sagir: Hill 260, Tekke Tepe—Kavak Tepe. Orders were accordingly issued for the Brigade to concentrate at Sulajik." (Diary 32nd Brigade.)

The line held by the 32nd Brigade at that time was from Scimitar Hill to Sulajik, with a gap north of that village to the right of the 6th York and Lancasters, who were in touch with the Dorsets on the lower slopes of Kiretch Tepe Sirt. Their original orders had been to take up a line between Sulajik and the Dorsets, but, owing to a "misunderstanding," the whole brigade, except one company of the West Yorks, and the York and Lancaster battalion had gone south of Sulajik. Brigade headquarters were on Hill 10, and "owing to the presence of snipers in the area between Brigade H.Q. and the battalions of the Brigade, the orders to concentrate took a long time in reaching units." The West Yorkshires, on Scimitar Hill, never received any orders at all.

It was not until 4 a.m. that the 6th East Yorkshire Regiment, supported by the 8th West Riding Regt. and the 67th Field Company R.E. moved off to occupy the heights. The 6th York and Lancaster Regt. remained at Sulajik, in reserve, pending the arrival of the West Yorkshires. The 6th Yorkshires were back at Hill 10, consolidating the position there. Brigade Headquarters moved up to Sulajik about midnight, and about 3.30 a.m. the 34th Brigade moved up north of Sulajik, on the left.

But the attempt to occupy the heights was made too late. One company of the East Yorkshire battalion (a Pioneer battalion by the way) reached the top of Tekke Tepe, led by Colonel Moore. But they were alone! They were captured, and, after surrender, their gallant commanding officer was killed by a bloodthirsty Turk.

"The force for the high ground north of Anafarta Sagir moved up to within a few hundred yards of the top, and was there met by a superior force of the enemy who drove them back down the hill. The 6th East Yorkshire Regt. and the 67th Field Company retired through the line held by the Brigade, whilst the 8th West Riding Regt. took up a series of positions and gradually retired to a position on the left of the 34th Brigade. At dawn, as the 3½ companies of the West Yorkshire Regt. were about to retire from Hill 70 (Scimitar) they were attacked in force from the direction of Abrikja, and were compelled to fall back with severe loss; a company of the 6th York and Lancs. was sent up to help, and a position was then taken up running south from the two huts in 105.b.3 (N. of Sulajik), the right of the line being in touch with the 33rd Brigade, and the left thrown back. The Turks worked round the left, and at one time were within 40 yards of Brigade H.Q., and had almost cut off the machine gun post situated in the huts. Major Wood, 9th West Yorkshire Regt., collected 30 men of the 86th Field Company, who were working about 100 yards south of Brigade H.Q., and made a counter attack and repulsed the Turks." (32nd Brigade Report.)

In fact the situation round about Sulajik was obscure. Obviously, units of the 32nd and 34th Brigades were well mixed up.

Meanwhile, the 33rd Brigade, on the right, was launched to the attack at 5 a.m. During the afternoon of the 8th, Brigadier General Maxwell had reconnoitred the position to be attacked from Chocolate Hill, and had seen troops in occupation of Scimitar Hill on his left; he had also been informed that the high ground overlooking Anafarta Sagir would be held at dawn. When he attacked the situation was otherwise. His left flank was not secure, Turkish reinforcements had arrived, and the slopes of Ismail Oglu Tepe were so steep, the dwarf oak scrub so thick that men could only advance along goat tracks in single file. At first, the attack progressed well on the right, then came to a halt, and gave way from the left.

This, then, was the situation at dawn and early morning of the 9th August, while the 53rd Division was disembarking on the shores of Suvla Bay.

. . . . .

THE LANDING OF THE 53RD DIVISION AT SUVLA BAY

At 7 o'clock in the evening of the 8th August, the 53rd Division Headquarters and the 4th Cheshires landed at Suvla Bay on C beach. The first order General Lindley received was to send two Brigades, less one battalion to be employed on beach duty, to the 11th Division. As only one battalion of his Division had landed, the order could not be complied with.

But units continued to arrive throughout the night, and the following day. There are a few points to be noted:—

Each man carried two hundred rounds of ammunition, but no reserve was landed.

In the original distribution to transport ships, the War Office had directed that units would take their vehicles with them, but animals would go on separate ships. The embarkation officer however, altered this arrangement, and the difficulties of organising on disembarkation were greatly increased. Only one Field Ambulance, with three officers, no transport, and no stores, arrived on the 9th; the Cheshire Field Company, Royal Engineers, were landed with no stores; the Signal Section did not arrive.

The Division had no wheels and no horses, and the question of supply was serious.

Divisional Artillery had been left in England under orders for France.

But the leading battalions of infantry were being landed, and far out to sea others were approaching. From those distant ships the troops saw the heights of Gallipoli thrown up in sharp relief against the red glow of dawn, for the morning of the 9th was drawing near. As the light increased the details of the coast emerged, the ruggedness of the low hills, scarred with gullies and deep ravines, and rough with scrub and stunted trees. The cliff line of the coast was broken where a rectangular plain thrust the hills back from the sea, but left a northern arm, Suvla Point, with the long ridge of Kiretch Tepe Sirt, while to the south, about Anzac Cove the retreat of the hills from the coast was more stubborn—one humpy spit, Nebrunesi Point, stuck out from this flat shore to form, with Suvla Point, the Bay. The Bay was two miles wide, and within its protecting arms a fleet of transports sat complacently on the sea, while fussy pinnaces and barges plied between them and the shore. In the far distance a rocky ridge fell in two well defined terraces to the almost flat plain.

"Along the edge of Suvla Bay runs a narrow causeway of sand, and immediately behind it lies a large salt lake, partly dried up in summer, but always liable to be converted by rain into a swamp. Eastwards of it the hills and flats are patched with farms and scrub, mostly dwarf oaks, and on the edge of the terraces the scrub grows into something like woodland; everywhere the plain is cracked with dry watercourses.

"Two villages are points in the hinterland—Kuchuk, or Little Anafarta, on the slopes at the north-eastern angle of the enclosing hills, and Biyuk, or Big Anafarta, two miles south across the watercourse of the Azmak Dere, and just under the northern spurs of Koja Chemen. The road connecting the two villages runs southwards to Boghali Kalessi, on the straits." (Col. Few.)

LANDINGS AT SUVLA

[*War Museum.*

"B" BEACH AND SALT LAKE, SUVLA.

LANDINGS AT SUVLA

[*War Museum.*

LALA BABA AND "LITTLE A" BEACH.

The Sussex and Queens battalions of the 160th Brigade landed on C beach between midnight and 2 o'clock on the morning of the 9th. This was the time when the 32nd Brigade was being assembled at Sulajik for the night march up the hill. These two battalions of the 160th Brigade bivouacked on the beach, and were under orders to proceed to a line running southwest from Hill 53 to construct a trench. But the crisis in the situation of both the 32nd and 33rd Brigades was reached about the same hour, and each brigade sent an urgent call to General Hammersley for reinforcements.

From this moment units of the 53rd Division were sent in all directions, and the story of their first day's experience of battle is a complicated one.

THE QUEENS

About 6.30 a.m. the Queens received an order, couched in urgent terms, to move forward to the northwest of Hill 53 and reinforce the 31st Brigade. The battalion advanced across the open plain south of the Salt Lake. By that time it was light, and they were in full view of the Turks who received them with artillery and rifle fire. They suffered a number of casualties before they reached Chocolate Hill.

Major Few, who was commanding the advance party, reported, as ordered, to the 31st Brigade on Hill 53, only to be told to proceed to the 33rd Brigade.

Brigadier-General Maxwell, commanding the 33rd Brigade, says that he saw Lt.-Colonel Watney, of the Queens, and ordered him to advance at once to the assistance of the Lincolns, on the left of his Brigade, and " push on the attack." But Colonel Watney states that the orders were given to Major Few by the 31st Brigade; that the position was pointed out and the battalion was directed to go round the north slope of Hill 53 and support the forward troops who were hard pressed; that the battalion was instructed to dig itself in and consolidate the position, but on no account to go too far forward. The words used were " Don't go off into the blue ! "

Colonel Watney moved his battalion at once, and at 9 o'clock found the battalion staff of the Dublin Fusiliers (6th). No map had been given him, and he consulted the Colonel and Adjutant of the Dublins, who said that when the battle started the Border Regt. were on the right, the Staffords in the centre, and the Lincolns on the left. These battalions were of the 33rd Brigade, 11th Division. The Dublins were of the 31st Brigade, 10th Division, and were in reserve.

While consulting with the Commanding Officer of the Dublins, a wounded officer came up to Colonel Watney, and told him of an old Turkish trench which he advised him to hold; and another officer, believed to be the Brigade-Major of the 33rd Brigade, also gave advice and directions. The whole thing seems rather like a nightmare—a confused situation, an extremely difficult country, no maps, and vague orders.

However, the Queens found the old Turkish trench, and advanced up the slope without serious opposition, until they reached the top of Hill 70, or Scimitar Hill. But here they came under severe fire from the enemy guns, and also, it is stated, from our own, which were firing short. Other troops were there, and, under the shell fire, all retired a short distance, but, later, advanced again to the crest. And then the brushwood on the hill caught fire and the position had to be abandoned.

At noon, the battalion was back in the old Turkish trench (105 H. pts. 3, 6, and 9.)

"I received no further orders that day, after the initial orders given verbally to Major Few at 8 a.m., and after 10 a.m., I saw no staff officer. In the absence of any orders the question was raised by officers of other units as to the advisability of holding our position or retiring. The senior officers of my battalion and I were unanimous and emphatic that we must remain where we were, and prepare to defend the position." (Col. Watney.)

The casualties of the Queens were about eight officers and 250 men.

THE SUSSEX.

At 11 o'clock the Sussex battalion was ordered up to support the 33rd Brigade, and arrived at Chocolate Hill about two hours later.

Brigadier-General Maxwell ordered Lt-Colonel Campion to "Push on to Hill 70 from the west." These instructions were followed, but the battalion was faced with the burning scrub, could not advance, and occupied the old Turkish trench, on the left of the Queens and with their right in touch with the Lincolns.

In the confusion that reigned, and the absence of written orders, it is hard to determine what these two battalions were expected to do. Although the right of the 33rd Brigade had, at first, advanced rapidly, the left had always been in difficulties, and the whole of the hillside was ablaze soon after the arrival of the Queens.

In a written report Brigadier-General Maxwell states that "Neither of these battalions, as far as I can see, accomplished anything, and did not appear able to go on after a few rounds of shrapnel, and remained in the low ground northwest of the word Burnu, and took little or no part in the operations."* It is, however, clearly established that the Queens did go up the hill, although they may not have reached the crest, and that by the time the Sussex joined them the hill was on fire, and no troops could go up.

Meanwhile, the 32nd Brigade, which was at dawn in a state of the utmost confusion, had also called for reinforcements, and was anxiously waiting for them. " Units of the 53rd Division were sent up, but they were all pushed in the direction of Chocolate Hill. The 6th Yorkshire Regiment was brought up from Hill 10, and that also was drawn off to the right. At dusk two battalions of the 159th Brigade were sent up on the right, near the hut, and the others acted as a connecting link between the left of the 32nd and the right of the 34th Brigade." (32nd Brigade Diary.)

One must always remember the fatality of bewilderment that accompanied this unhappy operation. Those brigades that had landed on the night of the 6/7th, unless they were on an easily recognisable feature, did not really know where they were; all are agreed that the country was most difficult. Units of the 53rd Division would, having only a few hours' acquaintanceship with the place, be in a worse case.

THE 4TH CHESHIRES AND 5TH WELCH

At 9 o'clock, after the departure of the Queens, two further battalions were called for, and left the beach to report to Brigadier-General Sitwell at Hill 10; these were the 4th Cheshires and 5th Welch Regiment, and the official report of their movements is brief. The 5th Welch cover the whole day with one line—" 0830. Advanced to attack Turkish position *and reached Anafarta Ova, and bivouacked there the night.*" The 4th Cheshires are a little more explicit. They received the order to report to the 34th Brigade at 9 a.m., and apparently did so at 11. " Gen. Sitwell, Cmg. 34th Bde., sent the battalion to support the 32nd Brigade in attack on Anafarta Sagir. The battalion pushed forward under heavy sniping fire." But, at 5 o'clock in the evening we are told that the 32nd Brigade " retired by small parties through our lines," and at 8 o'clock the battalion was re-organised and took up a position in some half constructed trenches.

The 7TH CHESHIRES AND 4TH WELCH

At 11 o'clock the remaining two battalions of the 159th Brigade were ordered to report to Brigadier-General Sitwell. There is no doubt that

* This places them over 1,000 yards west of Scimitar Hill.

these battalions started at the time stated, but what happened to them is not clear. The last two battalions, the 7th Cheshires and 4th Welch, were, apparently, at the 34th Brigade Headquarters with the 4th Cheshires and 5th Welch, for the 159th Brigade diary contains the note that the "two parties received different orders as to the direction of the advance, with the result that the Brigade Staff was quite unable to control the Brigade, and could do nothing. The battalions disappeared into the night, in rear of those of the 32nd Brigade, except the 4th Welch, which was kept in reserve." Captain Shuttleworth, Brigade-Major of the 32nd Brigade, says : " At dusk two battalions of the 159th Brigade came up, and were sent up on the right, near the hut in 105 H.3, and the others acted as a connecting link between the left of the 32nd and the right of the 34th."

At all events we know that Brigadier-General Cowans had been deprived of his command within a few hours of landing at Suvla, and Brigadier-General Hume had also lost two battalions. Later in the day, about 4.30 in the afternoon, Brigadier-General Lloyd was to lose the Herefords. This battalion was specially mentioned in Sir Ian Hamilton's despatch, but although they did well, and were well handled by Lt.-Colonel Drage and Major Carless, their experience was no happier than that of the other battalions.

THE HEREFORDS

General Lindley sent for Lt.-Colonel Drage, and told him that Colonel Bosanquet, of the Sherwood Foresters, was anxious about his flank, near Kaslar Chair, in front of which runs the dry water course of Azmak Dere. He said "Place yourself in communication with him. I don't think you will have much to do, or will get a dusting. Get away as quickly as possible!"

Later the order was given in writing; it is not extant. But the story of the Herefords is the story of the whole Suvla Bay operation, and can be studied with profit. Colonel Drage left D.H.Q. knowing nothing of the position of the enemy, and practically nothing of the position of troops to be got in touch with.

"I do not know whether I was singularly stupid or most unfortunate, but I had never been told anything about the Anzac position, and troops on the left of that position. This was most regrettable, as I know now that the Herefords were the extreme right of the IXth Corps, and should have been in touch, if possible, with Anzac. I can say with certainty that, bar the vague position of the Sherwood Foresters, no information as to

[*War Museum.*

VIEW FROM ANZAC, LOOKING ACROSS SUVLA BAY. THE LINE OF KIRETCH TEPE SIRT CAN BE SEEN IN THE DISTANCE.

[*War Museum.*

CHOCOLATE HILL, SUVLA.

operations and plan of action was mentioned, and no information was given as to what our side was trying to do."

Lt.-Colonel Drage moved off in half battalions. Major Carless led, with B and C companies, topped the shoulder of Lala Baba, and came under field artillery fire. The two leading companies extended and ploughed their way across rough ground which, though flat, was hummocky and covered with high brush wood; here and there were small arable patches, from which the crops had recently been taken. After advancing for rather more than a mile, some wounded men of the Sherwood Foresters directed them, and they turned half left and eventually got in touch with the Sherwood Foresters who were considerably more to the east than had been expected. The last part of the journey was completed under hot rifle fire, and by short rushes " in the approved Newmarket style."

But Lt.-Colonel Drage, keeping on the line that had been given him, lost touch with his second in command.

" It became increasingly difficult, owing to the dust raised by the shrapnel (enemy shrapnel) and the nature of the terrain, to see anything to the flank, as we approached the Azmak Dere. . . . We now came to a dried up watercourse with steep little banks about two foot high. This was the Azmak Dere, and I think we crossed exactly between the K and D, as ordered. We pushed on and eventually reached a low hill covered with scrub to our immediate front. . . . The position of the two second line companies was now at the foot of Damakjelik Bair . . . The left flank company commanders (Rogers and Capel) came to me for orders. I was in a quandary and confess I did not know what to do. I had lost touch with my two leading companies. In front was a jungle with, according to the map, an extremely difficult line of country at the back of it. No knowledge of the enemy's position and with a very vague idea of our troops on the left. It also seemed to me that I was over 1,000 yards in front of where I was told I might get in touch with our own side. (I know now that Captain Green had sent back a runner—from the leading companies—stating that they had met men of the Sherwood Foresters who had put them right as to the position of their battalion.)

" I decided to withdraw the supports to the Azmak Dere, whose left banks provided two feet of cover, in places, and a fairly open field of fire."

While discussing the situation with his officers a shell burst over their heads, and Colonel Drage, Captains Yates, Capel, and Nott, and Lieut. Bourne were all wounded. Nevertheless, Colonel Drage carried on, succeeded in closing up his two companies, and commenced to retire. Before he reached the sheltering bank of the Azmak Dere, he saw a horseman approaching at a gallop and waving his hand. "This was a staff officer from the 53rd Division, with a paper in his hand. He did not deliver it to me but told me I had to return to Lala Baba."

The object of this order is wrapped in mystery. Having gained touch with Major Carless, Colonel Drage withdrew his battalion, only to be ordered to report to the Sherwood Foresters the following morning at dawn! This the battalion did, but meanwhile the Commanding Officer had gone to hospital.

THE EVENING OF THE 9TH AUGUST

At nightfall, the situation was extraordinary and confusing. General Lindley found his division scattered in all directions. Divisional headquarters was at Lala Baba; the 158th Brigade had the Herefords "in action southeast of Lala Baba," while the three Royal Welch Fusilier battalions were bivouacked west of Lala Baba; the 159th Brigade was inextricably mixed up with the 32nd Brigade west of Sulajik, and their exact position was unknown to the Brigade Staff; the 160th Brigade had the Queens and Sussex in action about Hill 53, the Middlesex on beach duty, and the Royal West Kents still on board ship. There was no transport,* the Royal Engineers and one Field Ambulance were being landed without stores, and the Signal Company had not arrived. And the General received orders that he was to attack the next morning.

. . . . .

IXth Corps Operation Order, No. 2.

Ref. 1/20,000 Gallipoli.

(1) At conclusion of operations to-day, 11th Division and troops of 53rd Division attached hold the line Yilgin Burnu-Hill 50-I of Sulajik-A of Anafarta Ova.† 10th Division held line Bench Mark 200, on Kiretch Tepe Sirt—about 135 Y 6—about 118 A 7.

(2) Enemy has shown strength on ridges Ismail Oglu Tepe—Anafarta Sagir, and has opposed steadily 10th Division advance to present position to-day.

(3) The G.O.C. intends to attack the enemy's position on ridge S.E. of Abrikja, attack to be directed, approximately, right on point

---

* On the 10th August, the only transport ashore consisted of 500 mules, under the orders of IXth Corps.

† Not applicable to the sketch given.

where road cuts contour 100 about 105P5, left on point where road cuts contour about 106G half-way between point 3 and 6.

(4) The attack will be delivered by nine battalions of the 53rd Division, under the orders of General Lindley. Of these battalions, six which are now holding line north of Sulajik, under orders of G.O.C. 11th Division, will be withdrawn to-night, relieved by troops of 11th Division, and assembled as Major-General Lindley may direct.

The three battalions, 53rd Division, now at Lala Baba, will be also moved forward to a position of assembly selected by Major-General Lindley.

(5) G.O.C. 11th Division will be responsible for security of line now held by 11th Division *and* troops attached, as set forth in para. 1. He will place two battalions in Corps Reserve at Lala Baba.

(6) Artillery support of attack will be afforded—(*a*) by Field Mountain Battery of 11th Division ; (*b*) by Royal Navy, arranged by Brig.-General Smith.

The hour of commencement of artillery bombardment of position, direction of bombardment, and time of launching attack will be decided by Major-General Lindley in consultation with Brig.-General Smith, R.A.

(7) Water mules will be assembled at the " Cut " in Salt Lake, as arranged by D.A.A. and Q.M.G. IXth Corps and G.O.'s C. Divisions.

(8) Position of Corps report centre will be notified later.

9th Aug., 1915, 7.10 p.m.   H. L. Reed, B.G.G.S.

After Orders :

The G.O.C. 10th Division will remain in present position, and be prepared to cover left flank of Corps.

. . . . . .

THE MORNING OF THE 10TH AUGUST

General Lindley, however, found himself in the position of being able to use two brigades only—the 158th, which had the three Royal Welch Fusilier battalions bivouacked on the beach, and to which he attached the Middlesex battalion from the 160th Brigade in place of the Herefords ; and the 159th which was scattered about in the neighbourhood of Sulajik.

Brigadier-General Hume was now squatting on the beach with no command. The Royal West Kents disembarked about 3 a.m. on the 10th August, and were put on beach duty, to provide fatigues ; the Middlesex were employed as above. The other two battalions, the Sussex and Queens, remained with the 33rd Brigade until the 12th, and did good work. (In Brigadier-General Maxwell's report on these operations, in which he refers somewhat slightingly to these two battalions, and not, it must be said, with justice, he concludes: " Although the Territorial Regiments did not show up well in the advance, and at night are subject to wasting ammunition without cause, yet they have done exceedingly good and enterprising work sending out patrols and accounting for snipers, for which individuals deserve great credit. They have constantly patrolled the scrub, and accounted for many snipers; this was supplied to me by Lt.-Colonel Broadwick, Border Regiment, whom I placed in command of the right section of the line.")

The 53rd Division Operation Order No. 1 (a recapitulation of the Corps Order) directs that " The 158th Brigade, with the addition of the 10th Middlesex from the 160th Brigade, and the 159th Brigade will attack to-morrow against the ridge S.E. of Abrikja, etc. . . The 159th Brigade will commence the attack at 6 a.m. and advance from Sulajik with its left on the south of the Kanli Keupru Dere and its right on the track through 105, I.3, to 105, J.8. Its first objective is the line 105, I.3—Knoll at 105, D.8, just east of Kanli Keupru Dere. After making good this position, it will act as reserve to the 158th Brigade, which will pass through it and attack the ridge from 105, P.5, to 105, G, half-way between pts. 3 and 6. All troops must keep south of Kanli Keupru Dere, which will be shelled by our artillery."

THE ADVANCE OF THE 159TH BRIGADE

During the early morning of the 10th August, the 159th Brigade staff succeeded in locating the 4th Cheshires slightly north of Sulajik (on a north and south line sq. 105, B.5) and the 5th Welch in rear of them, both battalions on a frontage more or less favourable to the attack. " The most that could be done was to give orders to C.O.'s of three battalions who, however, were not in a position to say where their battalions were, except the 4th Welch." The staff of the 159th Brigade was also completely ignorant as to the whereabouts of the 158th Brigade, which, according to orders, was to pass through the 159th when the latter had captured the lower slopes of the Anafarta ridge. The Brigadier-General of the 32nd Brigade could give them no information whatever. It was an appalling situation, but a line of troops did advance at 6 a.m. and pass over the trenches of the 32nd Brigade; it included 1½ companies of the 7th Cheshires, and the 4th Cheshires and 5th Welch, who were not much stronger.

The comment in the 53rd Division report on these proceedings is that the 159th Brigade " had been fighting hard the whole previous day, and at nightfall were scattered. The Brigadier had much difficulty in collecting and re-organising his units in time for the attack next morning. This, however, was carried out, with the exception that a large part of the 7th Cheshires had not joined their brigade in the morning at the time ordered. The country over which the attack had to advance is flat and covered with scrub, trees, and hedges. There are but few landmarks, and it is extremely difficult to locate accurately either your own position or that of the enemy on the maps supplied, and there had been no time for previous reconnaissance. The keeping of intercommunication between units or even parts of units is extremely difficult. The communication between Divisional headquarters and units was also very much hampered owing to the non-arrival of the 53rd Signal Company."

The advance went slowly, with no cohesion, until 8.35 a.m., when all progress ceased, as far as the 159th Brigade was concerned. But the 158th Brigade had advanced from the beach and were behind them.

THE ADVANCE OF THE 158TH BRIGADE

The officers of the 158th Brigade had been given no opportunity to reconnoitre the ground; one company had, it is true, carried tools to the front line, but it was dark, and they were guided there like sheep. Probably the experience of all junior officers was much the same as that of Kenneth Taylor. He says:—

"We arrived in the Bay just as dawn was breaking (5th R.W.F.), and the sight was truly magnificent. In the darkness you could faintly see the outline of the ring of hills commanding the bay and the plain. In the Bay were the monitors and battleships, and a good and hefty battle was going on. You could see the flash of the guns, and bursting shells, the spluttering of rifles all round you, and in the hills. As it slowly grew lighter, the flashes turned to smoke in which the whole place seemed to be bathed. The monitors were paying particular attention to a farmhouse tucked away at the foot of hills on the left. As a first experience it filled us with delight. You could not see any movement ashore but the continuous rattle of musketry said that something was going on.

"The beach we landed on was afterwards known as C beach, and the ridge behind which we waited was Nebrunesi Point, though we did not know these things at the time. As a matter of fact, we had no map, and had not a notion where we were. . . . (Maps were afterwards issued).

"After dusk, one of our companies, A Company, under Bill Beswick, had to carry tools up to the line, otherwise we settled down to get what sleep we could. A battery of guns close behind us was rather noisy, but I slept like a log.

"Reveille was at 03.00, and we were soon awake and ready... The Colonel (Philips) called for company commanders and showed us on our maps the plan of operations; it all sounded so simple and easy. We were to move out over the left shoulder of Lala Baba, cross the Salt Lake, and the Brigade would rendezvous at Sulajik Farm, where final orders would be issued. Roughly we were to move half right, support the attack of the 159th Brigade on a certain ridge, and when they had made it good we were to pass through them and take the next ridge. We scarcely had time to impart all this to our officers and N.C.O.'s when the order was given to move.

"Our battalion led the Brigade with a small advance guard, and moving in companies in close column of route. When we were well into the Salt Lake we came under shell fire, fortunately light stuff and inaccurate. After a bit of this we opened out into artillery formation and plodded on. The Salt Lake was supposed to be dry at this time of the year, and it was to all appearances, but in reality we sank about six inches deep in it, in heavy, slimy, liquid mud. This, combined with heavy equipment, made progress very slow and exceedingly tiring. We got across at last without any damage, and we were making for a track which seemed to lead out of the Lake, when suddenly we heard rifle fire begin to crackle and found ourselves the target. This was quite unexpected, as we were some way off our rendezvous, and it rather upset our plans. The two leading companies were getting it rather hot, and we were all absolutely exposed to full view. The two companies in front of me extended, and moved half right. When I arrived at their point of deployment, I had no orders, but it was evident something had to be done, as we were now the heart's desire of Turkish bullets. Fortunately, I saw the General and Brigade-Major in a ditch, and so reported for orders. I was told to extend my company and push on up the hill in front as hard as possible, and I was to tell the Colonel to do this with the whole battalion; further that there was nothing in front of us but a few snipers—I thought if that was so, they must all have machine guns. I extended my company into two waves, and off we went. I delivered my message to the Colonel, when I passed him, and this was the last time I saw him.

"The hill, or rather ridge in front of us, had a gradual rise at first, which was covered with trees, hedges, bushes, and oak scrub, about waist high. It was practically impossible to keep any sort of formation or to keep touch, and we were soon split up and rather disorganised. All the time we were being pretty heavily shot at, where from it was impossible to tell, so the only thing to do was to go for the place where the bullets seemed to come from, as our original plan had evidently gone phut!

" The situation became more and more obscure until we suddenly emerged on a line of trenches in which were the 160th Brigade.

" We stopped here for a few minutes for a breather, and to glean as much information as we could. The situation became a little less obscure as we could now see the ridge in front of us and knew where the fire was coming from.

" The ridge must have been 150 yards to 200 away from us. About 50 yards away was a bank, and after that was all oak scrub.

" We started off again in waves with big intervals, and the first 50 yards was a hell for leather race, no cover, and every chance of striking eternity. We were getting a bit tired by now, and the Turk was having the best shooting he could wish for, unworried by fire from us as we could see nothing to shoot at, or by the guns who were blissfully silent.

" That 50 yards accounted for a good many, and my only recollection of it was the splendid way the men behaved. And so we arrived at the bank, and had another breather. Evidently there had been some dirty work here, as there were some ghastly sights of charred bodies. It looked as though they had been wounded and overtaken by a scrub fire.

" I was out of touch now with anyone on my left, although I tried hard to find them. Shortly the order came down to fix bayonets, and get ready to charge. I believe our own Colonel and Colonel Jones, of the 6th Battalion R.W.F., were together at this time, about 100 yards on my right, and soon the order came to charge. The density of the oak scrub absolutely ruined all chance of a decent charge, as we had to follow goat tracks and watercourses in single file to get through. Either the Turk could not see us or he was preparing to retire, as few bullets came over and we had little difficulty in getting to the top, and to my immediate front everything was quiet. But being split up into small parties by the scrub caused more confusion because so many parts of line were out of touch and it was impossible to tell how things were going on in other spots.

" After a while, I have no idea how long, everything seemed quiet except on the right. Soon we saw a retirement taking place on the right, and it gradually crept closer to where we were.

" I sent an officer off to find out what was going on, and he returned with the information that the order had been given to retire, so I withdrew my small party, and sent them back to the 160th Brigade trenches, as with no one on our right or left, and a field of fire of about two yards we could have done nothing.

" I was wandering slowly back when I met Tom Parry, who commanded B Company. He knew no more of the situation than I did. Eventually we arrived back to the trench, and I remember the kindness of a Queens officer giving us a most welcome drink.

" In a few moments the Regimental-Adjutant, Captain F. W. Borthwick, arrived and told us that the Colonel had been killed on the top of the ridge; he had raised himself on his hands to have a look at a road in front, and was killed instantly. So died a very fine man, leading the men he had trained in peace time.

" We could locate very few of our own men, as everybody was so mixed up—battalions, brigades and divisions all jumbled up together—so we decided to move to a big tree about 100 yards to the left and have a look round.

" We decided that we must find Major Head, who was now in command of the battalion, and get some orders and information, if possible. Borthwick went off in search of Head, Tom in search of a hospital (Captain Parry had been wounded) and I in search of the remainder of our scattered battalion. I found a few men and collected them behind a bank and hedge just in rear of our tree, a place Borthwick had decided on as our rendezvous. Borthwick returned later with a few more men, and the news that we were to collect all the men we could possibly find, and remain where we were in support, in case of necessity. Head, I think, knew less of the situation that we did, and was beating up stragglers in the rear. Later on we found Colonel Jones. Captain Porter had a few men of the 6th R.W.F. on our right, in the same boat as ourselves, and looking very miserable.'

The reports of this operation are very brief and non-committal. There was no communication between the 159th and 158th Brigades at the commencement, and the order that the advance should take place in two stages, with one brigade going through the other, was never carried out. No one knew exactly where he was. It is claimed that at noon the line was " almost " the first objective (105, I.3—105, D.8—E. of Keupru), but the 158th Brigade seems to have been on the right of the 159th. Again one finds bewildered troops falling back on occupied lines, and a paralysing mixing up of units. The two attacking brigades were mingled with those of the 11th Division, and what with the heat, the difficulty of getting water, and the soft condition of the men after three weeks at sea, all were well nigh exhausted.

At 1 o'clock General Stopford ordered the attack to be renewed at 5 p.m., and an attempt was made to reorganise, but with little success; there were not many officers and N.C.O.'s left. Still, at 5 o'clock, under cover of the Naval and Corps guns, an attack was launched and once more failed; the opposition was stronger than in the morning, and the effort resulted in no more than an average gain of some two or three hundred yards.

We now know that the three Turkish battalions defending Suvla Bay had, by the 10th August, been reinforced by two Turkish Divisions, approximately 12,000 rifles, but, of these, one division was south of Azmak Dere. There were also in action that day 35 Turkish guns.

At the conclusion of the days fighting the IXth Corps was ordered by Sir Ian Hamilton to entrench on a line from Azmak Dere to Hill 50 (to the east of Chocolate Hill), and so to the position held by the 10th Division on Keritch Tepe Sirt.

General Stopford divided his front, putting the 11th Division on the right, with the farm in the vicinity of Sulajik as their left; the 53rd Division in the centre, with their left on a point 300 yards south of Aghil; and the 10th Division on the left to the sea.

. . . . .

TRENCHES

The next day, the 11th August, the 158th and 159th Brigades moved to take over the Divisional front. After the shattering experiences of the 10th August, this simple manœuvre had become one of difficulty as units were still considerably mixed and a certain number of troops out of touch with their officers.

About 1 o'clock a start was made, and the 158th Brigade deployed, on the line given, to dig, or improve existing trenches. But the 159th Brigade, having been allotted the left of the line, found, when they attempted to extend in the direction of Aghil, an active enemy, instead of the flank of the 10th Division. They were met by a hail of bullets and had to turn their left flank to face north, and did not extend beyond Anafarta Ova.

Here was a new complication. Sir Ian Hamilton had proposed to attack the heights of Kavak Tepe—Tekke Tepe with the 54th (East Anglian) Division, which had arrived at Suvla on that same day (11th), but the uncertain position on the left of the 53rd Division had to be stabilised first.

The 163rd Brigade was, therefore, ordered to clear the wooded plain of Anafarta Ova.

On the morning of the 12th, Brigadier-General Cowans, commanding 159th Brigade, received the following order from the 53rd Division :—

"An attack will be carried out on Anafarta Ova this afternoon by the 163rd Brigade of the 54th Division under General Brunker. General Brunker will communicate with you at your headquarters. This attack will commence at 4 p.m., and will pass through your lines. After passing through your lines it is your duty to support this attack and to conform to any orders or instructions given you by General Brunker. This attack is a prelude to a bigger attack which will be carried out to-night by the whole East Anglian Division. You will confine yourself to the support of that made by the 163rd Brigade during the afternoon. If this is successful dig yourself in on a line as far east as possible, but not further than a north and south line drawn through the last A of Ova.* Under no circumstances must a shot be fired by your Brigade after dark. All men to be warned that troops and convoys will be passing through them during the night. Their passage is to be facilitated, and on no account are their loads to be touched."

It is extraordinary how situations in this Suvla Bay enterprise keep repeating themselves. Brigadier-General Cowans having received this order, heard nothing more. The 163rd Brigade made no attempt to communicate with him. He says that at 4 o'clock in the afternoon the 159th Brigade was ready to move, and that artillery commenced to search Anafarta and the ground east of it. Still no one came near him. At 5.30 p.m. "a thin firing line of the 163rd Brigade passed our line of trenches. As this firing line was unsupported by supports or local reserves, at 6.20 p.m. I sent a battalion to support it, followed by another half battalion." These were the 4th Cheshires and two companies of the 5th Welch, and they saw little of the troops they were supporting, and had no definite task given them beyond a vague order to entrench no further than the A in Ova; at dusk they returned to their original line.

The thick woods prevented anyone seeing what happened to the 163rd Brigade, but they did eventually establish themselves on the line towards Aghil. It was during this action that Sir H. Beauchamp, with 16 officers and 250 men, amongst which gallant band was a company of soldiers enlisted from His Majesty's Norfolk estates, pushed on, driving the enemy before them, with reckless determination, and vanished in the

* Not applicable to Sketch given.

mysterious depths of the close and intricate country—" Nothing more was ever seen or heard of them. They charged into the forest, and were lost to sight or sound."

Indeed, so difficult was the country that the right of the 163rd Brigade was not found by the 159th Brigade until August 15th. But, meanwhile, at 6.30 p.m., the Brigade Major of the 163rd Brigade arrived at Brigadier-General Cowans' headquarters, and the situation, as far as it was known, was explained to him. " He said he wished no further action taken till he had consulted his Brigadier in full. I sent a telephone line with him. . . . In the absence of any orders or information other than that contained in your G.68, it was difficult to operate. At this moment, 8.45 p.m., all firing has stopped and I have had no communication of any sort from General Brunker."

In this affair the 159th Brigade suffered about 200 casualties.

Nothing further occurred. The night march and attack of the 54th Division was abandoned, owing to difficulties of supplying troops with water, rations, etc., and this part of the line settled down to improving the trenches, a work in which the Engineers of the 53rd Division gave invaluable assistance. " The state of the line was indescribable. It consisted mainly of a shallow ditch behind a thin hedge and did not afford much more than kneeling cover. Our first job was to help convert this into a trench and at the same time secure the water supply for the battalion. (Queens). This was obtained from two wells which were heavily sniped, but two days and two nights work rendered them safe to obtain water by day. In three weeks time we saw the line grow from a shallow ditch into a quite passable trench system, and communication and support trenches."—(Lieut. Phillips, 1st Welsh Field Coy. R.E.)

All this time Brigadier-General Hume (160th) had remained on the beach without a command. The 4th Royal West Kents had been placed on beach duty on disembarkation, and the other battalions were attached to various units. The Queens and the Sussex returned from the 32nd Brigade on the night of the 12th August, and then the 160th Brigade, less the Middlesex, moved up and relieved the 158th Brigade on the night of the 13th. They were on the right of the line, and the impression made on Captain le Fleming was " At dawn we found that behind and in front of us were scattered fig trees and olive trees, excellent cover for those infernal snipers. The ground sloped up gradually in front until it culminated in Tekke Tepe, while away on the right lay Chocolate and Burnt Hills. The thick scrub in front hid all signs of the enemy. We spent a most unpleasant day, what with intense heat, flies, dust, sniping, a restricted water supply, and meagre rations."

The Herefords had also been withdrawn from the extreme right of the British line, on the 12th, to rejoin their Brigade, but, at the same time, the 158th Brigade lost the 7th Royal Welch Fusiliers, who were sent to Mudros on some harbour fatigue.

Excepting minor rectifications of the line, small enterprises to take houses which might be turned into machine gun posts, or the meeting of patrols (such as the Sussex experienced on the 11th September, when they scattered a Turkish party after killing five), the 53rd Division did not again attack. Their battle casualties, from the date of landing to the 14th August—five days—amounted to 123 officers and 2,182 other ranks. But dysentery, which had made its first appearance at Mudros, before troops landed at Suvla, now spread rapidly, and jaundice, too, became a serious matter; sick casualties rose to appalling numbers. The period of open fighting was over, and units settled down to a spell of trench warfare, with its wearisome routine, heat and flies.

When examining the Gallipoli operations one must not fall into the error of condemning the whole venture as futile from its inception, at the same time one must note that an evil fate seemed to have hovered over Sir Ian Hamilton, ready to visit regulars, territorials, and new army corps troops in turn. Sir Ian was, at times, so near success that one can almost call out to individuals by name to go on and snatch the victory which is within their grasp, that nothing opposes them! And yet one feels so much sympathy for these same individuals in their bewilderment. It is impossible to dip anywhere into the history of this enterprise, which seemed so promising and was such a dismal failure, without finding glaring evidence of faulty staff work; but it will suffice to insist here on the bewilderment of undefined purpose, which settled like a paralysing blight on the eager spirit of officers and men of the 53rd Division.

It was a curious business; one thinks of the bursting of a paper bag full of nuts.

GENERAL MARSHALL ASSUMES COMMAND

On the 19th August, General Lindley took command of Mudros and handed over control of the 53rd Division to General H. A. Lawrence until, on the 25th, General W. R. Marshall arrived and assumed command.

General Marshall had been in temporary command of the " incomparable " 29th Division, but he found little to complain of in the way the 53rd maintained their line. Under the expert advice of the divisional engineers, front and support line trenches were completed, and the water supply was organised. Also, thanks to the Sappers, the automatic distribution of rations was now simple; they had improved existing tracks and were constructing roads for heavy traffic. The latter was a difficulty along the sandy coast, and all manner of methods, brushwood, wire netting, even old clothes were tried; but the most effective proved to be sleepers laid about two feet apart, and the spaces filled with broken stone drawn from a quarry near Lala Baba.

To improve the water supply the Sappers sunk a considerable number of wells, some of them, on the edge of the Salt Lake, yielding a good supply of fresh water at six feet; on higher ground they had to sink 20 feet. One source was tapped by driving into the sandstone cliff at Lala Baba, and this tunnel, about four to five feet high and 15 yards long was the first shell proof shelter—needless to say, very popular at times.

The Division was becoming learned in the rules of trench warfare when, on the night of the 19/20th September, they were relieved by the 13th Division.

The change cannot be said to have been a pleasant one. The 159th and 160th Brigades were sent to Lala Baba, where the refuse of men and animals had accumulated and fouled the entire area, which had become a breeding place for a cloud of flies. The Rev. H. S. F. Williams gives a general description of the beach. " The area is tightly packed with mules, horses and men, streets and lanes of boxes piled 15 to 20 feet high, barges and lighters unloading at roughly thrown-out jetties, pyramids of baggage, mountains of forage! Above all the din and noise a faint moaning is heard, growing rapidly louder and deeper—thud—bang! and up goes a column of dust and debris. The air clears, heads bob up, and where there had been a pile of biscuit boxes there remains a shell crater, with a litter of scrap tin, matchwood, etc., and the work goes on."

The work allotted to troops was the preparation of winter quarters, and the inner defences of what was called the B area; but stricken by sickness—through flies and the climate—those who were not actually in hospital became so debilitated that General Marshall noted it was impossible for them to do a full day's work.

The 158th Brigade were, perhaps, slightly better situated beneath the slopes of Karakol Dagh, providing fatigues for beach duty, but, even so, their numbers dwindled.

" Our camping ground now was on the north-western slopes of Karakol

Dagh. The ground sloped steeply from the crest of the ridge until it fell away into the sea in a precipice which you could only climb down in certain places, and then with great difficulty. On the other side of the crest you got a most excellent view of the Bay, with A beach lying almost beneath you, then B beach with its hospital tents, and then Lala Baba, with the Salt Lake on the left, stretching away to Nebrunesi Point. C beach was hidden from view, but Anzac stood out with its bold heights and beach resting at the foot of the hills, and away in the distance was Achi Baba and Cape Helles. On the left of the panorama we had an excellent view of the plain, Anafarta Ova, as it is called on the maps, and the village of Anafarta Sagir just on the foothills. In the distance was the ring of hills from which the Turks could see you blowing your nose on the beach, and which we longed to climb but never did. Across the sea, to the west, you could see Imbros, looking so peaceful, and which was Army Headquarters... We had a fairly good rest in this camp, but some of the fatigues were rather heavy, particularly the water fatigue. Water had to be carried by hand from A beach twice a day in petrol tins, and as it was a long and steep climb up it was not at all a popular event. The morning party used to leave about 4 a.m. Another unpopular fatigue was the construction party for the new Corps Headquarters. I never saw them, but I heard it was a wonderful place, cut out of the solid rock, with fireplaces, etc., and it was about the only place on Suvla Bay that a shell could not hit."—(Ashton.)

In spite of this charming picture sickness continued. Apart from Colonel Philips, who had been killed, and Brigadier-Generals Lloyd and Cowans, and Colonel Swindells (4th Cheshires) who had been wounded, sickness had taken toll of Brigadier-General Hume, Lt.-Colonels M. Morgan (5th Welch), L. G. Backhouse (7th Cheshires), Jones (6th R.W.F.), H. Smithers (West Kents), and Campion (Sussex).

A story is told of the first visit by Brigadier-General Mott to the Herefords, on his arrival to take command of the 158th Brigade. Colonel Drage had not yet returned from hospital, and Major Holman was in command of the Herefords. It was in August, and the scene is a cowhouse just behind the front line. Everyone was very tired, and news had come that the new Brigadier would visit Battalion Headquarters after dark. He arrived about 9 o'clock. The commanding officer, tired out, was fast asleep, and his Adjutant seizing him by the shoulder, shook him violently and shouted in his ear that the Brigade Commander had arrived. Lifting his head for a moment, Major Holman opened one eye to gaze vacantly at the rude disturber of his slumber, and murmured " Tell them to go for a row round the Bay." His head fell back and he appeared to sleep again. Suddenly, however, in response to renewed shaking and pinching, he leaped to his feet and said " Good evening, sir, I'm glad to see you here," as if nothing had happened.

Numbers continued to dwindle, until it became necessary, for tactical purposes, to form composite battalions of the 4th and 5th Welch, under Major Southey, the Queens and Sussex, under Major Few, and the 5th and 6th Royal Welch Fusiliers, under Lt.-Colonel Rome.

It is curious that Major Austin Isaac, who commanded the Signal Company (and was attached to the 54th Division, while Lieut. Vickery worked signals for the 53rd Division with a Brigade Section) noticed that when he first landed flies were few, but the rate and extent of their increase was alarming. These vile pests were, of course, the chief carriers of disease.

THE FIRST TOUCH OF WINTER

The last phase of the Suvla Bay experience commenced on the 31st October, when the 158th Brigade left the Karakol Dagh camp and were attached to the 2nd Mounted Division. They had contended with Turks, heat, and flies, and now the whole division had to contend with cold and wet, which set in towards the end of November.

The Herefords had a particularly bad time. They were in a trench which ran into the Azmak Dere, not far from the scene of their first adventures after landing. The bed of the Dere had been barricaded by both Turks and British. Rain had set in, but, as yet, it was not very cold, and beyond the misery of being wet no one expected anything to happen. Suddenly a torrent swept down the dry watercourses, and filled the trenches waist deep !

Apparently the Turkish barricade had held up the water that drained from the hills into the Dere until it burst under the pressure, and the pent up force hurtled through everything it met. Some guns, comfortably sited in the stony bed, were immediately submerged, with nothing but the sights to be seen.

" I was in my little dugout, opening out of the rear line trench, and found the trench getting rather puddly, as I had only a waterproof sheet roof. I remember I had a sort of doorstep to prevent paper and mess blowing in, about a foot high, the floor level of the dugout being the same as the trench. Suddenly, without warning, my doorstep entirely dissolved, and a brown flood poured in. The water rose as you watched until it was about $3\frac{1}{2}$ feet deep, and then stopped. As I didn't want to drown I struggled out of the trench, and met the C.O. emerging from next door where the same thing had happened. It was quite obvious what had occurred. The very heavy rain, probably still heavier back in the hills, had suddenly transformed the Dere into a river again. The water had poured down from the high ground behind the Turks till it had got caught up behind their barricade. This, presumably, had held until there was a respectable weight of water behind it, when it collapsed and the whole tearing flood came rushing down at ours. It didn't gather, or pause for the twinkling of an eye at ours, it simply swept it away as if it hadn't been there, and swept on to the sea, a solid river, 20 yards wide and 8 or 9 feet deep. All our trenches opened out of the Dere, and though their floor level was higher than the bottom of the stream they were still deep enough to take in about four feet of water. As the ground sloped slightly upward towards the front line the rear lines were the worst.

" Our first consideration being the front line, I at once started off to see if it was still there . . . I went on till I got to the support line, about half way up it. As I couldn't cope with about three foot of rapidly flowing water any longer I got on to the top and reached the front line. There I found they had only about 18 inches of water, and though the first onrush had washed away a good deal of kit and some rifles there was nothing much the matter. After talking to Barker for a bit, I determined to get across to the other side where we had two vital machine guns. It wasn't possible to cross anywhere near the front line, so I went down stream about 300 yards, to a wide, pebbly place I remembered, and managed to get across. The water was about waist deep and running very strong. The R.E.'s two wooden bridges had absolutely disappeared. On my way down stream I heard something snorting and blowing in the dark in the water, and I found it came from a little Turkish ammunition pony, which had come down stream and got caught in a bush. I put two men on to get him out, and he continued his career in the British army.

" When I got across I walked overland to the front line, and found our two precious guns intact. It had now stopped raining and the Dere was running down fast."—(Ashton.)

It was then about 10 p.m. All the troops had got out of the trench and were wandering about " on top," but the Turks were doing the same and not a shot was fired. The night passed, and it was not too bad as regards cold; a general drop in temperature had occurred some days before, with occasional cold winds, but this night was not so cold. About 6 a.m., however, the wind changed, and it began to freeze, and continued all through the next day. About 9 p.m., the Fife and Forfar came up to relieve the Herefords, who received the distressing intelligence that they would have to bivouac amongst the open sand dunes about Lala Baba. It was blowing hard, and snowing—a regular blizzard.

"Men were pretty badly knocked up by now, as we hadn't had much food all day on top of the previous night, and they slept and fell all over the place. We even had some casualties from this. We arrived sometime, and were directed to a resting place, a bleak stretch of snow-covered sand dunes, with sundry clumps of a sort of gorse. When I had shepherded in the last straggler, I felt like lying down and dying. . . .

"Dawn, Sunday, 28th November, found it still snowing. We rose with considerable difficulty, and started a little circulation back in our frozen limbs. A great many people were unable to get up at all; Holman, for one, was practically unconscious, and we thought he was dead. But worse was to follow. Overnight our rations had been sent out to us in a lorry. The folk who sent them out, presumably sorry for those unfortunates in the snow, sent with them a double ration of rum. The wagon drivers, who brought the stuff, apparently before we arrived, finding no one to hand over to, had simply dumped the things by the side of the road and gone home. When morning broke men began wandering about, as men will, and unhappily found the dump. Instead of telling somebody, or even eating the food, which would have been sensible, they broke open the rum jars and started in. The effect on empty stomachs and in that cold was simply devastating. Filled with a spurious warmth, they lay on the ground, and in many cases took off coats, boots, even tunics!

"Those in the immediate vicinity of the dump were quickly put in the 'bag,' but, unfortunately the majority had filled mess tins, and water bottles, and crawled into the bushes to enjoy themselves. We fairly combed those bushes all the morning, but by the time we found them all a certain number were dead. I remember finding one man in particular in only his shirt and trousers, holding out an empty mug with a perfectly stiff arm, quite dead. Coming on top of everything else, it was heart-rending. Luckily, there were ambulances quite close, and we evacuated officers and men in a steady stream. When it was all over and the M.O. had gone too, there were left Rogers, 77 other ranks, and myself!"

Lt.-Colonel Drage had been in hospital when this disaster happened, but when news of it reached him he insisted on joining his battalion.

" In the afternoon who should come staggering in, to my great joy, but the Colonel, wearing his uniform on top of his hospital pyjamas !*

" For a real triumph of the spirit over the flesh it was magnificent."—(Ashton.)

Ever since the Division had been taken out of the line the construction of winter quarters had been the order, and all expected to stay on the peninsula till the spring; but evacuation had been under consideration since the 11th October. To Sir Ian Hamilton such a course was unthinkable, but he was recalled, and Sir C. Monro quietly commenced laying his plans for withdrawing the army.

The first suggestion was that the 53rd Division should have the honour of being the last to leave; but at the time of the blizzard, which reduced not only the Herefords, but every battalion of the Division, General Marshall's strength return was 217 officers and 4,522 other ranks (27th November), and these were physically fit for very little. So he represented that the troops should be sent to a healthy climate to recuperate, to be brought up to strength, provided with artillery, and generally completed as a division. He pointed out, too, the need of training these gallant but unfortunate troops to whom such meagre opportunities had been given. Reason prevailed, and the remnants of the Division started to embark on the 11th December.

"We packed up, not having much to pack, and embarked about 8 p.m. on a single 'beetle'—which is a barge with a paddle wheel in the stern. By a strange co-incidence we left from identically the same bit of beach, 103.U., as we had landed on just 18 weeks before. As I had been the first ashore I was also the last to leave. It was impossible to help noticing the contrast—that brilliant August morning, the battalion full of fight and high endeavour, 750 strong !—this dark cold December night, slinking away, under 100 strong, weary, dirty, blasé, disillusioned. And yet, I was sorry to go."—(Ashton.)

General Marshall remained to superintend the evacuation of Lala Baba, and did not rejoin the 53rd Division, but was ordered to Salonica, where he assumed command of the 27th Division.

* Denied by the Colonel. " I don't think there were any available in the Field Ambulances. I do remember my anxiety about my 'breeks' I took them off to have the flood and mud removed by a R.A.M.C. cook—he took my remarks as to the honesty of his noble corps in good part."

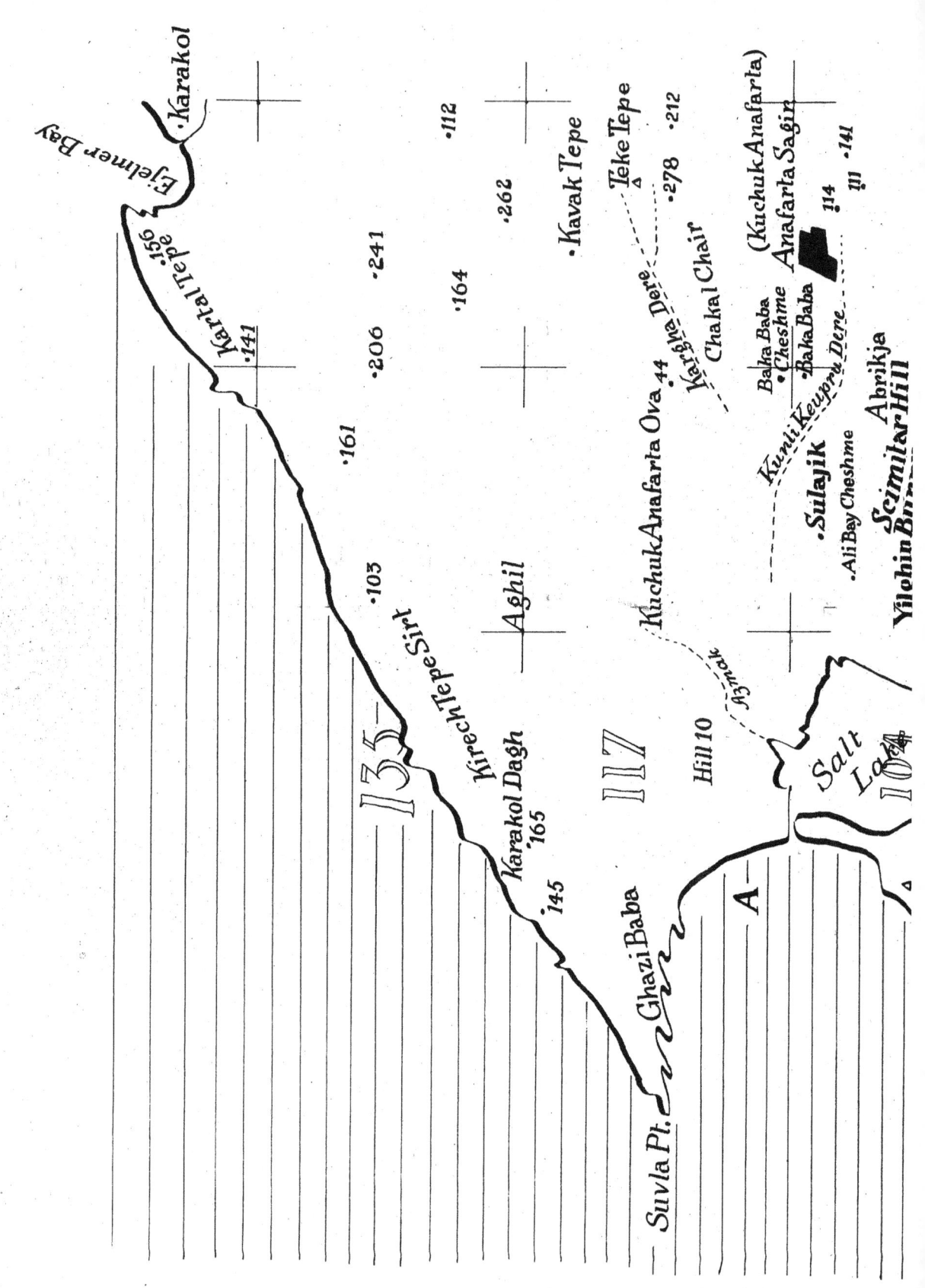

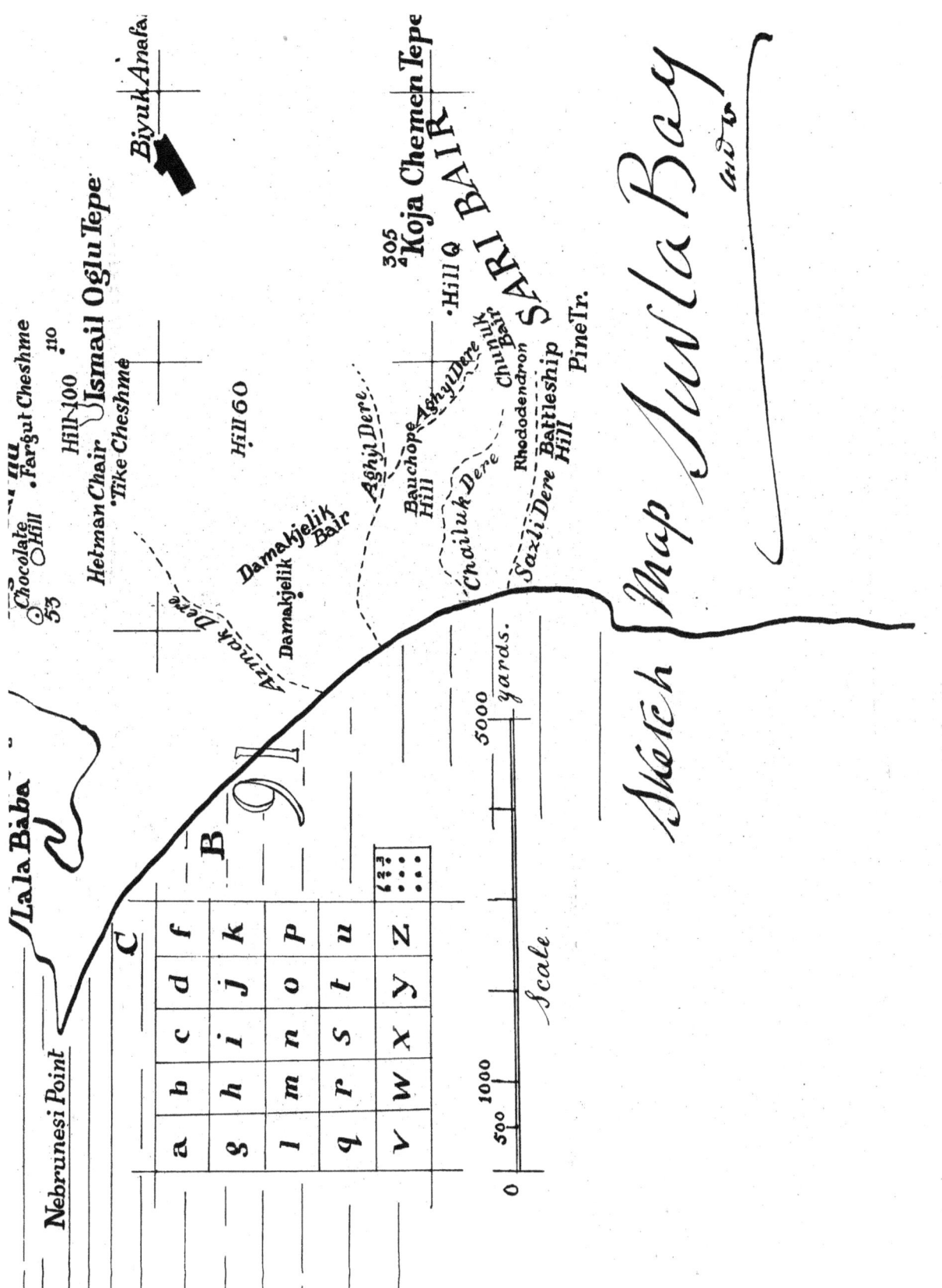

Sketch Map Suvla Bay

EGYPT

GENERAL WAR SITUATION

During the months of January—December, 1916.

Yaunde, in the Cameroons, taken by General Dobell's forces, 1st January.
First attempt to relieve Kut, 4th January.
Evacuation of Gallipoli complete, 8th January.
General Sir A. J. Murray assumes command of the Mediterranean Expeditionary Force.
Military Service Act comes into force in Great Britain, 10th February.
Russian attack on Erzerum begins, 12th February.
Fifth Battle of the Isonzo begins 15th February.
Capture of Erzerum by Russian forces, 16th February.
German forces in South Cameroons interned in Spanish territory, 17th February.
Battle of Verdun begins, 21st February.
German extended submarine campaign begins, 1st March.
Second attempt to relieve Kut, 8th March.
Germany declares war on Portugal, 9th March.
Sollum reoccupied by British forces, 14th March.
General Sir A. J. Murray takes over command of the force in Egypt from General Sir John Maxwell, 19th March.
Third attempt to relieve Kut, 1st April.
Russian attack on Trebizond, 6th April.
Constantinople and Adrianople attacked by British aeroplanes, 14th April.
Field Marshal Von der Goltz assassinated, 19th April.
Capture of Trebizond, 17th April.
Outbreak of Rebellion in Ireland, 24th April.
Capitulation of Kut, 29th April.
Allied blockade of the Hejaz coast, 15th May.
Rowanduz (northern Mesopotamia) and Khanaqin (north-east of Baghdad) taken by Russians, 15th May.
Turkish Army evacuates As Sinn and withdraws to Kut, 19th May.
Sultan of Darfur defeated by Sudan force, 22nd May.
Russian offensive (Brusilov) begins against Austria, 4th June.
Sherif of Mecca revolts against Turkish rule, 5th June.
Lord Kitchener drowned, 5th June.
Turkish offensive in West Persia begins, 5th June.
Turkish garrison of Mecca surrenders to Sherif, 10th June.
Battles of the Somme begin, 1st July.
Mr. Lloyd George, Secretary of State for War, 7th July.
Rumania declares war on Austria, 27th August.
Italy declares war on Germany; Germany declares war on Rumania, 28th August.
Hindenburg succeeds Falkenhayn as Chief of General Staff of German Field Armies, 29th August.
Turkey declares war on Rumania, 30th August.
Turkish garrison of Taif (Hejaz) surrenders to Arabs, 22nd September.
Mr. Lloyd George succeeds Mr. Asquith as Prime Minister, 7th December.
Rasputin murdered in Petrograd, 31st December.

EGYPT

WARDAN

ARRIVING at Alexandria on the 19th December, 1915, brigades proceeded to Wardan, about forty miles to the north of Cairo. "It was a thoroughly uninteresting place, with a small native village on the far, or east, bank of the Nile, the railway line, the usual canal crawling with bilharzia germs*, and nothing else but desert rising up to a ridge in front of us, some 3/4 miles from camp. We found that two of our most cherished illusions as to deserts were wrong; we had thought the desert would be flat whereas it is generally an everlasting tumbled mass of sand dunes and hillocks; and we had thought it always soft sand, whereas it varies and is generally fairly hard. . . . Wardan was a mixture. We found places hard enough to make passable football grounds, and others as soft as treading in flour."

Some, however, found an æsthetic charm about the place: "You know the paintings you see of sunrise in the desert?—They are not half so gorgeous as the real thing. . . . We crossed the canal at Wardan Station, secured some donkeys, and set off across the strip of desert that separated us from cultivation. We jogged along for about a mile, when we came to a rise in the sand followed by a sharp dip, and there we were, in as pretty a spot as you could wish to see, on both sides of us lay green crops of maize, and bersin (clover), groves of date palms and oranges, scattered sycamores, tamarisks and lebbek trees. Away on the left, amongst the trees, a white domed tomb. As we jogged along a narrow path, we passed between crops of broad beans. In the fields were goats, camels, donkeys, and water buffaloes innumerable. We soon came to a village (Beni Salama) a mass of mud huts, with a big, insanitary looking pond in front of it. All the women fled, but the children swarmed round demanding cigarettes and backsheesh."

The Division was to refit and reorganise. But as the original decision to attempt the forcing of the Dardanelles had meant a reduction of troops in Egypt, so the evacuation of Gallipoli caused, for the moment, an embarrassing inflow. Many divisions were refitting at the same time and considerable difficulty was experienced in getting stores: reor-

---

* The presence of these germs necessitated special precautions before water could be used for drinking or washing. All water was filtered or boiled, or collected from the canals and allowed to stand for 48 hours.—(Divisional Diary.)

ganisation proceeded leisurely. On 1st January the Division was informed that 6,000 troops were proceeding from England to reinforce the depleted battalions.

WADI NATRUN

There were, however, duties to perform, and the 159th Brigade was sent to Wadi Natrun, to the west. This Wadi contained a chain of narrow lakes of very salt water, and was considerably below sea level, consequently very hot. There was a small native village, and a salt and soda factory. The Brigade formed part of a mixed force which included the 3rd Australian Light Horse, a detachment of the Bikanir Camel Corps, a Machine Gun Section of the Egyptian Camel Corps, and some Egyptian Cavalry. Outlying posts had to be found at Khatatba and Bir Victoria.

The Khatatba Canal supplied Alexandria with drinking water, and a large part of Lower Egypt with water for irrigation purposes, and as the surface of the Nile was, at that time, ten feet below the bottom of the Canal any ill disposed persons could have made a breach in the side of the Canal and drained it in a few hours.

FAIYUM

In the middle of February, divisional headquarters and the 160th Brigade moved to Faiyum, and the 158th relieved the 159th at Wadi Natrun.

" We (160th) travelled southward all day, through Cairo and the palm shaded country west of the Nile to Wasta. Here we turned west and rattled through a few miles of particularly horrid desert, a lot of which came aboard the open trucks. Suddenly below and beyond us appeared the great green Oasis of Faiyum, a wonderful contrast to the ring of golden sandhills in which it is set. It was an enchanted land through which we swirled in the welcome coolness of the late afternoon. The reception we had from the inhabitants, who had strong Senussi sympathies, was anything but enchanting—the hostility of their actions, which included a certain amount of inaccurate stone throwing, was unmistakable. . . .

" I think Faiyum was the most picturesque of all the places we saw in our Levantine travels. Who will forget the great silvery palms, gently rustling as the cool evening breeze came softly breathing over the hot fields and sweltering villages—a sigh of relief after the grilling heat of the day ! Who will forget the lazy, querulous creaking of the water wheel, the sweet fragrance of the flowering bean fields, and the glorious sun-sets !

—silhouettes, black against an orange glow, then colour succeeding colour till the fast gathering purple dusk closed in ! The camp washes to laughter and song. There is a clink of glasses in the mess. Down on the canal bank innumerable frogs strike up their evening tune ! . . .

"Then again one remembers the dawn, when we marched along on those early mornings. On occasions, just as the day was breaking, we swung through a village, down an avenue of mulberry trees, and over the Bar Yusef, which reflected in its waters the gay pinks and yellows of the sky. . . .

"It was at El Azzab that we first experienced the horrors of a Khamsin. It was as though a giant oven door had been opened, and hot blasts of wind, bearing with it all the sand of the Lybian Desert, issued forth and overwhelmed the camp. 120 degrees in a bell tent is not a desirable temperature. . . . During our stay in Faiyum active work was impossible between the hours of 8 a.m. and 5 p.m., so we had reveille at 3 or 4 a.m. The normal way of spending the afternoon was to lie on one's bed, clad in a towel, with a bucket of water handy in which to damp the towel at intervals."—(M. R. Le Fleming, 4th Royal West Kent Regt.)

At Faiyum there was again a mixed force, scattered over a considerable area in that highly cultivated Province. The bulk was in camp at El Azzab, but there were mounted detachments, varying in strength from a troop to a cavalry regiment with a battery of Royal Horse Artillery, along the northern, western and southern side of the Province. All these troops (at this time one finds Staffordshire Yeomanry, Lincolnshire Yeomanry, East Riding Yeomanry, and, at Warden, the Welsh Border Mounted Brigade) came under the 53rd Division, command of which had been assumed by Major-General A. G. Dallas, C.B., on the 11th January.

On the 1st April, Major-General Dallas was appointed G.O.C. North-Western Force, and the Divisional Staff moved to Cairo.

On the 1st May, the 159th Brigade moved from Wardan to Sollum. The Division was then much scattered, but each brigade was busy training.

. . . . .

SOLLUM

The condition of Egypt gave cause for anxiety from time to time. It was known, at the outbreak of war, that the Khedive Abbas Helmi was a partizan of Turkey and the Central Powers; he was deposed on the 19th December, 1914, and Prince Hussein Kamel Pasha ruled in his stead as Sultan of Egypt.

But tribes in the Soudan were restive, and in the Province of Darfur the Sultan Ali Dinar formally renounced his allegiance to the Soudanese Government. The trouble spread to the Western front, where Sayed Ahmed, the Grand Senussi, who held much influence over the Arab population of Egypt, took up arms in August, 1915, and made a demonstration in the neighbourhood of the Tripoli frontier. Sollum Bay had, for a time, been evacuated. The Bedouin tribes of the desert required watching. Hence the posting of troops at Faiyum and the Wadi Natrun facing west, and the despatch of the 159th Brigade to Sollum. Brig.-General J. H. du B. Travers assumed command of the Coastal Section —Sollum, Matruh, Dabaa—on the 5th May, 1916.

. . . . .

THE CANAL DEFENCES

The distribution of troops administered by the staff of the 53rd Division prior to this move was given, on the 30th April, as follows :—

ALAMIEIN
: 1st Welsh Field Coy. R.E. (Detach.).
53rd Divn. Signal Coy. R.E. (Detach.).

MOGHARA
: 1st Denbighshire Yeomanry.

ABBASSIA
: H.Q. 53rd Divn. and 53rd Signal Coy.

WADI NATRUN
: 158th Brigade (less Transport Details).
1st Welsh Fld. Coy. R.E. (Detach.).
3rd Welsh Fld. Ambulance (Section).
53rd Divn. Train (Detach.).

BENI SALAMA
: 53rd Divisional Artillery (Less one Batty.).
Details 53rd Divn. R.E.
159th Brigade.
Transport Details 158th Brigade.
1st Pembrokeshire Yeomanry.
1st Montgomery Yeomanry.
2nd Welsh Fld. Ambulance.
3rd Welsh Fld. Amb. (less one Sect.).
53rd Divn. Casualty Clearing Station.
53rd Divn. Train Details and Bakery.
53rd Divn. Mobile Veterinary Sect.

FAIYUM
: 160th Brigade.
1st Welsh Fld. Ambulance.
53rd Divn. Sanitary Sect. (less Detach.).
2/1st Welsh Fld. Coy. R.E.
53rd Divn. Train Details.
53rd Divn. Cyclist Coy.

MAJOR-GENERAL DALLAS.
ON SECTION 2 CANAL DEFENCES, THE CAMP LINES WERE NEATLEY ENCLOSED IN BANKS OF SAND.

MINIA	4th Dismounted Brigade.
	4th Glamorganshire Battery R.F.A.
SOHAG	2/1st Cheshire Field Coy. R.E.
SUEZ	53rd Divisional Train.

Very soon, however, the bulk of the Division moved towards the East. On the 27th May, the Division was ordered to take over No. 2 Section Canal Defences from the 2nd Anzac Division, and Headquarters was transferred from Abbassieh, near Cairo, to Moascar, on the Suez Canal.

The Divisional Artillery had commenced to arrive at Wardan on the 12th February. There were four Brigades: the 1st, 2nd, and 4th Welsh, and the 1st Cheshire Brigades. They started from Bedford on the 19th November for France and were attached to the 32nd Division. After a short sojourn in the Somme area, in the neighbourhood of Vaux, they were ordered to Egypt, and left France on the 1st February, 1916.

During May the 158th Brigade moved to Zeitoun, near Cairo, and rejoined the Division on the Canal on the 21st June, so that in June the whole division was on the Canal, with the exception of the 159th Brigade, and the Cheshire Battery of Field Artillery, still with the North-western Force (the designation was changed on the 21st May to the Western Frontier Force).

SIR ARCHIBALD MURRAY'S TASK.

Sir Archibald Murray arrived in Egypt on the 9th January, 1916. At first his command was limited to the protection of Egypt against attack from the east, so that the 53rd Division did not come under his direction until a reorganisation on the 11th March gave him command of all Imperial troops in Egypt, and he took over those in the Nile Valley, the Delta and in the west, from Sir John Maxwell.

He found that—" the exigencies of the Gallipoli campaign had placed the force under my command in a serious state of disorganisation." His staff had not only to re-equip, reform brigades, divisions, and corps, but to create new units as well. In the case of the Australian units there was a further problem in a mass of unabsorbed reinforcements. Egypt became a gigantic depot for all the troops that had been engaged in Gallipoli. Gradually the congestion was relieved.

The re-embarkation of units for service elsewhere commenced in February, but the remaining divisions required, none the less, to be refitted and to have provision made for further training. A machine gun school was formed at Ismailia, which was later merged in the Imperial School of Instruction at Zeitoun. Here the officers and non-commissioned officers of the 53rd Division attended courses in machine gun, Lewis gun, hand grenades, trench mortars, artillery, and signals. And at Tel el Kebir a training centre was established for the Australian reinforcements which directly affected the 53rd Division inasmuch as Lt.-Colonel Cape, G.S.O.1, was whisked away as Chief Instructor, and was succeeded by Lt.-Colonel Robertson.

Sir A. Murray found that a scheme of defence had been prepared covering the Suez Canal, and a certain amount of work had been accomplished, but, generally speaking, the stationary defences were in a backward condition. The Turks had made a serious attempt on the Canal in January, 1915, when, without any elaborate preparation, they had dragged six-inch guns and steel pontoons across the desert, to the amazement of the military world. The storm centre had then shifted to the Dardanelles, and nothing had happened since, beyond an occasional skirmish with an odd detachment here and there. But, although Gallipoli had now been evacuated, there were no signs of an immediate advance by the Turks against Egypt, and Sir A. Murray was not anxious about the Canal Defences. The organisation of an offensive defence was another matter; it had not been approached and was pressing. A plan of campaign had to be drawn up, and mobile forces organised, entailing the collection of a large number of camels; above all, there was the water question! The obvious route across the Sinai Desert to the frontier of Palestine was the old high road along the coast, and through a chain of oases; more was, however, required before Palestine could be tackled, and the construction of the railway and water pipe line by Sir A. Murray gave a firm backing to the subsequent operations which opened the way to Jerusalem.

The advance across the desert was, of necessity, slow. Several sharp actions were fought, notably one at Qatia in April, but in May, although the strength of the enemy had increased, he remained behind the line of hills running north and south across the desert, about sixty miles from the Canal. During this month the Mahemdia-Romani district was occupied by British troops in some force.

The whole of June and part of July passed without any important operation on the part of the Turks. A column of Australian Light Horse raided and emptied the rock cisterns and pools in the Wadi Muksheib, and other reconnaissance parties penetrated far into the desert (on July 15th to Salmana) and found the country clear of all but a few Bedouin.

No Turkish troops were discovered nearer than Bir el Mazar, eighteen miles east of Oghratina, where there was a camp of 1,500 to 2,000.

On July 19th, the Royal Air Force discovered that a large body of the enemy had moved from El Arish, and on the morning of the 20th, cavalry reported that Oghratina was held by strong forces of the enemy, who were entrenching. Busy aeroplanes brought other information, and it was soon obvious that the Turks meant to fight.

The Turkish 3rd Division, with eight machine gun companies, officered, and partly manned by Germans, and some heavy artillery, manned by Austrians, advanced by deliberate bounds under Colonel Kress von Kressenstein.

On the night 27/28th July, von Kressenstein had pushed his line forward to Sabkhet el Amya-Abu Darem; and on the 2nd August, he made a strong reconnaissance towards er Rabah-Qatia-Bir el Hamisah, but his advance troops were driven back after several sharp encounters.

Up to this moment, Sir A. Murray was "still uncertain whether the ultimate assumption of the offensive would come from our side or the enemy's." But, on the 3rd, von Kressenstein advanced his line again to the semi-circle from "the immediate west of Hill 110, past the high ground east and south-east of Qatia, to the high ground north-west of Bir Hamisah," and it became evident that von Kressenstein had taken the initiative.

. . . . .

THE BATTLE OF ROMANI

The slow penetration of the desert had been going on for seven months, but the main line of defence lay along the Canal.

The Canal defences were divided into Nos. 1, 2, and 3 Sections. No. 2 Section, commanded by General Dallas, extended from the northern shore of the Great Bitter Lake to a couple of miles south of El Ferdan. The posting and reposting of units along the entire line was continual; the infantry brigades of the 53rd Division remained, however, within the command.

The 158th Brigade was in the neighbourhood of Moascar. "All these desert camps are much alike, in the routine of one's daily life, at least. Moascar was unusually good, from the comfort point of view, in that we had practically unlimited tents. It was part of the higher policy to induce enemy aeroplanes to believe that there was a large force at Ismailia, and to this end a large number of tents were pitched. . . . We began serious training in the digging of soft sand trenches, and found what immense labour was involved in throwing out enough sand to get any sort of depth. A trench had to be eighteen feet wide to get down five feet. When the required depth had been reached the walls of the trench, whether of hurdles or sandbags, were built, and then the sand was all shovelled back against them. The pressure of the sand would then, frequently, crush the whole thing inwards, and it all had to be done afresh, supplemented with heavy cross pieces (strutting) at the top and bottom."—(Ashton.)

The 160th Brigade were centred at Ferry Post. "Mile upon mile of rolling sand hills, a burning expanse unrelieved by tree or bush—such was our new home, some miles east of the canal. The Brigade was spread over a thirteen mile front, in a series of defended posts located on commanding sand dunes. Here it spent countless hours of toil, digging and sandbagging—and then destroying the fruits of hard labour, and starting all over again. Never was there such a pointless waste of time, temper, and energy. The heat was intense and the flies were a pest. Even in the "office," a large E.P. tent, the sweat poured off one to the papers, making the indelible pencil run in a disgusting fashion. Boils and blains added to the discomfort. . . The arrival of our horses and mules caused considerable excitement. The sight of some of us learning to ride was a joy to the rank and file. A couplet from the machine gunner's alphabet bore witness to this:—

> R is for riding—we see quite a lot—
> Some is quite good, and some is quite not!"
>
> (le Fleming.)

With the Turkish movement, life on the canal was rudely disturbed and the 158th Brigade, with the 160th Machine Gun Company, were sent through Qantara by train and route march to Romani; the 4th Sussex to el Ferdan; the 4th Welch from Dabaa to Ismailia. No. 2 Section then took over the 42nd Divisional front on No. 3 Section, and the extension was known as C Sub-section.

The 158th Brigade arrived at Romani on the 21st July. The 5th Royal Welch Fusiliers were attached to the 156th Brigade, 52nd Division, and the remainder of the Brigade was responsible for the centre section of the Romani line.

No. 2 Section Canal Defences also found two mobile columns. The first, despatched on the 28th July, under Lt.-Colonel Smith, V.C. (Camel Corps), contained a section of the 268th (4th Welch) Brigade, R.F.A., and was to strike at the left flank of the enemy. The second column was a smaller affair, and left on the 5th August led by Major de Knoop (Camel Corps), with a similar task.

The scene of action, the railhead, was an important oasis about eighteen miles from Qantara, with many wells and shady palms. To the east the country was broken and hilly, but dotted with wells and palm groves; south was soft sand, continually shifting and piling up into weird shaped hummocks and ridges. The line of defence was shaped like a fish-hook with a long shank, running from the coast and curling round the oasis of Romani. The 158th Brigade was responsible for five posts in the line, and the Herefords were detailed to hold them. Their extreme right was No. 6 Post, facing Qatia, before the first bending of the hook, and was held by 175 men under Captain E. A. Capel; next on the right was the 156th Brigade, to which the 5th Royal Welch Fusiliers were attached, and held in reserve.

Beyond the line of entrenched posts, out in the desert, was a cavalry screen. Ever since the 20th July, mounted patrols had been in touch with the enemy, as far afield as Oghratina, and when, on the 3rd August, von Kressenstein's intention was revealed, a strong cavalry outpost line was taken up from about Katib Gannit to Hod el Enna. The next morning the battle commenced, the cavalry retired, and the Turks attacked the bend of the fish-hook position.

In the time table of events, von Kressenstein launched his troops at 3.30 a.m. against the line of mounted outposts above the gullies that cut into the tumbled area of sand dunes south of Romani from the flatter desert. Our two cavalry regiments fell back from Hod el Enna to Mount Meredith, a high sand dune midway between Hod el Enna and Katib Gannit; here they repulsed a bayonet charge.

Again they fell back to Wellington Ridge, between Mount Meredith and Katib Gannit. Von Kressenstein's troops now worked south, the cavalry retiring before them.

General Lawrence, who was in command at Romani, seeing how the Turks were curling round his line, ordered two mounted brigades to move against the Turkish flank—one from Dueidar towards Hod el Enna, the other to follow from Hod el Aras, whilst infantry, from the 42nd Division, advanced from Pelusium Station. Also Sir A. Murray directed the mobile column under Lt.-Colonel Smith, V.C., to move from Ferdan against the enemy's left rear, towards Mageibra and Bir Aweidiya.

The party of Herefords in No. 6 Post were on the extreme left of this attack. They were first bombed by aeroplanes, about 5 a.m., and an hour later were subjected to heavy artillery fire. No enemy was seen until 7 a.m., when infantry was observed moving south. No direct attacks were made on the post, but it was again and again subjected to a heavy bombardment by six-inch guns, which caused a number of casualties.

At mid-day, Captain Capel was able to direct artillery fire on Turks seen massing in the distant desert; and a little later an attempt was made by the enemy to advance against Posts 4, 5, and 6. The 5th Royal Welch Fusiliers were ordered up by the 156th Brigade. But there was not much behind the Turkish attack, which threatened for about three hours, and then melted away. Isolated bodies tried to advance against No. 6 Post, but never got very close. This state of affairs lasted all the afternoon; our artillery fired at many and various targets, and the Herefords fired on any Turk within range, " but it became increasingly obvious that we were hardly in the picture."

Mid-day marked the high point of the Turkish advance. At that time they extended from Bir Abu Diyuk, along the southern part of Wellington Ridge, and then bent round the east and north facing our southern posts. The cavalry bore the brunt of the fight. General Lawrence had hoped that infantry reinforcements would be available at Pelusium Station, but there had been some delay in moving them up, and the full weight of the Turkish attack had to be sustained by the mounted troops. Some of those destined for the flanking movement had to be diverted to strengthen the line.

But, by four o'clock, two battalions of the East Lancashire Regiment had arrived on the scene, and with Yeomanry and New Zealand mounted troops were launched to a counter attack which swept the Turks from Mount Royston (a hill about two miles south of Pelusium Station), and from part of the Wellington Ridge. Darkness put an end to further manœuvre.

" As the morning light rapidly drove away the darkness, and disclosed the desert once more to the Turks on Wellington Ridge, this was the spectacle that presented itself. Immediately before them, across the Ridge, lay lines of the 8th Cameronians with bayonets fixed, prepared to assault. Behind the 8th Cameronians was a company of Royal Welch Fusiliers (D. Coy. 5th R.W.F.) being brought up in support to the right of the firing line. To the right flank of the Turks was a company of the 7th Cameronians, already working round either to enfilade or attack them in flank. Below, on the desert, to the west and south, were innumerable parties of mounted troops commencing to move eastward. . . . The Cameronians commenced to advance with the bayonet, and this decided the matter. The Turks

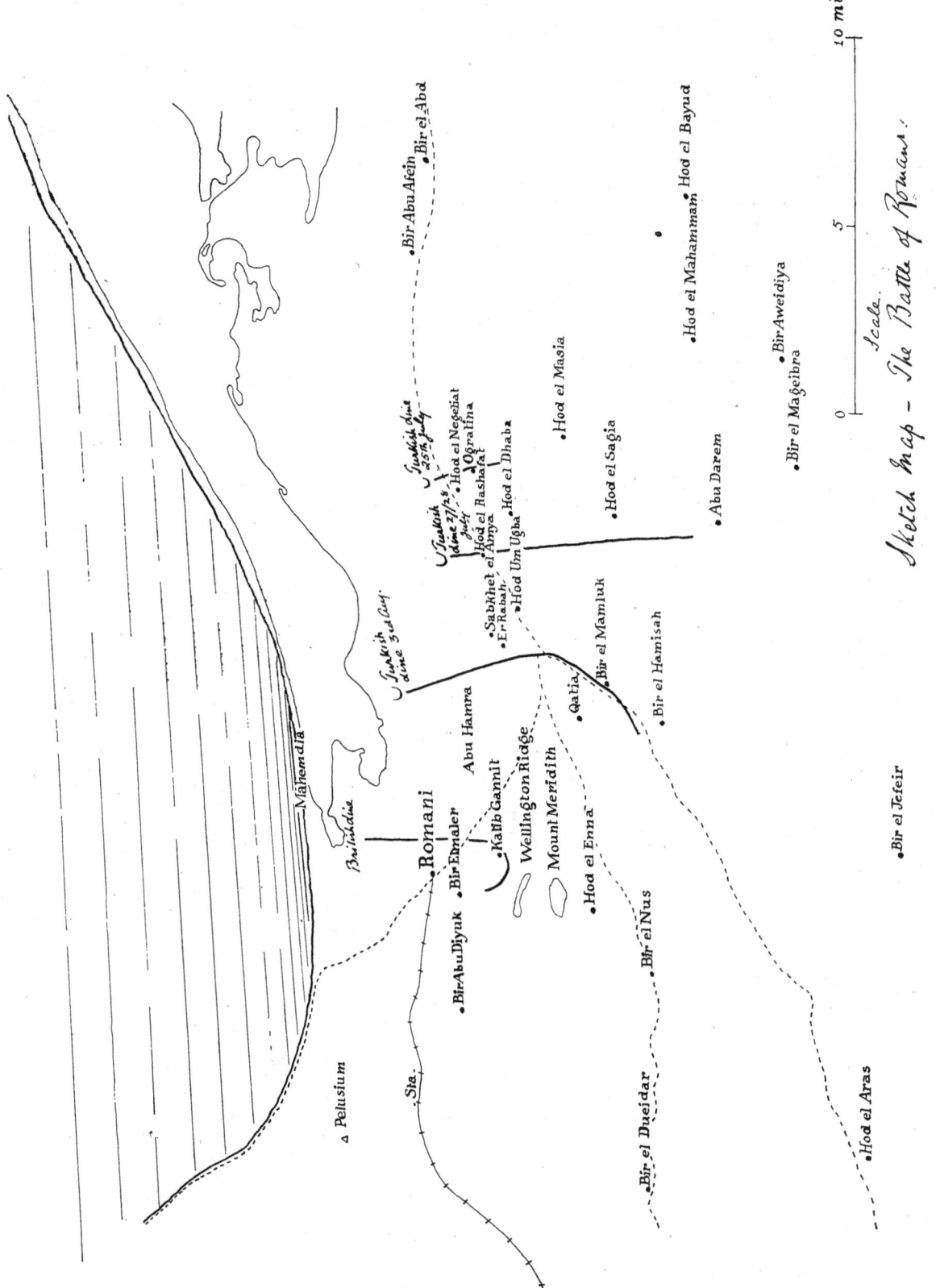

Sketch Map – The Battle of Romani

put up the white flag. . ." [The 52nd (Lowland) Division—Lt.-Colonel R. R. Thompson, M.C.].

Cavalry and infantry pressed forward in pursuit of the retreating Turks, but the 158th Brigade was ordered to remain in the Romani position.

The enemy fell back on the positions he had prepared during his advance. Smith's mobile column pushed forward from Ferdan to Bir el Mageibra, and hung on to the Turkish flank. And on the 5th Major de Knoop attacked Hod el Muhammam and captured a number of the enemy.

The Battle of Romani was the last serious effort to oppose a British advance across the desert, and inflicted heavy casualties on the Turks, also a loss of some 4,000 prisoners.

. . . . .

FERDAN AND QANTARA

On the 14th August, the 158th Brigade returned to the Canal, where the whole division (less a battery at Minia) was now concentrated, with headquarters at Ismailia.

Ferdan was the home of the 158th Brigade for the next three months. Battalions were some miles apart, but though Ferdan was nothing but a ferry, and a swing bridge, a certain amount of comfort was obtained through "security of tenure," Brigadier-General Mott having decided that it was not worth while changing the battalions round. Those who were on the edge of the Canal would sit on the banks in the cool of the evening and watch large steamers cautiously make their way up and down, with all lights on, orchestras playing, ladies singing! All ranks bathed daily. The weather, generally, was cooler and consistent. In the morning a slight breeze blew from the south-west, and dropped about 7 a.m. From 7 to 9 a.m. seemed the hottest part of the day. Then the breeze came from the north, and continued steadily until 7 p.m. The nights were absolutely calm.

The routine of duty may have been boring, but there were compensations. Thus the 160th Brigade :—" From Qantara we went occasionally to Port Said for the day. As we journeyed home the sun was setting. In the foreground was just the huge expanse of lake, scrub and salt pans. One laughs at the gold, sapphire and ruby idea, but I tell you the colours were deeper and beyond description. Yellow and orange sky, silver and blue water, green and grey scrub. Then, as the light changes, flame coloured sky, a silver band of water in the distance, a great tract of purple scrub, and the nearer expanses of water partly pink and gold reflections, and partly Cambridge blue. . . .

" The hospitable French Club at Ismailia !—Ismailia itself a perfect little French township, with appropriate two storied houses, plainly but tastefully built, tree shaded, with deep verandahs over which climbed innumerable plants. Bougainvillea, hibiscus and roses splash the gardens with rich colours. Through the trees is a glimpse of the Lake Timsah, a deep blue bounded by blazing golden sand. On moonlit nights, as one dined at the Club, or the Café Belge, the trees were silhouetted in filagree against the sky, sweet scents came stealing over from the gardens, and peace and content drove away the troubles of the moment.

" At Qantara, the town of tents, huts and dumps, bathing in the Canal, and riding along its banks, were the chief antidotes to care. Passengers on passing liners used to throw tins of cigarettes to the men in the water below."

" One curious duty was the keeping of the ' swept track ' This was a broad track in the sand along the canal bank, and was produced by dragging a very wide brush of branches by mules up and down to meet our next door neighbour. This was done each evening, and each morning a patrol proceeded along it to see if it had been crossed during the night by nefarious feet. The authorities were afraid that a very small enemy patrol might get through with camels and a mine, and drop it in the Canal."

MAGHARA

The only other active operation to note in the year was in October, when General Dallas was ordered to concentrate a special column at Bayoud and attack Maghara. " The fundamental principle underlying the organisation of the column was that every soldier had a mount, either horse, mule, or camel." The column included a machine gun, and Lewis gun detachment from the 160th Brigade. The Turks were encountered in the early morning of the 15th but, owing to a heavy fog which delayed troops and greatly hampered movement generally, no definite result was attained. Brigadier-General Mott commanded a part of the column.

. . . . .

THE WATER PROBLEM

The railway and pipe line pushed steadily forward, and in front of a labouring, sweating army, directed and helped by sappers, an ever-moving fan-shaped screen of mounted troops patrolled near and far. In November,

A CAMP SCENE. [*War Museum.*

[*War Museum.*
WIRE NETTING TRACK ACROSS THE SINAI DESERT.

when the railway reached Mazar, the outer edge of the protecting fan was three miles from El Arish.

In his despatch, which covers this half-year, Sir A. Murray draws attention to the hundreds of miles of road and railway that were built, and water piping that was laid; to filters dealing with a million and a half gallons of water a day; and to the quantities of stone that had to be transported from distant quarries. Qantara which had been a small and insignificant canal village, was now an important railway and water terminus; and laps across the desert were marked by standing camps of huts, by tanks, reservoirs, railway stations, aerodromes, signal stations, etc.

Water was the problem that had to be solved—water in abundance—together with direct and speedy communication across the desert. During November, before the pipe line reached Romani, water was brought up by rail, in tank trucks; when the pipe line delivered at Romani the situation was relieved, but difficulties again increased until the pipe delivered at Bir el Abd.

"But as the month advanced, the water question presented itself more insistently than ever," Sir A. Murray confesses. The enemy, at el Arish, covered all the local supply, and if the operation of dislodging him was to occupy two days, as a basis of staff arrangements, it would be necessary to forward very large quantities of water on camels for the men and animals engaged. No doubt the quantities appeared, at that time, alarming, but it is interesting to note that far more elaborate arrangements were made at a later date with complete success.

On the 20th December, Sir A. Murray was prepared to strike, but the enemy vanished; the Turks evacuated el Arish, and took up a position on the Wadi el Arish, where they were attacked by mounted troops under General Chauvel. The action was successful, but at one time the water question seemed likely to defeat the General's well-planned turning movement, for it was reported that unless Maghdaba could be taken within the day a withdrawal would be necessary as the horses had not been watered since the evening of the 22nd—the action being fought on the 23rd. Fortunately, all resistance was overcome by 4.30 p.m.

This success was repeated by the mounted troops under General Sir Philip Chetwode on the 9th January, when they captured an entire force in and about Rafah.

By the 31st December, the Province of Sinai was free.

By the end of February the continuous pressure of the mounted troops caused the enemy to withdraw from Khan Yunis and the field was ready for the first battle of Gaza.

REORGANISATION OF THE 53RD DIVISION

By the end of August, the whole of the 53rd Division was located on the Canal. In November, having been organised on a camel transport basis,* the 160th Brigade started to march across the desert, the Division, less this Brigade, remaining as general reserve to the Eastern Force at Moascar.

Christmas Day was celebrated by the 158th and 159th Brigades at Romani. A little extra food and a limited ration of beer had been brought up from Port Said. The 160th were not so fortunate at Bir el Abd, where they woke " to the sound of the Padre's chime of bells (a number of pipe rings on a stand), a frugal Christmas, perforce, as no one was allowed to go down the line to get Christmas fare, and the canteens had practically nothing. Then followed several days of rain, the men's only protection being their blankets, as they carried no waterproof sheets at that time."

Divisional headquarters spend Christmas at Mahemdia on the sea.

In December, the artillery settled down to its final state. The 2nd Welsh Brigade, which had been numbered 266th, was renumbered the 267th and reorganised into a two-battery brigade, six 18 pounders to each battery.† The 4th Welsh Brigade, had been numbered 268th, and was now renumbered 266th, and was given two batteries of six 18 pounders and one of four 4.5 Howitzers. The 1st Cheshire Brigade had been numbered 267th, and was now renumbered 265th, with two 18 pounder batteries and one Howitzer battery. The 1st Welsh (How.) Brigade disappeared, one battery going to the 265th and one to 266th (there were only two). The two howitzer batteries displaced the equivalent of two 18 pounder batteries, which were turned into Depot sections.

---

* The Transport animals of an infantry battalion were 12 horses (riding), 29 pack mules (or horses), 110 camels. The camels had 36 native drivers, and were allotted 102 fanatis (a receptacle for water—two to each camel).

A Field Battery of four guns (or hows.) had 37 riding and 96 draught horses; 17 camels, 7 drivers, 14 fanatis.

No. 1 Section Divisional Ammunition Column had 15 riding and 72 draught horses, 250 camels, 94 drivers, 18 fanatis. No. 2 Section: 15 riding horses, 324 camels, 120 drivers, 18 fanatis. A Field Coy. R.E. had 14 riding horses, 69 camels, 25 drivers, 18 fanatis. A Field Ambulance had 14 riding horses, 94 mules, 233 camels, 135 drivers, also 22 sand carts, and 150 pairs cacolets (a kind of pannier arrangements for patients, two to each camel).

† In April, 1918, this Brigade received a howitzer battery C/267.

Brigadier-General Short commanded the Divisional Artillery until October, when Brigadier-General R. E. A. le Mottee took over.

In the higher command certain readjustments had been made. Sir A. Murray had moved his general headquarters from Ismailia to Cairo, and Lieut.-General Sir Charles Dobell assumed command of the Eastern Force at Ismailia.

Later, at the commencement of December, General Sir Philip Chetwode arrived, and was appointed to command the Desert Column, under Sir Charles Dobell.

. . . . .

On the 20th January, 1917, the Division marched from the Canal in two columns, and on the last day of the month Headquarters arrived at el Arish, while the 160th Brigade, which had rejoined on the line of march and was leading, arrived at Bardawil.

The location of the Division on that day is given as el Arish, with detached troops as follows :—

267th R.F.A.	Southern Canal Section.
53rd Divn. Cyclists	(Tineh) Northern Section.
53rd Casualty Clearing Station	Northern Section.
53rd Artillery Depot	Qantara.
1st Welsh Fld. Coy. R.E.	,,
158th Brigade Transport Details	,,
53rd Divn. Artillery Depot	Romani.
53rd Divn. Depot Battalion	,,

GENERAL SITUATION

During the months of January-March, 1917.

Battle of Kut begins, 9th January.

German unrestricted submarine warfare begins, 1st February.

United States of America sever diplomatic relations with Germany, 3rd February.

Kut reoccupied by British, 23rd February.

Baghdad occupied by British, 11th March.

Russian Revolution begins, 12th March.

German retirement to Hindenburg Line begins, 14th March.

Tsar abdicates, 15th March.

Austria makes secret peace proposals to France, 31st March.

PALESTINE

FIRST BATTLE OF GAZA
"Y DDRAIG GOCH DDYRY GYCHWYN"

THE march across the desert "had nothing to relieve the monotony, so much in keeping with the surroundings; yet for some of us the desert grew to have a certain charm—the feeling of wide space, a horizon beyond which lay mystery, the amazing quiet and stillness around. It is not without a kind of wild beauty, especially at dawn and eventide, when the changing light catches the billowing sandhills, and shadows break up the burning waste. Then, when you come in from a ride which has taken you out of sight and hearing of human beings, there is something so homelike in the camp, something comforting about the twinkle of a fire and the snugness of tent or bivouac."—(Le Fleming.)

It was not always possible to see the scarce and welcome group of palm trees round a well. "We passed through three oases with date palms and wells, only about 200 yards square, and all completely hidden below the surface of the surrounding country. All the sand hereabouts is in ridges, all sloping the same way, N.W. to S.E., and one sees a huge sand dune and just below it, stuck away under the steep bank, the trees, or Hod, as it is called."—(H. E. P. Pateshall.)

The crossing of the Wadi el Arish, the old River of Egypt and nature's boundary, was an experience few will forget. The change was magical! From waste to growth, from sand to green grass. "For the first time, practically, since leaving England we were moving on grass again. The same main features of country persist right up to Gaza. Next to the sea there stretches a continuous band of high, soft sand hills, varying in width from one to five miles; next to the sand dunes comes a green valley, again of varying width, a corridor, as it were, up which runs the so-called road, trodden by innumerable soldiers from back in the dim past to Napoleon. Further inland high ground rises, passing to rolling downland, mostly cultivated, with patches of sand and scrub, gradually relapsing into desert again to the south-east. On the 25th (February) we marched on nine miles to Sheikh Zowaiid, and found the grass much better and the flowers brighter at every step. It really was like going on a holiday to have such surroundings to live in rather than the everlasting sand."—(Ashton.)

It must be remembered that this was the best time of year, after the rains, when grass and flowers grew strongly until they were scorched by the sun, and parched by the drought.

THE INVASION OF PALESTINE

At the beginning of March, General Chetwode had his headquarters at Sheikh Zowaiid, and his mounted troops were covering the construction of the railway along the coast to Rafah; Sir Charles Dobell had the Eastern Force in the neighbourhood of el Arish. By the middle of the month, the railway and pipe line were in Rafah, and Sir A. Murray considered the time had come to strike a blow at the enemy, who, after working for weeks on a strong position at Weli Sheikh Nuran, suddenly withdrew to the line Gaza-Tel el Sheria-Bir Sabe (Beersheba).

The mind of the Home Government had never been decided on the policy to be pursued in this theatre of war. Now, at the beginning of 1917, the order was for pressure on all fronts, but Sir A. Murray, while urged to press the enemy, was deprived of the 42nd Division, which was sent to France in February (less transport) and his instructions did not go so far as an advance into Palestine. Still, the matter had to be considered by him.

Brushing all local incidents aside, the general configuration of Palestine is a series of four parallel features. Between the sea and the great Arabian Desert there is a long Maritime Plain, a central range of mountains, the Jordan Valley and the eastern range of mountains. The only necessary modification to this broad view of Palestine is a break in the central range, where the Plain of Esdraelon connects the Maritime Plain with the Jordan Valley. From his position on the coast, at the edge of the desert, the whole of this country lay before Sir A. Murray.

The Turkish left was at Beersheba, away east, at the foot of the central range and on the edge of the desert; the British troops were collected at railhead, on the coast, with their lines of communication running back through the Province of Sinai along the coastal route. Sir A. Murray decided that it would be unwise to risk adventure in the direction of Beersheba, it would mean drawing his lines of communication across the enemy front. He considered that his communications would be more easily protected along the coast, that railway construction was faster, water more plentiful, and the enemy would be as effectively threatened.

So he reconstructed the Desert Column, which now consisted of the Australian and New Zealand Mounted Division, the Imperial Mounted

Division (each less one brigade), and the 53rd Welsh Division. With his other two infantry divisions, the 52nd and 54th, in the position of support, but not too far from railhead, and with a general re-arrangement of the transport he considered he could place Gaza within the radius of action of the Desert Column.

He decided to strike his blow at Gaza.

. . . . .

RECONNAISSANCE

The cavalry screen spread out far towards Gaza without molestation, and with it rode Brigadiers, Commanding Officers, and Regimental Officers reconnoitring the country. " They were rather jolly outings. One would make one's way slowly and steadily out all morning, till one reached the desired spot, when one would have a real good look with glasses and a map. A picnic lunch followed, and an hour's easy, and one would start off home again, and everything was so green and fresh with the ground fairly covered with little scarlet tulips."—(Ashton.)

" Forty mile rides, these mostly at a sharp walk with a five minutes' halt every hour, and half an hour for lunch. One swished through green barley, and jogged over newly scratched—one cannot call it ploughed—Bedouin tillage, skirted a Bedouin encampment, with barking dogs and murmuring women, while tall, dignified, and dusky men watched one go by with curiosity not unmixed with apprehension, though they were trying hard to hide both in the usual Arab fashion. Here and there were little patches of scrub, little groups of purple iris, perhaps an occasional tree. There was something most attractive about these reconnaissances. The Turks adopted the rule of watching rather than ' straffing,' which added to the attraction."—(Le Fleming.)

Reconnoitring parties found no difficulty in getting up to and across the Wadi Ghuzze,* one of the great features of the country. The soil, in those parts, is a sandy loam, and the volume of water, brought by the heavy winter rains, seeking its natural course from the inland heights of the Judean Hills has cut deep into this light soil. The Wadi Ghuzze is the most important of these great draining ditches, dry, of course, for the greater part of the year. It is wide, and has steep mud cliffs. From the coast the line of the Wadi runs in a south-easterly direction, and it receives, mostly from the rolling down-like country on its northern bank, a great number of minor tributaries; the longer tributaries have, in their

* The Royal Geographical Society gives the name Ghazzi.

turn feeding slots, all well defined, biting deep into the soil which, through centuries, has been unable to resist the wash of the gathering water. So, in the vicinity of the Wadi Ghuzze, there are innumerable nullahs cutting across the country up to the water-shed to the north of it. One great branch, the Wadi Sheria, strikes to the east, then forks towards Sheria and Beersheba; further inland a second branch, the Wadi Saba, leads to Beersheba itself.

As one journeys from el Arish along the high road to Gaza, before arriving at the steep banks of the Wadi, the high ground on the right culminates at In Seirat; and then, on the opposite bank, the ground rises straight from the Wadi to the el Sire Ridge, which runs along the right of the road to Gaza, the sand dunes being on the left.

On the highest point of the el Sire Ridge, overlooking Gaza, is the mosque of Ali Muntar. This marks the end of the ridge. The el Sire Ridge, with the green valley of the high road mark a definite line between the sand dunes of the coast and the gully strewn country inland. Hundreds of gullies drain the high ground that runs parallel to the Wadi Ghuzze, and at right angles to the el Sire Ridge. The left of this watershed is marked by Kh. Mansura, and the right by Sheikh Abbas: a curious sort of bank, like the edge of a dried up lake, runs between these two points. Looking over the edge of this bank one sees the Mosque of Ali Muntar and the slopes of the el Sire Ridge across an open valley. There is no cover of any sort for troops crossing this valley; they simply have to plug along down the hill and then up a long, bare glacis to the crest, and there, round the mosque, is the first cover, the cactus hedges that enclose the gardens and olive groves which encircle Gaza—the olive groves of Gaza are exceedingly attractive, and give to its outskirts a wooded appearance. But the line of advance from Mansura to the first cactus hedges, round Ali Muntar and east of Gaza, is not too good. To the right of Mansura is a wide, rolling plain.

The Turks held the two end high points of the el Sire Ridge—Green Hill and Ali Muntar—and another hill, not of the ridge, but which stands like a dot at the end of a line, Clay Hill; and to the west, on the far side of the ridge, they were entrenched amongst the cactus hedges, in what was known as the Labyrinth; and so across the sand dunes to the sea. The cactus hedges, tall, thick, and impenetrable, formed an important part of the defences of the town—they were most formidable obstacles, and gave excellent cover.

A great deal of all this could be seen by the reconnoitring parties.

[War Museum.

A TURKISH TRENCH AT GAZA.

CACTUS HEDGES, GAZA.

The operation contemplated by Sir A. Murray was similar to that which had been so successfully carried out at Rafah—a large, cutting out raid, which was to gather in the entire garrison of Gaza, but not necessarily to hold the place.

THE PLAN OF ACTION

The scheme, as set forth in a memorandum drawn up by General Dallas, was as follows :—

"On the night of the 25/26th (March) the position of the Desert Column and the 54th Division will be as follows : The 53rd Division east of Deir el Belah and north of the Rafah-Gaza road ; the 54th Division south of the 53rd Division holding the el Taire Hills ; the Australian and New Zealand Mounted Division, and the Imperial Mounted Division west of Deir el Belah.

"On the morning of the 26th inst., as soon as it is light enough to see clearly, the two cavalry divisions will cross the Wadi Ghuzze south of el Breij, and will press forward rapidly and take up a position east of Gaza as follows, vigorously brushing aside all resistance : The Australian and New Zealand Mounted Division from the sea, near Wadi Hesi, through Deir Sineid,* Negile, to Huj ; the Imperial Mounted Division from Huj, through Khirbet el Resum to the Gaza-Beersheba Road : They will establish their headquarters, the A. & N.Z. Mounted Division at Beir Durdis, and Imperial Mounted Division at Kh. er Reseim.

"The 53rd Division will push over the Wadi Ghuzze between the Rafah-Gaza main road and el Breij, for which purpose it will seize the necessary bridgehead.

"The 54th Division will follow the Cavalry Division across the Wadi south of el Breij, and go forward and occupy the Sheikh Abbas position. The Imperial Camel Corps will cross the Wadi near Tel el Jemmi, and clear the right front of the 54th Division.

"The Mounted Divisions will mask the attack on Gaza, which will be carried out by the 53rd Division. They will prevent the enemy from attacking the 53rd Division whilst operating against its objective,

* Deir Sneid, *R.G.S.*

and should the enemy move out from his position from Huj, Negile,* or from the Sheria-Hureira* region, they will counter attack and hold them in front, at the same time vigorously counter attacking him on his flank.

"It is intended to carry out the objective assigned to the 53rd Division as follows :—

(*a*) to hold the enemy to his works, which extend from Gaza to the sea, by a small force of one battalion, one cavalry regiment, and a section of artillery ;

(*b*) with the remainder of the Division to operate against the Ali Muntar position and the enemy's left.

"The bulk of the division will, therefore, cross the Wadi Ghuzze between el Sire and el Breij, having first seized the southwest end of the el Sire Ridge as a bridgehead. As soon as the bridgehead has been secured, and the crossing of the division can be pushed forward it will be necessary to secure the Ali Muntar-el Sire Ridge as far as el Sheluf on the north and the hills Tel el Ahmar-Mansura on the south.

"The Division, having reached the el Sheluf-Mansura position, visual reconnaissance will be made of the enemy's position about Ali Muntar, and arrangements made for the attack of that position.

"The Detachment already mentioned as operating in the sand hills west of Rafah-Gaza main road will consist of one cavalry regiment, one battalion of infantry, and a 60-pdr. section of artillery. The cavalry and infantry of this detachment will mainly demonstrate against the enemy's right from Gaza to the sea, with the object of preventing him reinforcing his left in the Ali Muntar region. Great vigilance will be exercised by the commander of this force, who will, if attacked, give stout resistence, to enable the 60-pdr. section to withdraw south of the Wadi Ghuzze. Should the enemy compel him to retreat, he will take up delaying positions and fight his way slowly back, reporting his action direct to divisional headquarters, repeating to his own Brigade commander. He will be supported by fire, if necessary, from the brigade operating on the Ali Muntar-el Sire spur.

"The mass of artillery will be employed in enfilading the enemy's works which face southeast and east of Ali Muntar which it is intended to attack. It is believed that Gaza is not strongly held, and it is therefore intended to push the attack with great vigour. The amount of

* Sometimes Hareira and Negileh.

ammunition available does not admit of any prolonged bombardment, and the intention, therefore, is to keep the Labyrinth well under fire, and to attack that portion of the works on the east and south-east after a short bombardment."

The supply arrangements were that the 53rd Division would move off complete with six days' rations. They were to be carried in three echelons.

> 1 day—A echelon, 42nd Divisional Train, temporarily allotted to the 53rd Division ;
> 1 day—B echelon—Train improvised from 53rd Division 1st Line transport (72 limbers and 10 G.S. wagons) ;
> 1 day—C echelon—camel convoy (600 camels from desert column).

A further three days' "emergency" ration was carried by certain 1st line transport camels which were temporarily withdrawn from units for that purpose.

In his despatch, Sir A. Murray explains that "the enemy's main body was in the Tel el Nejile-Huj area, south of the Wadi el Hesi, covered by detachments about Gaza, Sheria-Hureira, and Bir Sabe (Beersheba). His strength appears to be between two and three divisions.

" The object of this advance was three fold : firstly, to seize the line of the Wadi Ghuzze to cover the advance of the railway ; secondly, at all costs to prevent the enemy from retiring without a fight ; thirdly, if possible, to capture Gaza by a coup-de-main and to cut off its garrison." The last explains the nature of the preparations and the thought in the minds of the two Generals, Dobell and Chetwode. The garrison of Gaza was believed to be the 79th, 128th, and 2/81st Regiments with artillery, a total of 4,000 men. Actually, it was rather less. Liman von Sanders gives the strength, at the date of the battle, as 125th and 79th Regiments, and the 2nd battalion of the 81st regiment—seven battalions in all—two Austrian Howitzer batteries, two 10 c.m. guns from the Turkish warship Pasha I, and two Turkish field batteries.

When the Commander-in-Chief's plans became known the general atmosphere in the camp messes was charged with increasing excitement. The ordinary routine of life was disturbed. Staff Captains talked of supply echelons ; " G," absorbed in higher matters, found time to curse the inadequate supply of inaccurate maps ; Commanding Officers commenced to fidget and fume ; Quartermasters insisted on the hardness of their lot, and the magnitude of their tasks ; Adjutants were pestered with questions written and verbal—only the private soldier remained serene and undisturbed.

The whole division had assembled in the vicinity of Sheikh Zowaiid on the 27th February; they moved to Rafah on the 21st March.

THE ADVANCE MARCH

On the morning of the 24th March, "a mixed cavalcade cantered through the streets of the old frontier town of Khan Yunis, it was an advance party of British officers seeking out for their units hiding places in the shady fruit groves surrounding the town. It was our first real glimpse of the 'promised land.' On all sides were groves of fig trees, mish-mish, olives and oranges, protected by high impenetrable hedges of prickly pear. On the north this green gem ends abruptly in a bright golden setting of sandhills, beyond which lies the deep blue Mediterranean. An old crusaders' fort raises its tower above the surrounding squalor of mud huts. As we clattered through the lane, for it was scarcely a road, running through the centre of the town, savage looking but stately Bedouins gaze at us with curious eyes, and no doubt spies on the roof tops took a more technical interest in our passing."

The orchards and groves on the Gaza side of Khan Yunis extend for over a mile, and the 53rd Division, moving forward to take up its allotted position, found concealment there from enemy aircraft. Colonel Sinclair Thompson, the G.S.O.I., pointed out to each officer the definite area for his unit. Roads had to be cut through cactus hedges, and mud walls, and the troops moved in during the evening.

The two mounted divisions were already there, and that night the 54th Division marched into Rafah.

The next day, the 53rd moved on, late in the afternoon, to Deir el Belah. "On the evening of March 25th, the Division left its hiding place amongst the fruit trees of Khan Yunis. Slowly we moved across the plain, columns of infantry, winding lines of artillery, ambulance carts, camel transport and wagons. It was a beautiful evening with a blood-red sunset and strange but lovely colour effects. Soon the infantry were in thick yielding sand, plunging along, stumbling and cursing in the dark. At midnight we rested for two hours on a sand ridge, just above a tomato patch."

The whole army took up its final disposition prior to the battle; two mounted divisions and the 53rd at Deir el Belah, the camel brigade at

Abassan el Kebir; the 54th Division on the el Taire hill; the 52nd Division at Khan Yunis, with one brigade at In Seirat.

General Dallas' orders were that the division should move in brigade columns across the Wadi Ghuzze; first, the 160th Brigade (less 2/4 Royal West Kent), with one section of Engineers, and one sub-section of the Field Ambulance, were to cross the Wadi at 3.30 a.m., and "make good the el Sire Ridge for a depth of about 2,000 yards." This brigade was to be followed by the 265th Brigade R.F.A., and the right section of the 10th Heavy Battery R.G.A.

"On we went, across the cultivation, the silence only broken by the rustle of barley, the creak of artillery limbers and the clink of equipment." The crossing of the Wadi was completed some ten or fifteen minutes after the scheduled time.

Then the 158th Brigade, with a section of Engineers and a bearer detachment, followed by the 266th Field Artillery Brigade, was to cross the Wadi at 3.45 a.m. On the previous day (25th), the Brigadier (Mott) had reconnoitred the ground. "Brigadiers and their parties from all the divisions were present, and we sat on the forward slope of In Seirat while the Major General expounded in person, and finally allotted rôles to the Brigadiers. We then went down to the Wadi, and reconnoitred routes and crossings again, had lunch, and finally surveyed a route most carefully from our particular Wadi crossing back to the starting place, behind Druid's Hill, north of Deir Belah. It was an infernally difficult route, as various small wadis had to be crossed, but we got it pretty clear, with plenty of notes and compass bearings. However, we were not destined to use it. At 6 p.m., we got back to the Brigade's new area, and found the Brigade just in, having been marched off from Khan Yunis by old Green, as the senior officer left. At 9 p.m., after I had nearly wrecked the success of the whole operation by giving permission for fires to be lighted, which brought out an infuriated divisional staff, like wasps from their nests, we got a message that we were not to proceed by our carefully chosen route, but by one marked out by the C.R.E.—strips of canvas laid on the ground, and all picked up and thrown away by some light-hearted Anzacs—and that a guide would be provided. The Brigadier pleaded to be allowed to lead his Brigade, but was refused, as orders could not be changed.

"At 10.40 p.m. voluminous orders arrived, some nine pages of closely typed foolscap. We did our best to assimilate this mass of literature and snatch a few minutes rest, but without any particular success in either case. However, we hung up the Brigade's red lamp, and punctually at

1 a.m., the head of the brigade, 5th R.W. Fusiliers, appeared; not so the guide! It was a fine, clear starlit night, with no moon, but not dark, and as we were moving through nearly fully grown barley and green crops, and there was a heavy dew, we were literally wading, drenched from the waist downwards. Still no sign of the guide, and not till I had rushed vainly hither and yon, for some time, did he appear, very hot and bothered, half an hour late.

"The guide, poor soul, was as bad as I ever met. His canvas marks were not there, and he hadn't really reconnoitred the route properly. We marched in line of battalions, at 50 yards interval, battalions in column of route, and the guide completely and utterly lost his way. We alternately cursed and cajoled him, feeling our way along with numerous halts, until the Brigadier decided to march on a compass bearing which eventually brought us to the rendezvous, the el Breij hut, a tumble down place with a few evil looking Bedouins living in it, about half a mile from the Wadi. Even then our guide lost his way again before we reached the Wadi crossing. However, we did find a crossing of some sort, and got over at 4.35 a.m., nearly an hour late, and dawn breaking."

THE FOG

After that beautiful starlit night there came, with the dawn, a rolling fog from the sea that effectively postponed the light of day. Colonel Pateshall, in a letter written on the 24th, mentioned a thick fog that morning which lasted until 10 a.m., so that it was not a phenomenal occurrence. It caused delay, and a great deal of anxiety, but whether its effect was fatal to the operation is a moot point. Apparently, two fighting hours of daylight were lost; but, on the other hand, the first news that reached the Turks of the advance was at 8 o'clock, and it was brought to Tel es Sheria.

The order for the mounted divisions was to cross the Wadi "as soon as it was light enough to see clearly," and they were already on the move when the fog rolled in—it does not seem to have hindered them to any extent.

The 2nd Light Horse Brigade, riding on a compass bearing, were able to gallop a Turkish patrol in the neighbourhood of Sheikh Abbas, just before 8 o'clock, and they saw aeroplanes on the ground a few hundred yards off which succeeded in taxi-ing away. This Brigade was at Beit Durdis at 9 o'clock, and had occupied Jabalieh by 10.30. At that hour the whole of the Anzac Division may be said to have been in position; and they had captured the G.O.C. and Staff of the Turkish 53rd Division who were driving quite quietly and comfortably into Gaza.

In rear of the Anzac Division the Imperial Mounted Division were delayed over broken ground, but were in contact with the enemy near Kh. el Baha and Hureira about 9.45 a.m.

The masking of Gaza by the cavalry had been done swiftly and successfully.

The fog did not affect the movements of all infantry units. The 160th Brigade, with the Sussex leading, had occupied a favourable position on the el Sire Ridge by 5 a.m., but the 158th Brigade were retarded—the fog caught them before they had crossed the Wadi.

"Having got across and orientated ourselves by a building which we had noted the day before, we took a compass bearing, nearly due east, and started for Burjaliye. The Brigadier (Mott) produced the most amazing fine leading. Dashing off on a horse, and aided by a natural sense of country, he led the Brigade, 5th R.W. Fusiliers leading, straight to our next objective, my job being to keep touch between the Brigadier and the head of the 5th Fusiliers. It was quite a feasible route, too, for we took with us the signallers cable wagon, a large heavy affair.

"We occupied the high ground at Burjaliye, and reported our safe arrival to the Division. As they had nothing to say we pushed on to Tel el Ahmar, a small, flat hill in the middle of the most desperately broken country, and arrived there at 7.45 a.m. The fog had now lifted. Two Turkish aeroplanes rose from the flat ground ahead of us, and the sound of trumpets was heard in the direction of Gaza (at 8.30), although the alarm was probably given by Bedouins whom we bumped up against in the fog. Here we waited for a spell, and got into touch with the 160th Brigade, up on the ridge to our left, who had got as far as el Sheluf. The Major-General arrived, very full of life and spirits, and had a look round. Finally, at 9 o'clock we advanced again, and came to a rest at the cliff edge of Mansura, with the open plain to the east of Gaza in front of us. It was like being inside an enormous and very shallow gravel pit, and looking over the side the ground stretched practically flat, straight away from the level of our eyes. It was a most excellent place, completely hidden from view of Gaza and its defences, and the Brigade sat down and took a long breath."—(Ashton.)

The 159th Brigade had crossed the Wadi in rear of the 158th, and were in a covered position by half past six. The Brigadier (Travers) asked repeatedly for orders to move, but was met by the reply " no orders to move." At 9.30 he was ordered to go to a conference at Mansura, and after instructing Colonel Kinsman (4th Welch) to lead the Brigade, he joined the Divisional Headquarters.

The conference called by General Dallas was according to plan, for all orders to the infantry beyond the Mansura-Sheluf line were to be issued after a "visual reconnaissance." At the conference, General Travers pointed out that his brigade could not possibly get to Mansura under 1½ hours, and the C.R.A., General le Mottée, when asked how long it would take to get his guns in position stated "two hours," from which it appeared probable that the attack would start about 12.30 p.m. As a matter of fact, both artillery brigades were in position when the question was asked.

"The Major-General again allotted jobs to brigades, ours being to 'attack from the east on Ali Muntar,' with the 159th Brigade to the north-east, beyond us. C.O's were produced in their turn, and shown their respective jobs. All was, apparently, proceeding according to plan, and I had a desperate struggle to keep awake—suddenly the atmosphere changed!"—(Ashton, 158th Brigade.)

The change was due to the natural anxiety of General Chetwode. He had established his headquarters at In Seirat, next to those of General Dobell, with whom he was in constant consultation. He knew that the mounted troops were well on their way to the north of Gaza, and probably in position (as indeed they were), but he had no news of any advance by the infantry. About 10 o'clock, while General Dallas was holding his conference, and the Anzacs were closing in on the northern side of Gaza, he sent a telegram urging speed on the part of the infantry divisions. General Dallas replied that his guns were not up, but that a start would be made about mid-day.

The short written order for the attack was then issued—it does not tell very much :—

OPERATION ORDER NO. 26. 26/3/17.

The Division will attack the Ali Muntar position as follows :—

"160th Brigade along the main ridge from the southwest on Ali Muntar;

158th Brigade from the east, also on Ali Muntar;

159th Brigade, less one battalion, on the hill northeast of Ali Muntar, indicated to G.O.C. 159th Brigade, at the same time covering the right of the 158th Brigade.

The artillery of the division will support the attack under order of the C.R.A.

The G.O.C. 159th Brigade will detail one battalion in Divisional Reserve at Mansura."

General Dallas also asked the Eastern Force Command for the 161st Brigade, and the 271st Field Artillery Brigade which were being held to support him, if necessary; but the messenger he sent to lead them up could not find them—they had already moved, intending to go to Mansura, but had lost their way.

As time went on General Chetwode became more impatient, and at 11.30 sent another telegram, in more emphatic language, and it was then that the " atmosphere changed "—Brigadier-General Mott, who had not contemplated moving until 12.30, was abruptly ordered to advance.

THE ATTACK

The 5th Royal Welsh Fusiliers, with a strong patrol out ahead, led the 158th Brigade, while on the el Sire Ridge, General Butler advanced with the 160th Brigade.

At the time the attack was launched the Artillery was not in action, and the 159th Brigade which should have advanced on the right of the 158th had not yet arrived.

The 5th R.W. Fusiliers, after leaving the protecting rim of Mansura, had to march on a line parallel with the Ali Muntar defences until they were opposite their objective; they then wheeled left, and advanced on a two company front. They were followed by the 6th and 7th Battalions, each wheeling left when five hundred yards beyond the point of deployment of the last. The advance was over bare country, and across the open valley which lies between Mansura and the el Sire Ridge, and so up the long, smooth, glacis to the crest, and the Mosque of Ali Muntar. The country was so open that the whole manœuvre could be seen, not only by the Brigade staff, and the Turks, but by the mounted troops of the Anzac Division picquetting the hills on the far side of the Gaza-Beersheba road, in the direction of Huj and Beit Durdis.

" The three battalions moved out in fine style, and when opposite the various objectives, wheeled left handed and proceeded northwest towards the heights. The 5th R.W.F. naturally completed the wheel first, and advanced rapidly down a slight slope till they reached a small cactus encircled garden, about 800 yards from the crest of Ali Muntar. Thinking that the other two battalions were getting too far to the north, the Brigadier sent me out after them, and I passed the time of day with Rome and Harker, both full of spirits. The only sign of enemy opposition, so far, had been some very high shrapnel. Now rifle fire broke out from Green Hill and Ali Muntar, and the advance slowed down."—(Ashton.)

It seemed clear, from the volume of fire that had been opened, that Ali Muntar and Green Hill were strongly held. Colonel Borthwick (5th R.W.F.) found his battalion rather in the air—there was no one on his immediate left, and the battalion on his right was not yet up—so he decided to wait by the cactus garden.

" As the other two battalions (6th and 7th R.W.F.) got up in line, firing became general. It was then found that the Brigade had struck in too far to the north—too far for a fair and square frontal attack, and not far enough for a turning movement—with the result that the 5th were being fired on from the immediate front and also from Green Hill, their left front. After consultation with Colonel Borthwick, the Brigadier sent him up sundry sections of machine guns, and finally ordered the Herefords to attack Green Hill, past the left of the 5th R.W.F. At 1.45 the Herefords moved out."*

Meanwhile the 159th Brigade had arrived at Mansura, half an hour after the attack had been launched, and the 5th Welch and 4th Cheshires, straining every nerve to catch up and take their position on the right to attack Clay Hill, hurried down the slope, now and again at the double.

As the Herefords moved off to go in on the left, the 6th and 7th R.W.F. came up on the right of the 5th R.W.F. and the whole line of the 158th Brigade advanced; the 159th Brigade streaming in a diagonal line across their rear, making to extend the attack yet further to the right.

THE 160TH BRIGADE

While this was going on the 160th Brigade had come to a standstill. The three battalions advancing along the el Sire Ridge had a task hardly less formidable than the 158th and 159th Brigades. On their left was the Labyrinth, a system of trenches in and about a good deal of cactus hedge, and much cultivation—olive groves and so on. The Brigade advanced with the Sussex on the right and the Middlesex on the left—Queens in reserve.

* Lieut.-Colonel Drage denies that he was actually ordered to attack Green Hill. It may be that the difficulty of pointing out features caused an order to be given to prolong the left, although the clear intention of the Brigadier was that the Herefords should attack Green Hill. It will be seen that it took the whole of the 161st Brigade, with additional and fresh artillery support, to capture the hill later in the afternoon. The importance and actual physical size of this feature had been under-estimated.

At 1.30 the Middlesex reported that they had captured the whole of the Labyrinth, and had established themselves on a grass ridge about half a mile from the town, which places them down the slope of the main ridge towards Gaza; but their position is not really clear. They got into the cactus hedges and groves, and the artillery observers of the 265th Field Artillery Brigade report that " the initial assault seemed to be successful, and the Labyrinth and hedges seemed to be taken, but progress ceased about 2 p.m."

On the right the Sussex did not fare so well; they got into broken and difficult ground and suffered heavy casualties. Colonel Ashworth was killed, and they were unable to advance.

THE ARTILLERY ACTION

For the first three hours of the battle artillery support had not been good. Colonel Rome (6th R.W.F.) had sent repeated messages for artillery support against the crest of Ali Muntar, and comments that " the artillery was very slow indeed in picking up targets, and it is suggested in future that a Forward Observation Officer in direct communication with his battery is sent with each battalion commander."

The 266th R.F.A. Brigade at Mansura, and the 265th between the el Sire and Tel el Ahmar ridges, had commenced to fire about mid-day;* while on the banks of the Wadi Ghuzze one section of the 10th heavy battery was in action at the end of the el Sire Ridge, and the other near the Gaza-Rafah road. Their task it must be admitted was not easy. Because of difficulties of ammunition supply, only the Cheshire Brigade (265) and the 4th Welsh Brigade (266) were brought up to support the attack of the three infantry brigades,† and the dispositions were such that the 266th had to support two infantry brigades in line. There was no pre-arranged plan beyond that " the mass of the artillery will be employed in enfilading the enemy's works, which face southeast and east of Ali Muntar, which it is intended to attack "—enemy positions which were unknown.

The 265th R.F.A. Brigade had crossed the Wadi Ghuzze in rear of the 160th Infantry Brigade. Their instructions were that they would have to work through divisional headquarters, but they do not seem to have done so; they had officers forward, and were in communication with the

* Both these Artillery Brigades were in position, and had registered on Ali Muntar by 10 a.m.
† The third artillery brigade, deficient of a How. Battery, was kept on the Canal.

infantry Brigade Headquarters; they had no further orders from or communication with divisional headquarters, or the C.R.A.

Captain Barton, acting as Forward Observation Officer for B/265, says that there was a shortage of telephone cable. " I reported to Colonel Pearson (Middlesex) and when the order to advance was given followed the battalion, laying my cable and pausing from time to time to send information to the battery which was shelling the Labyrinth. For a time all went well; then I found myself at the end of my cable and no reserve to call for. We tried running out an extension by means of an enamelled wire, the thickness of stout thread and about as much use. Finally, I went on ahead of the telephonist and signalled back to him, but the difficulty of getting orders through in time to be effective by this means will be easily understood. During the battle my battery occupied no less than six different positions, lying far apart, and in exceptionally difficult country. Getting guns round or across the numerous wadis was the devil of a job." They expended 1,511 rounds during the day.

The 266th R.F.A. Brigade had the more difficult task, with two brigades of infantry deployed in front of them. Perhaps it was for this reason that General Dallas " gave personal instructions to the B.G.C. (Mott) that the artillery support would be under Divisional control, and that all requirements were to be made to Divisional Headquarters through brigade." On the other hand, the diary of the Divisional Artillery Headquarters states that " time did not admit of any detailed programme. All that could be done was to trust to information from the F.O.O.'s to bombard whatever parts of the enemy's works were holding up the infantry's advance. Neither the full extent of the enemy's line, nor his flanks had been accurately located." The complaint of all Commanding Officers of the 158th and 159th Infantry Brigades was, however, that the F.O.O.'s were conspicuous by their absence, and it is not to be wondered at, with seven battalions in line! It seems as though all information came from the infantry through Brigade, and so to the artillery. The diary complains that " during the whole afternoon conflicting reports as to the position of our infantry were received. Owing to this fact, and the fact that the amount of equipment available for communication between Divisional Artillery Headquarters and units was altogether insufficient, and to there being no accurate maps on a fairly large scale, it was very difficult to keep units informed of the situation. The method of communication during the afternoon was as follows :—

> 265th Brigade, by cable, laid by Divisional Signal Company;
> 266th Brigade, verbally."

Resting in Wadi Ghuzze, before the First Battle of Gaza.

Colonel Pearson's R.F.A. Brigade firing, at the First Battle of Gaza.

The Divisional Signal Company declare that they laid cables to four infantry brigades, two artillery brigades, and divisional ammunition column.

Be that as it may, the 159th Infantry Brigade had no artillery officers forward, and were much hampered by the lack of support at critical moments.

THE ATTACK HELD

About 2 p.m. the 158th Brigade was definitely held up before the cactus hedges crowning the summit of Ali Muntar Hill, and were being raked by flank fire from Green Hill, against which the attack of the Herefords had been unavailing—they had edged to the right. The time coincides with the check in the advance of the 160th Brigade on el Sire Ridge. But the 159th Brigade came up on the right of the 7th Royal Welch Fusiliers, with the 5th Welch and 4th Cheshires leading. As these two battalions advanced—the 4th Cheshires on the northern side of the Gaza-Beersheba road—a gap appeared between them, and the 4th Welch were sent to fill it. There was a good deal of overlapping, and the three battalions became mixed. The 159th Brigade carried the advance a bit further, but lacking artillery support of any kind, battalions were held up by Turks concealed behind the thick cactus hedges between Clay Hill and Ali Muntar —the machine gun fire was very heavy.

The attack of the 53rd Division had now come to a standstill.

REDISTRIBUTION OF MOUNTED TROOPS

Naturally, all these movements, the wheeling of battalions from the top of Mansura into line facing Gaza, took time. Already General Chetwode had been much exercised in mind over the effect the fog might have had on his plans. Soon after his exchange of messages with General Dallas he had placed General Chauvel in command of both the mounted divisions which were covering the advance of the infantry on Gaza, and had ordered him to attack the town.

The order necessitated a redistribution of troops, and General Chauvel directed the Camel Corps to take over from the Imperial Mounted Division who, in their turn, took over from the Anzac Division.

Troops had to move over a wide circle; hours passed. Again telegrams were despatched by General Chetwode, urging speed. But it was 4 o'clock before the Anzac Division commenced to move on the town—at 4 o'clock came the first news of Turkish movement, a long way off.

. . . . .

THE CAPTURE OF ALI MUNTAR

Meanwhile the 161st Infantry Brigade, which had been applied for by General Dallas about 10 o'clock in the morning, arrived at Mansura at 3.30 p.m. Apparently they had been ordered up by Eastern Force before General Dallas' messenger arrived, and had lost their way in the fog, which still hung about at that hour in the valleys, and had, eventually, found themselves at el Sire.

The arrival of this Brigade, with the 271st R.F.A. Brigade, enabled General Dallas to release the 7th Cheshires, held in Divisional Reserve, and also to give the much needed artillery support to the 159th Brigade.

The centre of resistance to the 159th Brigade was in the cactus hedges on Clay Hill and in the hollow below Ali Muntar Hill, where nests of machine guns had been distributed. It had not been possible to give General Travers any of the artillery assistance he called for so persistently, and rifle and machine gun fire was not enough to dislodge the enemy.

The 5th Welch on the flank of the Brigade, joining with the 158th, had suffered most heavily. Colonel H. R. Bowen, Major H. Southey, the Adjutant, and three Company Commanders were amongst the casualties. The 7th Cheshires were sent up to help them, while the 271st R.F.A. Brigade prepared to bombard the hedges.

But, before the effect of this reinforcement could be felt, Captain Walker, of the 7th Royal Welch Fusiliers, with Lieuts. Latham and Fletcher, and about 40 men, together with two officers, Captain A. H. Lee and Lieut. R. H. Taylor, of the 5th Welch, and an equal number of their men, organised on their own initiative a dash at the enemy's line. They rose suddenly from the ground and sprinted forward in a most gallant and inspiring fashion. The rush was so determined that they must succeed or be annihilated, and they pierced the Turkish line east of the Mosque. Some fierce hand to hand fighting took place amongst the cacti, but the Welsh men overcame all resistance, cleared the line, and secured a number of German, Austrian and Turkish prisoners.

The 7th Cheshires arrived on the scene, most opportunely, as this feat of arms was accomplished, and, under Colonel Lawrence, the position captured was organised, and fire directed on the Turkish trenches to the west.

Captain E. W. Walker's account of this noteworthy incident is interesting.

He says he advanced with a half company on the right of the 6th Royal Welch Fusiliers, " overlapping with the 159th Brigade, and got on to the ridge running northeast and southwest. On obtaining this position, I found myself facing directly towards the Mosque. I therefore continued that advance in conjunction with the other half of the battalion and the 6th R.W.F. on their left. I advanced very rapidly as the fire on this line of advance was very slight. I did not stop for any length of time till I was 800 yards from the enemy's position. I then called up supports; an officer of the 5th Welch Regiment then brought up two platoons, a Lewis gun and Mr. Latham's platoon. I then continued the advance to within 600 yards of the objective. Up to this time, I had had only one casualty, as I had drawn no machine gun fire. I lost Mr. Thomas, wounded, who had given me great help in every way. I sent a written message to Captain Evans for supports; as a result Mr. Westcombe succeeded in joining me. I here again began to suffer casualties, and signalled for further support. Two platoons of the 5th Welch Regiment came up on my right—the remaining two platoons of this company had already come up. I then signalled again and again for support, and eventually sent a written message for support which was delivered to the Captain of the 4th Welch Regiment, all my own battalion supports being already up; no supports however came up. I ordered the two platoons on my right to fix bayonets and move up on to the high ground on my right, where there were some sniper posts which appeared unoccupied, and so proved to be. This enabled me to move forward to within 200 yards of the position. I now sent back a written message to my C.O., stating that with help of supports I was in a position to assault, and asking that bombardment be lifted. I afterwards learned that this message did not reach him. This was about 14.30, and I waited in hope of support for about an hour. This delay caused me many casualties, but we were not under machine gun fire. Mr. Westcombe was hit during this time after excellent work. I was greatly helped by overhead machine gun fire from the ridge behind me, and by the Lewis gun with me, brought up by 5th Welch Regiment. Mr. Roberts from D company here came over to me, and I found that he was suffering more heavily than I was, and could obtain no support. All the supports of his own Brigade behind him had come up. Apart from the machine gun in the gully, which I could plainly see firing to my left, there was extraordinary little fire on our position. Just after this there was a direct hit on the machine gun in the gully, and the artillery bombardment seemed mostly on foreside of the position. I saw Mr. Roberts, Mr. Lastin, and an officer of the 5th Welch Regiment, and we assaulted. I was here separated from Mr. Latham, who assaulted through the prickly pear hedge, while I went up the gully to machine gun, which, however, offered no resistance.

"I then sent parties round the trenches, and turned out and collected about 20 Austrian and German prisoners, some of whom were officers, and about 12 Turks. Unfortunately, a second machine gun managed to get away into the trenches further to the left, from where it caused us several casualties. I reported capture of hill, machine gun, and prisoners to my C.O. in duplicate, but I learned that neither message reached him.

"The time was, as far as I remember, 15.50, but I subsequently lost my note book. At this time, about five minutes after the capture of the hill, I was reinforced by a strong party of the 7th Cheshires, under Colonel Lawrence, who then took command, and consolidated position."

Lieutenant C. Latham, after charging through the prickly pears, says that "we continued clearing cactus gardens, and rounding up all prisoners under heavy fire from snipers. I then met a Major of the Cheshire Regiment (Major Pemberton), who asked me to organise all men I could get hold of, and build up a line of defence along the prickly pears running northeast, and commanding a good view of Gaza town, which was a splendid position for a counter attack. This position was held at night by several units, men reporting from all quarters of the fighting area, and were all put on duty to strengthen the defence, and re-organised into their own units, which chiefly consisted of the 7th R.W.F., 5th Welch Regiment, and 7th Cheshire Regiment."

Captain Lee, who described his command as a mixed grill from all units in the Brigade, his own, the 5th Welch, predominating, gave a fuller account of the charge through the cactus hedges. "Our great concern was a certain cactus hedge, from which machine guns might wipe us all out as soon as we got level with it. A small party was sent off to investigate, and all being reported well we got on a few yards further, leaving some behind (hit) at every rush forward. Worn out and heavily laden (besides their packs the men carried extra rations, a second water bottle, and extra bandoliers of ammunition) the prospect of having to rush the entrenched and steep slopes was not a pleasant one, but with bayonets fixed and revolvers cocked, off we went with a cheer. The Turks vacated their trenches and ran. The top of the hill was reached and we rounded up many Turks. Those who ran were fired at and some bowled over. On looking round we found ourselves behind Turks who were still firing on other oncoming troops, and we got some fine firing at their backs, until they withdrew. Our party had reached the top, I suppose unobserved, at any rate for a while, for we were troubled by British shells and rifle fire from converging troops. These troubles soon ceased, and Colonel Lawrence of the Cheshires came along and took command of the situation. . . . Water shortage was serious, and parties were sent off to collect water bottles from the dead, and ammunition from the wounded and dead."

On the latter point, Captain F. S. Harries wrote " the lack of water and only seven hours' sleep in nearly four days were almost the worst features . . . . The men were splendid and up to a point it was more like a sham fight, but the machine guns stopped us and as we lay we suffered terribly."

.   .   .   .   .

While this fighting was going on round the Mosque, the 271st Field Artillery Brigade, having brought their guns into action, smashed the cactus hedges which concealed machine gun nests on the 159th Brigade front. Immediately, the result was apparent. The 5th and 4th Welch, with the 6th Cheshires, jumped forward as the artillery lifted, and captured Clay Hill.

This success, led by the 7th R.W. Fusiliers, and the 5th Welch, coincided with the advance of the Anzac Division from the north; the New Zealand Brigade, coming from Jabalieh in the direction of Ali Muntar, became involved in hand to hand fighting, while the 5th Welch and 4th Cheshires were making their final advance on Clay Hill.

The Turks were being hard pressed on the north-east and north of Gaza, but there had always been a gap between the 160th Brigade, who were held on the el Sire Ridge although they had captured the Labyrinth, and the left of the 158th Brigade. The enemy on Green Hill had inflicted severe casualties all day, driving the Herefords by machine gun fire to the right, and the Sussex, reinforced by a company of the Queens, were unable to help from the el Sire side. In consultation with the two Brigadiers, Travers and Mott, General Dallas ordered the 161st Brigade to attack Green Hill. The attack was launched at 4 p.m.

Thus it will be seen that the culminating point in the day's operations was reached between 4 and 5 o'clock. Brigadier-General Doddington's 4th and 5th Essex Battalions advanced rapidly and successfully on Green Hill, and enabled the whole line to advance; the Turks fled into Gaza.

By 6 o'clock, Clay Hill had been cleared by the 159th Brigade, Ali Muntar by the 158th and 159th, Green Hill by the 161st, and the Labyrinth was still held by the 160th. At the latter place only was there any uncertainty, although it does not seem to have been reported.

The gunners of the 265th Artillery Brigade had seen some of the infantry retire across the open, south of the cactus hedges and gardens, at 4 o'clock, and were in some doubt as to the actual state of affairs. Colonel Pearson, commanding the Middlesex, says, " Owing to the extraordinary broken nature of the ground, which was covered with deep pits, ravines and water courses, it was impossible to see what were the movements of our troops except for a few yards at a time. Urgent appeals were made for S.A.A., water and stretcher bearers. Wounded were lying about with little prospect of removal. The troops were growing very weak from want of water. . . . At 6.30 p.m. there was little change in the situation though several small mixed detachments were organised from stragglers and pushed into the line. Any attempt at advance immediately drew heavy concentrated machine gun fire from enemy guns concealed in the cultivation on the left flank." But, though precarious, the position gained was still held.

Only on the sand dunes did the Turks remain in their original trenches, before Colonel Money's detachment. The Royal West Kents had taken up the position allotted to them without opposition—their total casualties during the day being eleven.

· · · · ·

THE ORDER TO WITHDRAW

This was the moment for a great decision. Time had been impressed on all concerned as a governing factor. The morning fog, and the delay in developing the infantry operation had caused the greatest anxiety, which does not seem to have been allayed by the tardy movement of Turkish reinforcements; no news was heard of them until 4 p.m., when an air report stated that a small body of Turks was advancing on the north of Gaza, about seven miles away. Later, about 5 p.m., while the Imperial Mounted Division was occupying some of the positions from which the Anzac Division had been withdrawn, they came in contact with the enemy north of Beit Durdis, and were driven from a hill—but the Turkish advance was held. Aeroplanes reported this enemy force to be 3,000 infantry and two squadrons of cavalry.

Later still, just before sunset, a further report from the air estimated 7,000 men advancing from Abu Hureira.

But, before this last news came in, General Chetwode, in consultation with General Dobell, had decided that if Gaza was not captured before 6 o'clock, the mounted troops would be withdrawn. In reaching this decision, General Chetwode seems to have been greatly influenced by the necessity for watering the horses of the mounted divisions. He did not know that a considerable number of units had found water during the day. Also, at that hour, he did not know of the 7,000 enemy troops advancing from Hureira. In his despatch, Sir A. Murray says "the majority of mounted troops had been unable to water their horses during the day, and it appeared that, unless Gaza were captured during the day, they would have to withdraw west of the Wadi Ghuzze in order to water their animals." He then mentions that strong enemy forces, with guns, were advancing (the subsequent information) and continues : " It was at this moment that the loss of two hours daylight made itself particularly felt, since, had two more hours daylight now been available, there is no doubt that the infantry would have been able to consolidate the position they had won, and for arrangements to have been made by which the 54th Division could have effected junction with the 53rd. It is, perhaps, possible that, if General Dobell had at this stage pushed forward his reserve (the 52nd Division) to support the 53rd, the result would have been different, but the difficulty of supplying water for men and horses would have been immense, and impossible to realise by those who were not on the spot."*

General Dobell had, of course, always watched his right flank with care and doubt. At about 5.30 p.m., when the first news of a Turkish advance from the north-east came in, he ordered the 54th Division to move from Sheikh Abbas and occupy a line from Sheikh Nebham to Burjaliye, through Mansura, to a point a mile north of that place. This movement had a great effect on subsequent events.

Punctually at 6 o'clock, General Chetwode gave orders that the mounted troops should be called in. And, although news of the first success on Ali Muntar was in his possession before the orders went out, he did not modify his decision. The situation at that moment pointed to the town

---

* As a matter of fact, the mounted units had found water during the day, but the position of such small supplies was, of course, unknown to the Higher Command. Later water was developed in the Wadi Ghuzze. On this particular day the 437th Field Company had put down Norton Tubes and dug shallow wells in the bed of the Wadi, and "it was depressing to hear of the shortage of water and the sufferings of the advanced troops when we, in the Wadi, had lashings of perfectly good water, but no means of getting it up to the positions. I was amazed, late in the evening of the 26th, when I saw Brigadier Wiggin at the head of the 5th Mounted Brigade returning across the Wadi. He hailed me and told me his orders were to return to Belah for the purpose of watering. I pointed to five or six canvas troughs, brim-full, but he had to carry out orders and passed on. When the order for withdrawal came we had to pull up all our tubes and dismantle all our gear, emptying some thousands of gallons out on the bed of the Wadi." (Phillips.)

being captured, certainly by dawn. The 160th Brigade were nervous. "At 7 o'clock the left flank was thrown back still more, in order to save surprise by small bodies of the enemy. I considered that, unless large re-inforcements were pushed forward both to my left flank and to the general line held by the 160th Brigade, the position would become untenable."—(Pearson). But this was merely a local condition in a rough bit of ground. On Green Hill it was otherwise "The Brigadier (Mott) sent for horses, intending to ride up and consolidate the position gained. Unfortunately, before he could start he was told by the Divisional Commander to hold fast, as General Dobell, who had just taken over from General Chetwode, (*he did not do so till next morning*) was about to pronounce on the situation. General Dallas also mentioned the possibility of withdrawing, a suggestion which filled the Brigadier with horror and amazement. However, he sent the whole Brigade staff, Price, myself, and even Hampson, the signaller, up to Green Hill to do what we could to organise the position. We found a strange scene of turmoil, masses of dead and wounded of both sides, a lot more people nearly frantic with thirst and excitement, and a great mixing of units—Green Hill in the hands of the 5th R.W.F., Herefords, and part of the 161st Brigade, while Ali Muntar was held by the 6th and 7th R.W.F., and the 5th Welch and 7th Cheshires from the 159th Brigade. A certain amount of desultory firing was still going on, on the far side—though it was now quite dark—where a certain amount of the enemy were still sticking in the gardens and cactus hedges which cover that side (*opposite the Middlesex Regiment*). We tried to get permission to send water and ammunition up to the parched heroes on the heights, but the Division would not allow camels to be sent. The evacuation of the wounded was also an enormous job." Water, food, and ammunition had been brought up near Divisional Headquarters during the afternoon. The Queens had water and ammunition dumped at their headquarters.

There was naturally some confusion, but the whole of the el Sire Ridge was clear of Turks, as was Clay Hill, and the Anzac troops were well into the gardens on the north side of the town. Water could, no doubt, have been sent up during the night—and, refreshed, all that units had to do was to stand fast. But it was not to be.

It might be said that the real accidents of the day, which robbed the troops of the fruits of their victory, were not so much the result of the sea fog in the morning as the fog of war amongst the higher command in the evening. Neither General Chetwode nor General Dobell knew the extent of the successful effort of the 53rd Division and the 161st Brigade, or that the Turks had retired, helter skelter from the ridge into

Gaza. It was 11 o'clock before General Dobell knew it. On the other hand, General Dallas was never informed by General Chetwode, or General Dobell, of the move made by the 54th Division. Consequently, when having issued his orders to the mounted divisions to retire, General Chetwode spoke to General Dallas on the telephone and told him of the cavalry retirement, and that the 53rd Division must, being left in the air, withdraw and connect with the 54th Division, the effect of this startling communication on the Commander of the 53rd Division can well be imagined.

Neither General knew what the other was talking about, and neither received any enlightenment on the true situation from the other. General Dallas, thinking of the vast distance which separated him from the flank of the 54th Division which was, as he thought, at Sheikh Abbas, asked that the cavalry might be used to fill the gap; General Chetwode, unaware of the fact that patrols were actually feeling their way into certain parts of the town, and thinking of watering his horses, refused to accede to the request. General Dallas, in despair, pleaded for time to consider, and received a peremptory order to draw back the right of the 53rd Division to connect with the 54th.

Meanwhile, information on the true state of affairs began to filter through to General Dobell. He knew how his troops stood round Gaza, he knew that the Turkish reinforcements were still some way off, and not pressing forward; he also received an intercepted wireless from the German, Major Tiller, commanding at Gaza, describing his desperate situation.*

He therefore ordered General Dallas to dig in where he stood, with his right on the 54th Division, imagining that the 53rd Headquarters knew all about the move of the 54th. General Dallas merely read this order as a confirmation of General Chetwode's order, which he was, at that moment, carrying out.

General Dallas, in no better temper it may be presumed than his Brigadiers, ordered the 53rd Division to occupy the line Sheikh Abbas—Mansura—rather north of el Sheluf—Tel Ajjul, and so informed General Chetwode, at 9.30 p.m. No comment was made. No glimmer of light was perceived by the staff—after all, at the root of this misunderstanding, if one could trace it, there probably stood a member of the staff.

* The first of these intercepted messages ran: "Your telegram received please attack at all costs at 2 o'clock to-night." This was timed 23.00 hours and addressed to Sheria. A later message was more despairing: "Position lost at 19.45, I am still in possession of town, help required at once or it will be too late."

"However, orders were orders, and the necessary instructions were sent to units, and at midnight the withdrawal was begun. As a matter of fact, small parties of heroes had pushed down the slope into Gaza, notably one under Walker and George Latham of the 7th (R.W.F.) and never got the order, only coming away at dawn, when they found that there was no one else about. One such party met some Anzac cavalry, who had come right through the town, from north to south. It showed to what a pitch the Turks had sunk. The whole remnant of the garrison and Gaza itself was like a large plum, and no one to pick it. . . We got back behind our cliff edge at Mansura somewhere about 2 a.m., and literally fell asleep in a heap across each other."—(Ashton.)

The 159th Brigade occupied their new position by 3.30 a.m., the 160th and 161st by 4 and 5 a.m.

"At one o'clock in the morning," General Dallas says in his report, "I learned from my own staff that troops of the 54th Division had appeared in the open plain north of Mansura, having apparently closed in on my right for some two miles. . . . Further, at daylight I learned, for the first time, that the 54th Division, less the detachment that had been placed at my disposal, had been withdrawn during the night from Sheikh Abbas to the line Mansura-Tel el Ahmar-el Burjaliye-el Adar. Had I known that the 54th Division was moving to close in on my right, I should have held on to the positions gained, possibly with the exception of the hill north east of the Mosque Hill (Clay hill), and have consolidated the ground gained. I would also have followed my intention of pressing down into the gardens and town, and so of widening and strengthening my position."

Of course, in the morning, when General Chetwode understood what had happened, he ordered General Dallas to re-occupy Ali Muntar !

. . . . . .

ACTION ON THE 27TH MARCH

The high moral of the 53rd Division responded to the order. The 160th Brigade had had no rest—they were the last to reach their position after marching all night, and had barely got there when they were ordered to go forward again.

The 7th Essex (161st Brigade) re-occupied Green Hill and Ali Muntar, and Brigadier-General Butler ordered the Queens to push forward on their left, while Brigadier-General Mott detailed the Herefords to advance on the right and take up the old position of the 158th Brigade—the 5th and 7th Royal Welch Fusiliers were to prolong the right, but bent back, across the valley, to conform with the Divisional order to join with the 159th Brigade " which will fill the gap between it and the 54th Division."

As the Herefords were moving forward—the leading company was actually on Ali Muntar Hill—it was found that the Essex were retiring. An order to retire was apparently passed to the Hereford companies, and a Turkish attack, sweeping through the cactus hedges, carried not only Ali Muntar but Green Hill as well. It was the second attack the enemy had made—the first having been repulsed by the Essex—and, from Mansura, where General Mott was watching, the situation looked extremely grave. The 158th machine gun company abandoned seven guns in this unexpected break. Brigadier-General Doddington ordered up reinforcements from the 161st Brigade, and Brigadier-General Mott galloped over from Mansura to lend the influence of his presence against the tide. The retirement was checked.

But the 5th and 7th Royal Welch Fusiliers, isolated in their position across the valley, had eventually to fall back and conform to the new line. These two battalions continually reported the presence of considerable enemy forces in the cactus hedges, and also that a large body of enemy troops was advancing rapidly on Gaza—this about 4 p.m.

At 8.30 a.m. General Dallas had wired to Desert Column : " Captain Tollemach, liason officer Eastern Force, has come to my Headquarters to find out situation. It is this. The enemy has appeared on Sheikh Abbas, and he is shelling my reserves and back while I am holding and fighting on the line Ali Muntar-Sheluf. The 54th Division is facing Sheikh Abbas on line N.E. of Mansura and along the line Tel el Ahmar-Burjaliye-el Adar. We are in a bottle neck, but can hold our position provided Ali Muntar can be retaken by fresh troops. Enemy has only recently appeared on Sheikh Abbas and cannot have yet deeply entrenched. I presume I am still under your orders till I hear to the contrary. Am arranging close co-operation with General Hare, who is, as you know, under Eastern Force Command. Orders regarding our movements, until Sheikh Abbas is taken, should be addressed to both of us."

The position at that early hour was far from satisfactory. The artillery units of the 53rd and 54th Divisions were actually firing back to back—or trail to trail—the gunners being able to speak to each other. There was also a great congestion of traffic behind Mansura Ridge as all the camel transport that had moved forward during the night was trying to get back.

Orders transferring the 53rd Division from General Chetwode's command to Eastern Force, under the direct control of General Dobell, came into force at 8 a.m., and General Dobell placed the 54th Division under the orders of General Dallas.

Although the Turks, after retaking Ali Muntar and Green Hill, made, for the time being, no further effort, the day was exceedingly trying for troops. The hot wind, the Khamsin, was blowing from the Arabian Desert and its effect was most exhausting. Towards the evening, General Mott asked if he might have the camel transport sent up to get food and water to the men as soon as possible, but General Dallas said that an event of great importance would happen shortly, and no camels were to be sent up.

There had been constant communication between General Dallas and Brigadier-General Dawney, the B.G. General Staff of the Eastern Force; and General Dobell had decided that as the position then held was not a good one for further operations, he would retire behind the Wadi Ghuzze. He directed that the 158th Brigade should cover the retirement of the 53rd Division which would commence at 7 p.m.

Just at that time the Turks launched another attack against the 161st Brigade on the el Sire Ridge, and a feeble attempt against Mansura—both efforts were repulsed.

The retirement was carried out without incident, the 158th Brigade arriving at the Wadi Ghuzze at 1.15 a.m. on the 28th March.

· · · · ·

Sir A. Murray, commenting on the situation prior to the final retirement to the Wadi Ghuzze, says in his despatch: "If it had now been practicable for the General Officer Commanding Eastern Force to advance with his three infantry divisions and two cavalry divisions, I have no doubt that Gaza would have been taken and the Turks forced to retire, but the reorganisation of the force for a deliberate attack would have taken a considerable time, the horses and cavalry were very fatigued, and the distance of our railhead from the front line put the immediate maintenance of such a force with supplies, water and ammunition entirely out of the question."

He says, "The total result of the first Battle of Gaza, which gave us 950 Turkish and German prisoners, and two Austrian field guns, caused the enemy losses which I estimate at 8,000, and cost us under 4,000 casualties, of which a large proportion were only slightly wounded, was that my primary and secondary objects were completely attained, but that

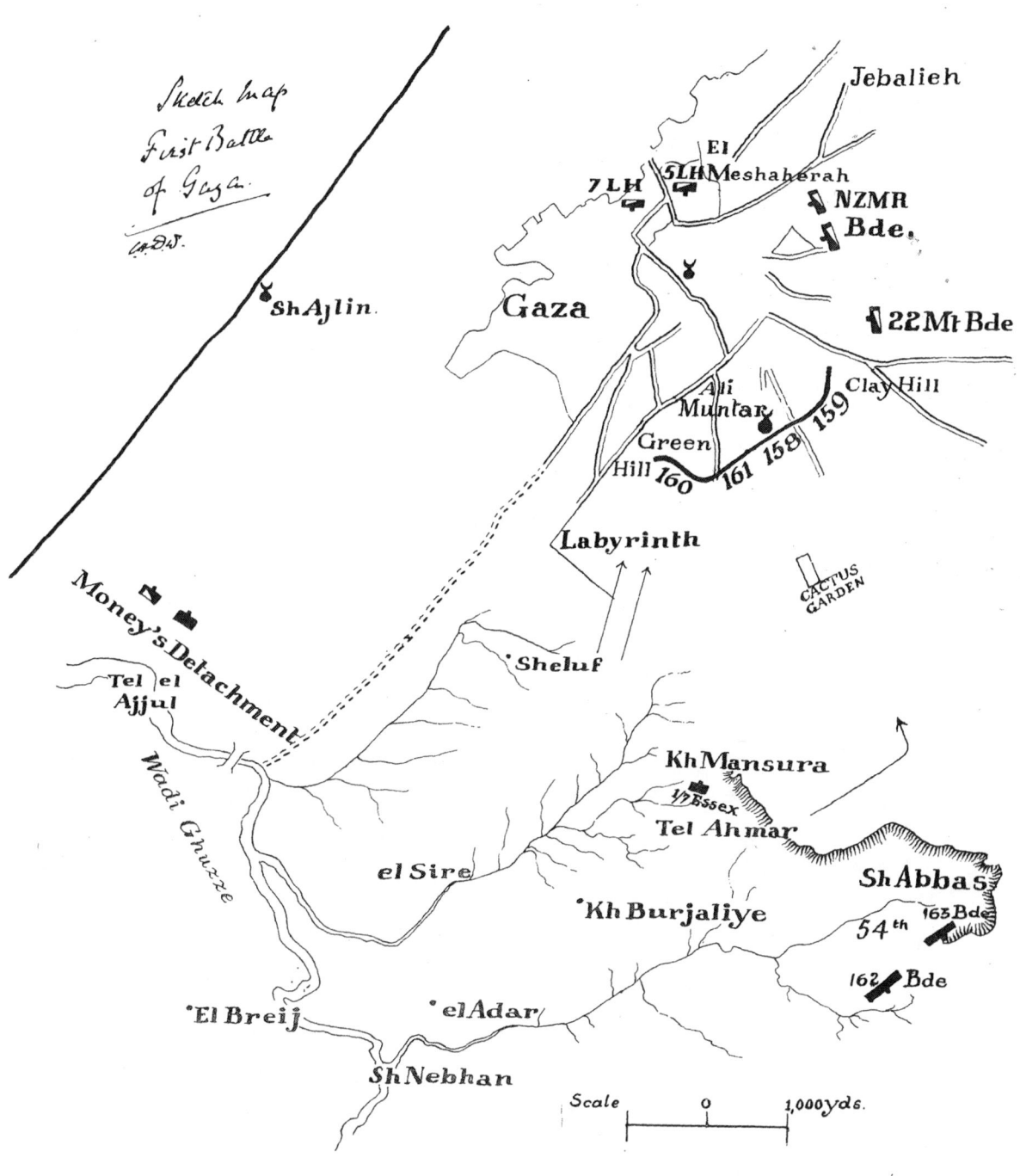

March, 1917   PALESTINE : FIRST BATTLE OF GAZA   97

the failure to attain the third object—the capture of Gaza—owing to the delay caused by the fog on the 26th, and the waterless nature of the country round Gaza, prevented a most successful operation from becoming a complete disaster to the enemy."

For the rank and file it was a most disappointing affair. They considered they had captured Gaza, and that they had been dragged, like a dog on a leash, from their prize.

Our total casualties were 397 killed, 2,900 wounded and 200 missing. The enemy casualties were greatly over-estimated by Sir A. Murray, the official Turkish return shows them as 2,447, which includes prisoners.

In the 53rd Division, casualties were :—

	Killed.		*Wounded.*		*Missing.*		*Total.*
	OFF.	O.R.	OFF.	O.R.	OFF.	O.R.	
158TH BRIGADE.							
5th R.W.F.	2	33	9	186	–	9	239
6th R.W.F.	2	14	11	138	–	3	168
7th R.W.F.	9	38	7	219	–	15	288
Herefords	4	13	11	181	2	24	235
TOTAL	17	98	38	724	2	51	930
159TH BRIGADE.							
4th Cheshires	–	6	9	96	–	10	121
7th Cheshires	4	14	5	108	–	–	131
4th Welch	1	32	12	150	–	31	226
5th Welch	4	29	16	210	–	39	298
TOTAL	9	81	42	564	–	80	776
160TH BRIGADE.							
Queens	1	4	18	88	1	5	117
Sussex	4	24	12	154	–	57	251
Kents	–	1	–	9	–	–	10
Middlesex	4	14	5	108	–	26	157
TOTAL	9	43	35	359	1	88	535

G

GENERAL WAR SITUATION
During the month of April, 1917.

United States declare war on Germany, 6th April.
Cuba and Panama declare war on Germany, 7th April.
Battles of Arras begin, 9th April.
French offensive begins, 16th April.
French offensive stopped, 20th April.
Samarra (Mesopotamia) taken by British, 24th April.

SECOND BATTLE OF GAZA

THE 53rd Division now held a line on the banks of the Wadi Ghuzze, from the Khan Yunis-Gaza road to the sea. The Turks made no further move, and a general reconnaissance on the 1st April was able to cover a depth of over a mile without opposition.

General Dallas resigned his command, and Brigadier-General Mott assumed command of the Division on the 10th April.

Brigades were grouped as follows:—

158TH GROUP.	159TH GROUP.
Brig.-Gen. C. S. Rome.	Brig.-Gen. J. H. du B. Travers.
Bde. Signal Sect.	Bde. Signal Sect.
158th Inf. Bde.	159th Inf. Bde.
158th Machine Gun Coy.	159th Machine Gun Coy.
436th Fld. Coy. R.E.	437th Fld. Coy. R.E.
3rd Welsh Fld. Amb.	2nd Welsh Fld. Amb.

160TH GROUP.
Brig.-Gen. W. J. C. Butler.
Bde. Signal Coy.
160th Inf. Bde.
160th Machine Gun Coy.
439th Fld. Coy. R.E.
1st Welsh Fld. Amb.

The artillery could not, as yet, be included in the grouping, there being only two composite brigades.

So far as the situation of the line was concerned, it was not unpleasant. Apart from the labour of digging trenches in the sand, troops were not unduly worried, while just behind the line one brigade headquarters speaks enthusiastically of "a shady grove of pomegranates, spangled with scarlet wax-like blooms, citrons and large Eucalyptus trees!" this was known as St. James' Park.

The men were able to bathe, and—a curious situation—the coast being straight and flat, without headlands, parties of the enemy could be seen bathing at no great distance.

But rumours of a second attempt on Gaza ran through the Division.

. . . .

THE SITUATION

In the first battle of Gaza the bulk of the enemy forces had been to a flank, away out east; Gaza itself was not strongly held. Now, however, realising the intention of the British command, there was a redistribution and reinforcement of the Turkish Army. Gaza was incorporated in a strong defensive line, and was no longer a post on the Turkish flank. It was believed that the garrison had been increased to five regiments (18 battalions), two Austrian Howitzer batteries, two German long range guns, and a Turkish battalion of artillery (8 guns), and there were more troops in reserve, and more artillery.

The second attempt would have to be a battle on a different scale—no cutting out operation was possible.

Although Sir A. Murray had a harder problem in front of him, and could hope for no reinforcements other than he could squeeze out of Egypt, he was not in such bad case. He had only used the 53rd Division; the 52nd and 54th were practically untouched, and the newly constituted 74th, made up of dismounted Yeomanry, but without artillery, was at his disposal. Also the work of supply was made easier by the advance of the railway to Deir el Belah, so that not only were the field artillery brigades of the 53rd and 54th Divisions which had been left on the Canal released for service, but the remaining heavy batteries, and four heavy howitzers from the Canal were now available, and in a position to be supplied with ammunition.*

Sir A. Murray says in his despatch that, after the first battle, " preparations were immediately begun for a second attempt in greater force on the Gaza positions as soon as possible, though I instructed the General Officer Commanding Eastern Force, that upon no consideration was a premature attack to be made. . . . The troops were all concentrated, ready for an advance, and reconnaissances for artillery positions east of the Wadi Ghuzze were completed early in April, but the chief factor in fixing the date of advance was our continual source of anxiety, the water supply. It was necessary for the next advance that two divisions should be able to water in the Wadi Ghuzze, where the prospects of obtaining water by well sinking were small. Tanks, therefore, had to be set up in the Wadi, and arrangements made to pump rail-borne water from Deir el Belah

---

* The 267th Brigade arrived from the Canal Section early on the 19th, and was in a position of readiness on the east bank of the Wadi Ghuzze, but does not seem to have fired a single round.

over the In Seirat Ridge to fill them. . . . Meanwhile, the enemy in front of me had been considerably reinforced, and had abandoned all intention of further retirement. It became clear that five divisions and a cavalry division had now appeared on our front with an increase of heavy artillery. Not only were the Gaza defences being daily strengthened and wired, but a system of enemy trenches and works were being constructed southeast from Gaza to the Atawineh Ridge, some 12,000 yards distance from the town. This put any encircling movement of our cavalry out of the question, unless the enemy's line in front of us could be pierced. . . . ."

Of Gaza itself he says there were now " strong defences known as the Warren, the Labyrinth, Green Hill, Middlesex Hill, Outpost Hill, and Lees Hill, running southwards along the ridge from Ali Muntar. This position, which commands all approaches to the town from the south-west, south, and south-east, has been very strongly fortified and well wired, in addition to the natural obstacles formed by thick cactus hedges, and had been made into a nest of machine guns, largely manned by Germans. The right of the line, between Gaza and the sea, ran in the arc of a circle west and south-west of the town. This section consisted of a double line of trenches and redoubts, strongly held by infantry and machine guns, well placed and concealed in impenetrable cactus hedges built on high mud banks, enclosing orchards and gardens on the outskirts of the town."

To tackle this job a redistribution of the forces under his two subordinate commanders was necessary, and so General Chetwode's Desert Column was made up of mounted troops only—the Anzac Mounted Division, the Imperial Mounted Division, and the Imperial Camel Brigade—while Eastern Force was given the four infantry divisions, one without artillery (the others with one howitzer battery short), the 10th, 15th, and 91st heavy batteries (60 pdrs.) the 201st Siege Battery (two 6-inch and two 8-inch howitzers), and 8 tanks.

The Tanks, although their crews fought them in most gallant fashion, became the subject of jest; they were part worn instructional machines, and had been shipped " in error."

Up to the last moment General Dobell hesitated between an attack on Gaza itself, and breaking the enemy line about Atawineh with his infantry and so letting his mounted divisions through; finally, he decided on the first course, which fell into two phases.

THE FIRST PHASE

The first phase was carried out on the 17th April with practically no opposition. The 54th and 52nd Divisions occupied the Sheikh Abbas-

Mansura position. The 53rd Division completed on this date a new line, well forward on the coast and running back to Kurd Hill. While the advance of the 54th and 52nd Divisions was in progress, two Companies of the Queens moved forward on the flank in the direction of Heart Hill, keeping touch with the 52nd and reconnoitring the valley that runs between the El Sire Ridge and the sand dunes.

The 18th was spent in preparation for the second phase of the battle. The " gunners " had an exceedingly busy time. " My battery, B/265, occupied four separate positions on four consecutive nights ; each night we dug four large cavities in that infernal sand, and dragged four unwilling guns into them " (Barton), and then built a rampart of sandbags round each gun. And the signallers, on their metal, worked all night laying innumerable cables over the sand dunes—amidst the doleful howling chorus of jackals, which was unearthly in the darkness. It was hoped that communication between artillery and infantry would be perfect. At the last moment the Tanks, moving to their positions, crossed most of the lines, wound the cables round themselves, and all the work had to be done over again !

. . . . .

THE GENERAL ACTION

On the extreme right of the British line was the Desert Column with an outpost line from el Gamli to the right of the 54th Division ; at Sheikh Abbas the 54th and 52nd infantry divisions then carried on the line through Mansura to Kurd Hill; the 53rd Division lay across the sand dunes to the sea.

Zero hour was 5.30 a.m., and the rôle played by the 53rd Division can best be appreciated by following the movement of troops from the extreme right of the line.

The two mounted divisions advanced with the object of engaging the enemy in the direction of Abu Hureira and along the Gaza-Beersheba road. On the right flank, one brigade of the Anzac Division went to Tel el Fara, one towards Abu Hureira, and two were held in reserve ; this division did not dismount.

The Imperial Mounted Division attacked on foot, with varying fortune. They had some hard fighting, but on the whole were successful in their object of holding and diverting enemy troops. They advanced to within a short distance of Abu Hureira and occupied the Kh. Sihan in conjunction with the Camel Brigade which was working with the right battalion of the 54th Division.

The Desert Column was, therefore, flung out over a wide front from the Wadi Ghuzze to Kh. Sihan, protecting the operations of the main infantry force from an enemy flank attack.

The infantry attack followed a two hours preliminary bombardment by the reinforced artillery. All available batteries were used, while, from the sea, the French battleship "*Requin*," and two British monitors lent the weight of their armaments.

The heavy guns fired on selected strong points, the "*Requin*" on Ali Muntar Ridge, one monitor on the Labyrinth, the other on the Warren; the 201st Siege Battery turned its 6-inch guns on Outpost and Middlesex Hills, and its 8-inch on the Labyrinth and Green Hill, the 91st Heavy Battery dealt with the el Arish redoubt and Magdhaba trench, which affected the front of the 53rd Division, and the 10th and 15th Heavy Batteries on other points opposite the 54th and 52nd Divisions.

At 7.30 a.m., the three infantry divisions advanced.

The field artillery was insufficient to cover the entire front in the manner of massed artillery in France, but ten minutes after the infantry moved to the attack an 18-pdr. barrage was put down on certain trenches.

THE 54TH DIVISION

The 54th Division moved down the slopes of Sheikh Abbas and Mansura on a two brigade front, its right directed on Kh. Sihan, its left on the point where the Mukkadam crosses the Beersheba road. Immediately in front of them was the bare plain; on the far side of the Gaza-Beersheba road undulating brown hills rising to what is called the Shephalah, a distinct range of hills lying close against the dark Judean mountains in the background. Without sufficient artillery to sustain fire on the line of enemy trenches, the position was entirely favourable to the machine gun and rifle defence of the Turks. Moreover, the counter-battery work of our heavy guns seems to have been futile; the Turkish artillery was well directed and sustained, and took an immediate toll on the British infantry descending from the Sheikh Abbas-Mansura Ridge and followed them to the glacis where the Turkish and German machine gunners were able to add their hail of bullets.

These are not idle excuses as a comparison of the casualties will show. The field artillery gunners did their best—soon they were ordered to husband their ammunition—but the weight of metal was not there to hurl against the entrenched positions held by the Turks. Except on the extreme left of the 54th Division, where the 11th London Regiment captured a front line trench astride the Gaza-Beersheba road, the infantry got no nearer the Turkish defences than 200 yards. The tanks were equally unsuccessful.

THE 52ND DIVISION

The advance of the 52nd Division was a more complicated manœuvre. It was led by the 155th Brigade along the Es Sire Ridge, with the 156th Brigade echeloned on the right rear. When the 155th had cleared sufficient ground on this difficult front the 156th were to wheel to attack Green Hill and Ali Muntar.

Led by a tank (which fell into one of the steep sided Wadis and was replaced by the one in reserve), the 5th K.O.S.B. captured, lost, recaptured, and again lost Outpost Hill. The 156th Brigade started their wheel on Green Hill and Ali Muntar, but soon found that until Outpost Hill was firmly secured they could not advance. This was never achieved. There was one dramatic moment, when Major Forrest, an international football player, led forward, on his own initiative, two companies of the 4th K.O.S.B., and was followed by an irresistible rush from all the other battalions of the Brigade—the Turks were swept off the position but concentrated their artillery fire on the restricted area so that the gallant stormers were isolated for a considerable time. The sacrifice was of no avail—the 156th Brigade could not advance.

THE 53RD DIVISION

On the coastal sector, General Mott, with Brigadier-Generals Travers and Butler, had made a personal reconnaissance of the approaches to the enemy's advanced line. For 1,500 yards to the west of the Gaza road there was little cover; the line of advance along the sea coast was in the nature of a glacis; the centre was more broken and afforded a certain amount of cover, and this was the line of advance decided upon. He attacked with two brigades—160th on the right, 159th on the left. The new line which had been dug since the 17th was held by the 158th Brigade; but the attacking Brigades formed up in rear, between Money Hill and Cliff Fort, and their orders were to go through the battalions of the 158th Brigade and move, the 160th against Samson Ridge, the 159th against the high ground between Samson Ridge and Sheikh Ajlin. One battalion of the 160th was to make a subsidiary attack along the valley between the Es Sire Ridge and the sand dunes, keeping in touch with the 52nd Division.

THE ADVANCE OF THE 7TH CHESHIRE FROM SHEIKH AJLIN,
SECOND BATTLE OF GAZA.

RUINS OF GAZA.

"In attacking the first objective, it is essential that all units march direct on that portion of the objective which is allotted to them. Samson Ridge must be taken before the advanced works east of Sheikh Ajlin are stormed, but close contact with these works should be gained by the 159th Brigade in order to assist the 160th Brigade."—(O.O.35.)

A second objective was given, to be attacked in conjunction with the advance of the 52nd Division.

A "female" tank was allotted to the 160th Brigade and a "male"* to the 159th.

The two attacking brigades advanced from their rear position at 7.15 a.m. Owing to the soft and deep sand it was deemed advisable to start the advance a quarter of an hour before the set time, so that the attack of the 53rd might keep level with that of the 52nd Division. Following the action of battalions from the right, the Queens who had, on the 17th, reconnoitred the ground with two companies, carried out the subsidiary movement in touch with the 52nd Division. The battalion drew up behind Brown Hill, and then followed a covered line of advance along the Wadi in Kurd Valley. One company and the two machine guns allotted to this battalion took up a position which had been previously selected on Softly Hill. At 9.30 the advance guard came on Heart Hill, under heavy rifle fire, and the battalion left the cover of the Wadi.

The main attack of the 160th Brigade was given to the Middlesex and West Kents, each on a 500 yards frontage. The first check was experienced soon after passing through the outpost line. They were in full view of all those gardens and groves outside Gaza, which run down the slope of the Es Sire Ridge on that side, and long range machine gun fire was very troublesome. Samson Ridge itself was under fire from the 266th Field Artillery Brigade, and also at this time from the guns of the French battleship, "*Requin*," and the gardens were having special attention from the gunners in the shape of gas shells; unfortunately, the gas took no effect.

At 10 o'clock the Middlesex were some 300 yards from the redoubt on Samson Ridge, but reported that the artillery support was insufficient for further advance.

General Mott urged the necessity for assaulting the position as soon as possible, and the Sussex moved up from reserve to the right of the Middlesex. About this time, too, the Queens, on receipt of an order from

---

* The distinction was in armament. The "male" carried two small calibre guns and machine guns—the "female" only machine guns.

Brig.-General Butler, moved to attack the eastern slopes of Samson Ridge, but found the rifle and machine gun fire from the gardens and cactus hedges on their right flank so intense that they were held, strung out, facing Gaza, about a thousand yards on the right rear of the Sussex. The machine guns attached to this battalion moved up to Heart Hill and did some useful work on that flank.

Meanwhile the West Kents, who had lost their Commanding Officer, Colonel Money (wounded), and their Adjutant (killed) reported, through the second-in-command, Major Höhler, that they were in a position to assault. The guns lifted at 11.15, but the enemy machine gun fire was too severe and no assault took place.

By a quarter to one, the Middlesex and West Kents, and the Sussex on their right, had crept forward to within 200 yards of the redoubt, and the Brigadier was ordered by General Mott to fix a time for assault.

The artillery then lifted, and the Sussex, Middlesex and West Kents rushed up the slope and carried the position.

A few hundred yards beyond Samson Ridge, cactus hedges, scrub, and some cultivation began. The enemy defences were sited on the very edge of this cultivation on a slight upward slope, where solid ground allowed the digging of better trenches, and the cactus and cultivation gave a certain amount of cover. The Ridge was only a forward post, held by the Turks for observation and annoyance; its capture in no way embarrassed their main line of defence on the extreme edge of the sand dunes area.

Under such conditions the line held was, naturally, sketchy; there were gaps and in some places a poor field of fire. Colonel Pearson (Middlesex) reported that, owing to casualties and disorganisation, two battalions would have to be sent up to carry on the attack. The Herefords were ordered forward and occupied, after overcoming some resistance, a ridge running southeast from Samson Ridge, which was afterwards known as Hereford Ridge.

The tanks were not successful; but in spite of all handicaps one of them, the "Tiger," with the 160th Brigade, did good work.

The crew knew nothing of the terrain, and as the view obtainable from a tank was exceedingly limited, Lieut. Dunkerley, of the Royal West Kent, had been detailed to act as guide. He found the tank at Money Hill, with its machinery clogged by fine sand, and the crew working desperately to get it going in time for the attack. It could not be moved until after the advance had started, and then crept forward in rear of the infantry, who were struggling up and down the long slopes of heavy sand. Eventually it passed through the infantry, but the links of the "track" again became clogged within a few hundred yards of the Turkish position; the crew got out and cleared the tracks under a brisk rifle fire.

When the tank moved forward again, Dunkerley, who had hitherto walked in front, now entered the machine. With the April sun beating down on the steel shell, and the engine nearly red hot, the temperature inside was torrid. Leaving the infantry behind, the "Tiger" struggled right up to the el Arish Trenches. One of the two gunners was hit in the stomach and collapsed. Two of the crew fell across the engine and were badly burned. Dunkerley, slightly wounded himself, found that he was the one man able to stand, but knew neither how to work the machine guns nor the engine.

Turkish shells were bursting all round the "Tiger," doing considerable execution amongst their own infantry, but by good luck she (it was a female) was not hit. A Turk seized the projecting barrel of one of her machine guns, and was shot by Dunkerley with his revolver. Fortunately, the wounded gunner, lying on the floor, was able to give him instructions, and Dunkerley found to his delight that he scould fire the guns. Turks had gathered round the tank, but in a few seconds the survivors were scampering for cover.

Following further instructions from the crew, Dunkerley succeeded in reversing the engine, and the battered "Tiger" struggled back to our lines. Finally, one of the crew recovered sufficiently to take charge of the engine, and the intrepid Dunkerley got out to walk in front and drag our own wounded out of the way of the unwieldy machine.

The 159th Brigade had an easy task, as it proved. According to orders they halted about eight hundred yards from Sheikh Ajlin until Samson Ridge was taken, and then the Turks in front of them ran, and they occupied their objective without opposition.

Battalions of the 158th Brigade were moved up in support—the 6th Royal Welch Fusiliers to be under Brigadier-General Travers, and the 5th and 7th on the right flank under the direct control of General Mott.

More could not be done by the 53rd Division. To attempt a further advance with all those cactus hedges and orchards filled with Turkish riflemen and German machine gunners would have been madness. Moreover, General Mott had already found it necessary to put in his reserve brigade to capture Samson Ridge and the final objective allotted to him, and though the coastal brigade had suffered very slight casualties any further advance beyond what was contemplated by the higher command would have made no impression, and would not have helped the 52nd Division at that late hour of the day—the only result would have been to extend the line in the sand dunes, already very long. In any case the 53rd Division could make no advance of this nature without orders from Eastern Force.

Up on the Es Sire Ridge the remnants of the 155th Brigade were still hanging on, but precariously, to Outpost Hill, where the situation was such that the 156th Brigade could not move on their right; fresh troops were necessary to give impetus to the fight, and the reserve brigade was on the point of advancing when Sir A. Murray gave orders to stand fast and continue the attack the next morning.

Something of the unvarnished truth, that the Eastern Force attack had been beaten to a standstill, was realised later. So far as Sir A. Murray knew, the situation at 4 o'clock was that the desert column was meeting with all the success anticipated in the containing attack; the 54th Division could hold on to what was gained (in reality little), " until further progress by the 52nd Division should render practicable a renewal of the advance "; and the 53rd were also waiting for further progress by the 52nd.

He says in his despatch: " Middlesex Hill, and a large area of extremely broken ground west and north-west of it, had been made by the enemy exceedingly strong. The nests of machine guns in the broken ground could not be located among the narrow dongas, holes and fissures with which the locality is seamed. Partly owing to this, and partly owing to the extent of the area, the artillery fire concentrated on it was unable to keep down the enemy's fire when the Brigade on Outpost Hill attempted to advance. (*The 53rd Artillery was turned on the hill as well as the 52nd.*) The reserve brigade of the 52nd had not been employed, and the remaining brigade was in a position to attack Green Hill and Ali Muntar as soon as the progress of the brigade on Outpost Hill on its left should enable it to do so. Up to this time, therefore, only one brigade of the 52nd Division was seriously engaged. The conformation of the ground, however, was such that the attack on Outpost Hill and Middlesex Hill could only be made on an extremely narrow front. It is possible that if the General Officer Commanding Eastern Force had now decided to throw in his reserves, the key of the position might have been taken with the further loss of between 5,000 and 6,000 men. . . . As it was the General Officer Commanding Eastern Force, in view of the information received that our attack had not yet succeeded in drawing the enemy's reserves,

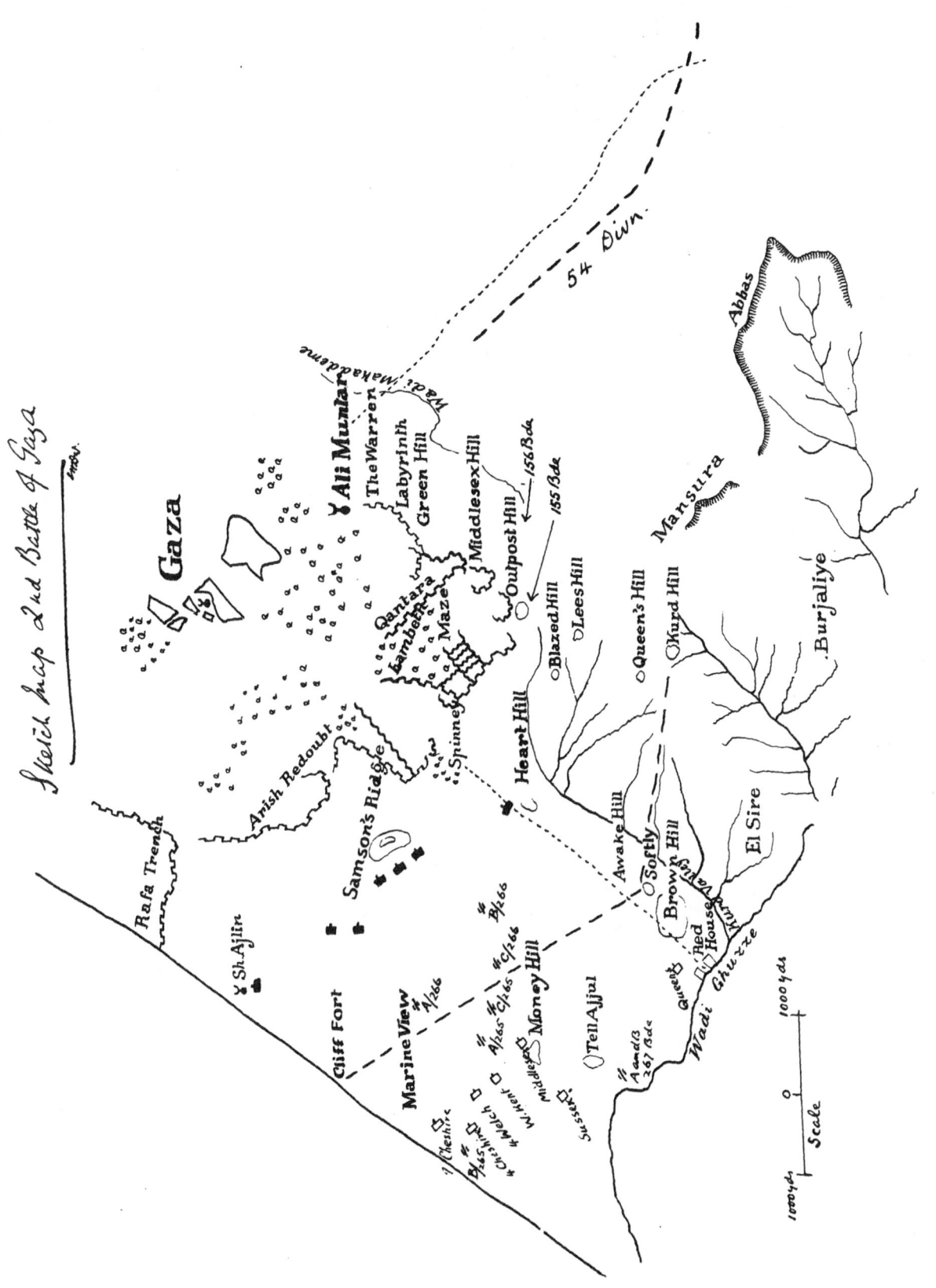

decided that the moment had not come for an attempt to force a decision by throwing in the general reserves."

At six o'clock the 155th Brigade was forced to evacuate Outpost Hill, and some idea of the casualties and the general situation filtered through.

The 52nd Division had lost 1,365, the bulk of the casualties being in the 155th Brigade; the 54th, 2,971; the 53rd, 584; the Camel Brigade, 345; the Anzac Division, 105; the Imperial Mounted Division, 547; there had been, too, a heavy loss of animals.

There was, however, an untouched division, the 74th, and these casualties alone would not have altered plans. "During the night 19/20th," Sir A. Murray states, "I received a message from General Dobell to say that, after careful deliberation and consultation with all the divisional commanders, he was strongly of the opinion that the resumption of the attack, ordered for the following morning, did not offer sufficient prospect of success to justify the very heavy casualties which such an operation would, in his opinion, involve. He, therefore, urgently requested my sanction to cancel the instructions previously issued, and my approval for the substitution of orders for the consolidation of the position already gained to be carried out on the 20th with a view to a further attack on the enemy's line at some point between Gaza and Hareira, as and when the opportunity might offer. In view of the strongly expressed opinion of the General Officer Commanding Eastern Force, supported by the General Officer Commanding Desert Column, and the Divisional Commanders, I assented to this proposal."

So the three divisions dug in where they stood.

"By 7 p.m.," says Von Kressenstein, "the Turks had won the battle." "Only on the coast, among the sand dunes, had the British an important success. Here they won a good deal of ground, and captured one particularly high dune which was very important as an observation post, south-east of Gaza."

The Turkish General Staff gave their casualties as 48 Officers, and 1,965 other ranks.

The disappointment of the army was echoed in the War Cabinet at home. Sir A. Murray's telegram, after the first battle of Gaza, had been couched in glowing terms. The operation, he states, had been most successful, and only fell short of a complete disaster to the enemy through the accident of the fog. His troops were never at any time hard pressed, and had " proved conclusively that in the open the enemy had no chance of success." The troops felt the same, but they also felt that they had not been given a fair opportunity, and as the battle was unsuccessful it was easy enough to criticise.

At the time it was not generally known that the second attempt on Gaza was the opening of a new policy. The first battle, designed as a dramatic and damaging " coup de main," was part of the offensive defence which followed the expulsion of the enemy from the Province of Sinai, a raid into his territory with no immediate intention to invade and conquer; but the second battle was planned under instructions from the War Cabinet to capture Jerusalem.

PALESTINE

GENERAL SITUATION
May-November, 1917.

Russian Provisional Government issue a declaration repudiating a separate peace, 19th May.

Battle of Messines, 7th June.

Mutiny in the Russian Black Sea Fleet, 21st June.

First contingent of U.S.A. troops arrives in France, 25th June.

Russian Summer Offensive begins, 29th June.

German Counter Offensive on Eastern Front begins, 18th July.

Kerenski, Premier of Russia, 19th July.

Battles of Ypres begin, 31st July.

Siam declares war on Germany, 22nd July.

Liberia declares war on Germany, 4th August.

China declares war on Germany, 14th August.

Battle of Riga begins, 1st September.

Kornilov heads revolt against Russian Provisional Government, 8th September.

Russia proclaimed a Republic, 15th September.

Brazil declares war on Germany, 26th October.

Arrival of British troops in Italy, 4th November.

Bolshevik revolution in Petrograd, 8th November.

General Sir S. Maude dies at Baghdad, 18th November.

Battle of Cambrai, 20th November.

THIRD BATTLE OF GAZA
"OFNER NA OFNO ANGAU"

THE 53rd Division then proceeded to make the new line across the sand dunes secure; second line works were made, and a careful siting of machine guns, Stokes trench mortars, and artillery. There were rumours of a great Turkish counter-stroke, but it did not materialise. The enemy, whose losses had been comparatively slight, were brought up to strength, and reinforced by additional troops—Sir A. Murray's estimate was eight divisions in all—but the Turkish Command was content to defend.

Both sides settled down to trench warfare. The right of the British line was away at Shellal, thence to Sharta, and the Sheikh Abbas Ridge. There was a wild stretch of country dividing this section of the line, and the Turkish line Hureira-Beersheba. But from the Sheikh Abbas Ridge to Sheikh Ajlin, a distance of some fourteen thousand yards, the two forces were in close touch.

Sir A. Murray made arrangements for the construction of a new branch railway from Rafah to Shellal.

In order to establish a regular system of reliefs, the line was divided in two sections, and on the 8th May, the 53rd Division moved into the back area, the 52nd taking their place in the line. It was during this relief, while marching to the neighbourhood of Sheikh Nebham, that one of those disasters occurred which are always remembered as fearful even in the midst of a general holocaust. The Turks, at this period, held the supremacy in the air, having the better machines, and carried on a great deal of bombing in the back areas. The West Kents were on the march during one of these air attacks, and a bomb fell in the centre of a company, killed 31 other ranks, and wounded two officers and 36 other ranks.

It happened in the middle of a moonlight night. The scene can be imagined!

A less tragic attack took place at the same time on Eastern Force Headquarters, and as was usual, though hard to explain, was watched by troops with the greatest amusement. The following day General Chetwode told how he was debating in his mind whether he should have

H

a second glass of port when an agitated bugler put his head in the tent and said : " They're 'ere, sir ! " and how, in the general *sauve qui peut* for the dugout, he was ruthlessly elbowed out of the way by his staff and the mess waiters.

The " rest area " behind the Mansura line, was very dusty, the light soil being churned up by the traffic, and was infested with fleas and flies ! —mostly flies. " Rest " meant innumerable fatigue parties, and a certain amount of training, also reorganisation on the new platoon system, with rifle, Lewis gun, bomb and rifle grenade sections. The Division was not long in this uncomfortable area ; they moved to el Israain on the 18th and 19th May. The march was eastwards—into the dusty and arid plains that lie between Gaza and Beersheba, wide expanses of undulating, almost treeless country, broken by little deep, dry wadis—and was very hot and dusty.

There occurred, at this time, changes in command ; General Chetwode assumed command of the Eastern Force, and General Chauvel of the Desert Column ; General Chaytor succeeded to the command of the Anzac Mounted Division.

On the 23rd and 24th May an Anzac brigade carried out a successful raid on the Beersheba-Auja railway, with the object of destroying material which the Turks might be using in the construction of the branch line they had started to build between El Tine and Mejdel, north of Gaza. Two days later (26th), the 53rd Division took over the right sector of the British line.

The line, which followed the south-eastern bend of the Wadi Ghuzze, consisted of a series of redoubts on the right bank, covering the water and crossings at Gamli, el Fara, el Shellal, and Hiseia. It was the Desert Column sector, and by day mounted troops made wide sweeps into the rolling country towards the distant Turkish lines ; at night, they had standing patrols at important points. These mounted patrols sometimes got in touch with enemy parties, but the infantry were so little troubled that they were able to supervise gangs of natives who were allowed to harvest their crops beyond the line of redoubts.

The line was considered rather pleasant, sited on the far lip of the broken ground beyond the Wadi, with battalion headquarters and reserve companies back in the crevices and crannies of the Wadi itself. It was over seven miles from end to end and Brigadiers did their rounds in Ford cars—" a marvellous car, which consisted of the chassis, a box for the driver to sit on, and a flat tray behind. It used to grind through the foot thick

A Sniper.

British Trench, Coastal Sector, Gaza.

[*War Museum.*

dust at four miles an hour, and boiling so fiercely as to be in danger of spontaneous combustion. Still, it was better than miles of riding in that heat."

In the Wadi there were a number of long pools of water. Sand grouse came to drink every morning and evening at these pools.

The whole line of the Wadi Ghuzze became a busy thoroughfare which, as Engineers constructed pumping stations and wells, railways, and pipe lines, assumed an air of permanency—the camps might have been a series of villages.

In spite of the extreme heat, training was carried on persistently by the brigades in reserve. General Mott " is very addicted to night operations. The usual procedure is a wire, about 6 p.m., to stand by to move at a moment's notice, followed by another to march out and take up a certain position and dig in after dark. We get back to camp in the middle of the night."

The long period of uninterrupted routine was not contemplated with equal satisfaction by all the officers and troops of the 53rd. " The long spell without leave, the bitterness of two defeats, heat, flies, scorpions, played havoc with liver and temper. The fleas from near-by native villages added a somewhat unlooked for burden to the discomfort. To such straits were we reduced that among the so-called amusements was the indulgence in anthems and hymns based on famous advertisements. In the evenings we might be heard proclaiming in harmony that " Hudson's soap it is the best," etc. Occasionally, we were pleasantly stirred by a thrilling air fight. Then came leave. Cairo, clean linen, lashings of beer, motors, clubs, books, new clothes, Shepheard's grill—how good they seemed after that seven months away from civilisation!"

On the 1st August, the Division was relieved by the 60th Division* and moved to the sand dunes once more, where they took over from the 54th Division.

Trench warfare was more active here, although there were no operations of importance during the three weeks' tour of duty. It was found that the Turks had changed their tactics in the interval of time, and no longer indulged in sniping by day, but a heavy desultory fire was kept up all night. Also at night, larger parties, between twenty and forty strong, sometimes with a machine gun, would lie out in No Man's Land. One patrol of the 53rd, under Lieut. E. L. Lindzell, of the Herefords, was caught by such a party of the enemy, but the prompt order of Lieut.

* Arrived in Egypt on 1st June from Salonica.

Lindzell to charge through the Turks extricated the patrol with the loss of but two men.

A smart little affair was carried out by Lieut. K. Raynor, of the Middlesex, who with a party of men rushed a Turkish picquet on a sand dune known as Sugar Loaf hill, sixteen of the enemy were killed and twenty wounded—the Middlesex party lost two killed and six wounded.

The 4th and 5th Welch, and the 5th and 6th Royal Welch Fusiliers also had successful patrol encounters which yielded a few prisoners.

As for the artillery, batteries became expert in " test support." " It was a daily occurrence for an infantry officer to appear, suddenly, at our observation post, thrust a paper into the Gunner officer's hand on which was written a map co-ordinate, and murmur ' test support.' The round was supposed to reach the point indicated within a minute. Really it was amazing how this little device speeded up the machine, and all hands thoroughly enjoyed it."—(Captain Barton.)

For the rest, the protective wire was strengthened, and large working parties were employed nightly in digging slits for protection against bombardment, in burying cables, in constructing gun emplacements, and in widening communication trenches.

The relief of the Division, by the 54th, commenced during the night 23/24th August, and occupied four nights. Battalions then concentrated in what was known as the Southern Reserve area, beyond the Wadi Selka, behind Deir el Belah, and training for open warfare commenced on the 28th August.

· · · · ·

GENERAL SIR E. ALLENBY ASSUMES COMMAND

Great changes took place during this period of trench warfare and training. Sir A. Murray was recalled, and on the 28th June General Sir E. Allenby assumed command of the Egyptian Expeditionary Force. A vast amount of important work had been carried out under Sir A. Murray. The maintenance of a large force on the borders of Palestine was made possible by his organisation and construction. The striking range of the Army was no longer confined to a short radius from railhead on the coast. The supply of water had been increased and material had been accumulated.

Pondering over the situation, General Chetwode prepared an appreciation and a plan which he placed before the new Commander in

Chief on his arrival. The plan, in its broad conception, was accepted, and Sir E. Allenby cabled to the War Cabinet, giving details of his proposed operations. "My plan of operations," says Sir E. Allenby, "was based on his (Chetwode's) appreciation of the situation, and on the scheme which he put forward to me on my arrival in Egypt."

The width of the enemy front remained the same, Gaza to Beersheba, a distance of thirty miles—but every week that passed made it stronger. It had always been held by a series of entrenched localities, and these were now being joined up and improved. The attacks on Gaza had resulted in that place being transformed into a modern fortress, capable, as General Chetwode knew, of protracted resistance. There was still a big gap of some four miles between the Abu Hureira—Arab el Teiaha trench system and Beersheba, which stood by itself though covered by strong works. The Turkish front was wide, but their lateral communications were good, and enabled any portion of the line to be reinforced quickly.

The shifted balance in disposition of troops now left the Turks with one vulnerable flank only, and the plan was to capture Beersheba, deploy a force on the high ground to the north and north-west of the town and attack the Hureira-Sheria line.

"This front of attack was chosen for the following reasons: The enemy's works in this sector were less formidable than elsewhere, and they were easier of approach than other parts of the enemy defences; when Beersheba was in our hands we should have an open flank against which to operate, and I would make full use of our superiority in mounted troops, and a success here offered prospects of pursuing our advantage and forcing the enemy to abandon the rest of his fortified positions, which no other line of attack would afford." (Allenby.)

There were still, however, great difficulties to be overcome. The supply problem, when worked out, showed that the whole transport of the army, including thirty thousand pack camels, would have to be allotted to one portion of the force. Water was always a great anxiety. There was a supply, dependent on the success of the attack, at Beersheba and Sheria, but meanwhile it would have to be developed at Esani, Khalasa, and Asluj.

For the execution of this plan the Eastern Force was doubled in strength, receiving the 10th Division (Irish) consisting of three regular battalions and nine New Army battalions,* the 60th Division (London

---

* 10th Division arrived in Egypt from Salonica 30th August, 1917. The 75th was made up on the spot.

Second Line Territorial battalions), and the 75th Division (Territorial and Indian units).

And the Army was reorganised. We have now to deal with the Desert Mounted Corps, under Sir H. G. Chauvel; the XXth Corps, under Sir Philip Chetwode; and the XXIst Corps under Sir Edward Bulfin.

During these months of paper planning and preparation the 53rd Division did some excellent training in the back area, behind Deir el Belah. In the desert wastes that lay there, field firing could be carried out on a grand scale, with overhead machine gun, and artillery fire. " Oh, those days of divisional and brigade training, with their early starts, their ghastly greasy breakfasts, hurriedly pushed down in the glare and heat ! Our great relaxation was an evening ride to the sea, with a glorious bathe at the end of it ! But canteens were well stocked, concert parties were started, and leave to Cairo was plentiful." The Divisional Concert Party called itself " The Welsh Rare Bits."

There were other jaunts too—a kind of parade reconnaissance—a regular pageant that rode out in the direction of Beersheba containing the General Staff, the " Royal Party " in many motor cars.

" These reconnaissances were most interesting outings, and the programme was always the same. We would start from Belah in Ford cars about 10 a.m., and driving via Shellal (about 25 miles) arrive at el Buggar, our usual rendezvous, about 1 p.m. Here we would take to horses, which had been sent over to Shellal the day before and out to el Buggar during the morning, and reconnoitre various parts of the allotted line behind the cavalry screen from Toweil el Habari down to Wadi Saba one way, and through Point 820 to Point 810, and forward, nearly as far as Point 790, on the other. We would potter about, dodging a few shells generally, then back to el Buggar and the homely Fords, and finally home to dinner about 8 p.m." There were also new aeroplanes " stunting " from Belah Aerodrome.

Certain changes in Brigade Commands took place, Brigadier-General Rome, a gallant and popular figure, was given a cavalry brigade (he was a Hussar), and the 158th Brigade passed to Brigadier-General H. A. Vernon; Brigadier-General Butler was invalided home, and the 160th Brigade was taken over by Brigadier-General Pearson (Middlesex Regiment); finally, after all the training and preparation were completed, Brigadier-General Travers fell ill, and Colonel N. E. Money (West Kents) assumed command of the 159th Brigade.

"All is stir and bustle—equipment is overhauled, surplus baggage is despatched dumpwards, camel and limber loads are culculated to a nicety. One night, in the middle of October, the whole Division melts away, leaving a dummy camp to amuse Fritz. Allenby's first offensive has begun!"

. . . . .

THE CONCENTRATION

The first move of any unit towards the concentration area for battle was made by the 158th Brigade. On the 20th October, at the close of a beautiful autumn day, the Brigade crossed the railway below Belah, marching east. General Mott stood near by and took the salute.

The greatest secrecy had been enjoined. In a personal letter to his Divisional Commanders, General Chetwode asked them to give their careful attention " to every device by which enemy airmen may be deceived, such as leaving your present bivouacs and areas looking as much occupied as possible by leaving tents standing and digging holes wherever you have had blanket shelters, by not pitching Brigade Field Ambulances, or showing their flags, and by not allowing new ground to be used. I would ask that the troops of the 60th, 74th and 53rd Divisions when east of the Wadi should keep concealed as much as possible in Wadis, gardens, near buildings, etc., etc." Added to which the 10th and 60th had to move, the Desert Mounted Corps had to move, and the whole vast army had to prepare. The arrangement for supply to the XXth Corps alone meant the organisation of an army of camels.

After a fifteen mile march, the 158th Brigade took over Kent Fort and Shellal Defences from the 161st Brigade, 60th Division.

Here they remained for a few days, studying orders, and thoroughly reconnoitring the routes into and out of the Wadi and the country round Imara. On the 24th, they were relieved by the 159th Brigade, and moved into the bed of the Wadi for the night—" a grisly squash, hot and dusty, and entirely airless."

The whole Division arrived, and steel helmets were issued. A certain number of these headpieces had been given out for trial at Belah, and some units, after laying them on the sand for an hour found that they were too hot to touch and reported adversely on them. The consensus of opinion, however, seems to have been that they were good.

On the 25th October, the 158th Brigade moved forward into No Man's Land and took up an outpost position from Goz el Basal through Goz el

Geleib, and back towards the Wadi, covering the other brigades of the division, and also the construction of a railway towards Karm.

THE "BACKSHEESH STUNT"

On the 27th the Division, covered by the 5th Royal Welch Fusiliers and Herefords, and one battalion of the 229th Brigade attached, advanced to occupy a line through el Buggar and el Girheir. The attached troops were the 91st Heavy Battery (60 pdrs.), 378th Siege Battery (6-in. Hows.), 229th Inf. Brigade (74th Division), and one company of the 5th Royal Irish Regiment (Pioneers). The position to be taken up was already occupied by the 8th Mounted Brigade, Brigadier-General Rome's new command, and the infantry were on the move, when "a most unpleasant little battle, always known as the 'Backsheesh Stunt,' presumably because it was so unnecessary" commenced.

The two main points of the outpost line were Hills 720 and 630. Brigadier-General Rome did not think the Turks were making any serious attack, but he asked that one battalion and a battery should move on Hill 630, on his left. The 5th Royal Welch Fusiliers were sent, a distance of some eight miles.

The sounds of battle had commenced at dawn, and at 7 a.m. there seemed to be no improvement, so Brigadier-General Vernon despatched the Herefords to assist.

Soon after nine o'clock the order was received for the whole Brigade to march on Hill 630, and for the 160th Brigade to march on Hill 720.

"At 10.15, the Brigadier and I rode to Rome's headquarters," says Captain Ashton, "Here we saw the most melancholy sight—the fall of both Hills 630 and 720. As they were about four miles away, and the air was very clear, we could see the Turks, infantry and cavalry apparently mixed, swarm up and over the threatened positions. Both defences were entirely wiped out, except a small party which managed to hold out in a cruciform trench in rear of Hill 630, and which was eventually extricated. The 5th Royal Welch Fusiliers, followed by the Herefords, were moving up quickly, but the distance was too great.

"The situation was now distinctly unpleasant. We were operating in a large saucer, so to speak, of which the Turks, through their capture of these posts, held the eastern edge. Consequently, they had perfect observation of our every movement. We understood that they were holding their line in some strength—an aeroplane message said 2,000 rifles—and, though the 5th Royal Welch Fusiliers were in touch it was obvious that they could not attack a position of such strength alone, and without any artillery support. The Herefords were some distance behind, followed by the 6th and 7th Royal Welch Fusiliers. The Howitzer Battery of our artillery brigade was, for some obscure reason, still back in Shellal, and had to be fetched up, while the other batteries were in action on a flank.

"About 3 p.m. the Turks started to shell us. The situation was perfectly ludicrous. The whole plain was crammed full of troops—for the 160th were crossing our rear—there were batteries, camel convoys, ambulances, General Mott in a motor car, and every conceivable kind of target. The enemy artillery observer must have lost his head in the multiplicity of things to aim at, with the result that he nearly missed the lot.

"Finally, we got out some sort of orders, and at 4 p.m. the attack began. As soon as things got really going, the Turks slipped away, and we re-occupied the line of hills without difficulty."

This strong reconnaissance by the Turks—Sir E. Allenby gives their strength as between two and three thousand infantry and two regiments of cavalry, with guns—was a curious affair, for it does not seem to have enlightened the enemy on the true plan of attack at that moment in preparation before their eyes. But while this "affair" was in progress, the bombardment of Gaza commenced, and the cannonade seems to have given the final touch to a clever ruse played by an Intelligence Officer on the Turks. The story bears repeating. This officer rode towards the Turkish lines with the object of inducing one of their mounted patrols to pursue him. He succeeded, and as he galloped away he pretended he had been hit, swayed in his saddle, and dropped his haversack. The conscientious Turks picked up the haversack, and found in it a letter to the officer's wife, telling her, amongst other things such as a husband might write to his wife, that the attack on Beersheba was a feint, Gaza being the real objective. He also enclosed a five pound note to pay a pressing account. The Turks, and Germans, found the "fiver" absolutely convincing. The letter played an important part in the surprise that was effected.

The outpost line, running along the ridge which masked all movement to the west of it from the Beersheba lines, was occupied by the 53rd Division, and the engineers worked feverishly on the railway line until it reached Karm.

Meanwhile other troops concentrated for the attack.

THE OPENING OF THE BATTLE

The opening movements for the great battle that followed are contained in the following extracts from orders :—

"The XXth Corps, in co-operation with the Desert Mounted Corps will attack and destroy the enemy's detachment at Beersheba. The Desert Mounted Corps will co-operate on the right of the XXth Corps and attack the enemy's defences from the south-east to the north-west of Beersheba and the town itself. The XXth Corps, less one division in reserve, will carry out the main attack.

The 60th Division will attack the Beersheba works on the right of the 74th Division, while the 53rd Division, with attached troops will cover the left flank of the Corps from a position on a general line Kh. el Sufi and el Girheir. . . .

The following troops, attached to the 74th Division, will be known as 'Smith's Group,' under the command of Brigadier-General C. L. Smith, V.C.—the Imperial Camel Brigade (less two companies), two battalions of the 158th Brigade.* The rôle of these troops is to hold the ground from the Wadi Saba . . . to the right of the 53rd Division, to deal with any counter stroke against the left of the 74th Division, to prevent the transfer of troops to reinforce the enemy on the front of attack of the 60th and 74th Divisions by holding the enemy in his trenches north of the Wadi Saba."

The attack on Beersheba, the defences of which it will be remembered were widely separated from the general Turkish line, was divided into two phases, the first against some advanced works on the 60th Division front (right), the second against the main line. While the enemy was held by this attack, the Anzac Mounted Division, and the Imperial Mounted Division, now renamed the Australian Mounted Division, were to make a wide encircling movement from Asluj, and charge into the town from the south-east.

On the 30th October, the left of the 53rd Division front was taken over by the 30th Infantry Brigade of the 10th Division, and, after dusk, a slight advance was made across the Hanafish. During the night the 74th and 60th Divisions moved up and deployed on the right of the 53rd for the attack.

In the successful battle of the 31st October, the 53rd Division guarding the left flank was unmolested by the enemy. The 158th Brigade was more concerned than the others, it was split in two parts.

* Actually it was the 158th Brigade, less two battalions, in Smith's Group.

"We in Smith's Force, *i.e.*, the Brigade, less two battalions, marched at 5.30 p.m. (30th) to our old haunt, el Buggar, and then east, along the Beersheba-Fara track, in rear of the 229th Brigade, till we got to Taweil el Habari, which is at the top of the slope whence the ground runs gently to Beersheba. The 5th and 6th Royal Welch Fusiliers then turned right handed and marched down to their allotted positions. There was some shelling away out on the right and occasional rifle fire, but otherwise all was silent in front of us—but not so behind us ! The noise of tractors bringing up guns was overpowering, as if the whole British army was on the move, and sounded like the roar of London traffic from a little way off. The whole plain behind us hummed with mechanical noises, and I marvelled that the enemy in their trenches could not hear it. They afterwards told us they were taken by surprise, but it is indeed hard to believe.

"The attack by the 60th and 74th Divisions began at dawn, and by 11.30 was entirely successful. Our rôle was purely demonstrative, and, although the 5th Royal Welch Fusiliers advanced in touch with the 229th Brigade on their right, and did what they could with long range machine gun and Lewis gun fire, we were not really in the picture. As the attack was designed only against the defences south of the Wadi Saba, the enemy in front of us in trenches across the road, where there was a particularly nasty-looking, heavily wired place, called the Barricade, was not being disturbed."

Actually the defences of Beersheba were not entered until about 12.30 p.m. At that time the 2nd Australian Light Horse were astride the Hebron road, to the north of the town, but it was not until about six in the evening, that the 4th Australian Light Horse galloped over several lines of trenches and entered Beersheba itself.

At one o'clock General Mott ordered Colonel Drage to send forward a few patrols in order to ascertain the situation on his front and right, and the 160th Brigade was warned to be ready to push a battalion to the north to threaten Irgeig. The Barricade was still reported held, but an advance in this direction had to receive the sanction of General Chetwode; it was received about four o'clock.

Colonel Drage was ordered to " demonstrate " with his two battalions, while the 230th Brigade attacked northwards and took the trenches in enfilade. It was, however, considered that the Herefords and 7th Royal Welch Fusiliers could not get in a position to help the 230th Brigade until 8.30 p.m., and the order was, therefore, cancelled. The 230th Brigade as a matter of fact found no opposition.

The 5th and 6th Royal Welch Fusiliers then took up an outpost line along the Beersheba-Fara road, across the Barricade and in touch with the 230th Brigade in Beersheba.

THE MARCH INTO THE HILLS

The first move in Allenby's offensive was completely successful. But, in order to ensure elbow room, the 53rd Division was ordered, during the night, to move at dawn, relieve the cavalry pickets on the hills to the north of the town, and occupy the line Towal Abu Jerwal-Muweileh, the Camel Corps would operate on the right.

"The chilly hour of 5.30 a.m. found us all present and correct at the Barricade, but with no instructions for a further move. After some delay General Mott arrived, a most wonderful sight, in a torn cardigan jacket, no tunic, a steel helmet, and riding a policeman's horse, with the rifle in the bucket, all complete. He was also very cross, as his car had broken down, and everything had gone wrong. However he had, as usual, a complete grasp of the tactical situation."

The General sat by the roadside and gave verbal instructions which were afterwards confirmed.

"The 53rd Division will move east, and then north to-day with the object of seizing a line from Towal Abu Jerwal, along the spur running west and north of Muweileh, with the I.C.C. on the right of Towal Abu Jerwal.

Troops will march in the following order :—

Advanced Guard—158th Brigade (less two battalions).
1 Section R.E.
1 Battery R.F.A. (266th Brigade).
Detachment of 3rd Welsh Field Ambulance.

Main body—Starting point Barricade on Beersheba Road.
0630 I.C.C. Brigade.
0700 Divisional H.Q.—Signal Company.
0710 Divisional R.E.
0730 Two Battalions 158th Bde. (under Col. Drage).
0745 266th Bde. R.F.A. (less 1 battery).
0800 159th Inf. Bde. and Detachment 2nd Welsh Field Amb.
0830 H.Q. Artillery and 265th Bde. R.F.A.
0845 267th Bde. R.F.A.
0900 Trench Mortar Batteries.
0905 160th Inf. Brigade and Detachment 1st Welsh Fld. Amb.
0930 Field Ambulances (less detachments).

"The 5th Royal Welch Fusiliers started off through Beersheba, which proved to be a small and fairly modern town, with Abraham's Wells still functioning, and then turned off north-east, with the 6th (R.W.F.), conforming to their movements about a mile to their left; 'A' Battery 266th Brigade under James Gammel, came with us, but we very soon got into such hilly and broken country that they had to go right out to the right to find a passable track. By 11 a.m. we reached our first point, Hill 1020, where we were joined by Colonel Drage and his army, which had marched straight across country from their late position. We climbed on and up, and successfully occupied Towal Abu Jerwal at 2 p.m. It was a long march, about 16 miles over a terribly mountainous and trackless country, particularly the last few miles. In many cases the men, who suffered considerably after living so long on sand and soft going, had to proceed in single file—we were marching on a bearing and could not deviate to any extent. The passage of limbers was appallingly difficult, but a limber can go in most places, and finally we arrived intact, not having dropped a man."—(Ashton, 158th Brigade.)

The 158th Brigade took up an outpost position beyond the Lekiyeh Caves, with the Camel Corps on the right and the 159th Infantry Brigade on the left, slightly in rear. The night passed quietly, perhaps gloomily, as the ration convoy had lost its way and the men had no food or water. At one time the question of water for the whole Corps was acute, but the 53rd Division were the real sufferers.

The 159th Brigade, which had been following the 158th, had branched off about Khashm el Buteiyir and marched on Muweileh as a separate column. The 160th Brigade, on relief by the 30th Brigade, on the Wadi Hanafish, had marched ten miles to Beersheba, where they were ordered to rest and feed, and only moved forward again during the afternoon.

The administrative difficulties now commenced. The nearest water was seven miles away, at Beersheba. This difficulty became serious later on, as the Division advanced to the Khuweilfeh Heights, eleven miles from Beersheba. Under arrangements made by the XXth Corps, water was sent up by Camel Convoy, but the convoys seldom arrived at their destination up to time, owing to the great distance they had to cover, and also to their guides losing their way in the roadless, hilly country. Prior to the operations, two water bottles were issued to each man, and undoubtedly eased the situation; but the only solution to the horse question was sending them back to Beersheba for the night, and keeping them there till it was necessary to move guns and vehicles forward. This first march into the hills was a very trying one. From point to point the Division had moved

14 miles in the day, over a mountainous and roadless country, which added miles to the map distance.

General Mott reported that the Turks had appeared opposite the Abu Jerwal Hill about half-way between Beersheba and Khuweilfeh, shortly after it was occupied by the 158th Brigade, " and it appeared likely that had they not been forestalled by the rapid advance of the 53rd Division, they would have established themselves there to impede our further advance. Finding the cavalry were working north, in the direction of Khuweilfeh Heights and Ras el Nagb, they retired to the Khuweilfeh Heights. During the night the 10th Division had occupied Irgeig, and my left was in touch with this Division."

. . . . .

THE SITUATION IN THE HILLS

Ever since the 27th October, the bombardment of Gaza had been proceeding with consistent severity, and the Turks and their German advisers were convinced that the blow would fall there. After the capture of Beersheba there was a pause of one day in the infantry attack, and then, on the 2nd November, General Bulfin attacked on the coastal sector, captured Umbrella Hill, and advanced to Sheikh Hassan. The whole of the Gaza positions were now threatened.

But the Turks had also moved. Colonel Garsia, at a later date G.S.O.1 to the 53rd Division, visited Berlin in 1920, and had an interview with General Kress von Kressenstein, who good-naturedly answered certain questions. He was asked the following : " When you realised that Allenby's main attack was against your left flank (he had already told me that he had, right up to the last minute, expected it via Gaza), what did you do ? " His reply was that "*he moved his general reserves to strike the outer flank of the turning movement, his object being to get outside it,*" but the whole of his plan failed through the occupation by British troops of some hills, from which he was unable to dislodge them. The troops were, of course, the 53rd, and the Imperial Camel Corps, under " Camel " Smith, who were attached to the 53rd Division and played an important part in the battle.

Early in the morning of the 2nd November, aeroplanes reported a large number of enemy columns moving east from the plain. At ten o'clock General Chetwode visited General Mott, and it was decided that the 53rd Division should remain on the defensive for that day, and dig in, and that one brigade of the 74th Division should be attached to the 53rd to take over the left of the line, the whole of which covered six miles.

The situation had necessitated a change in the original plan for the further advance after the capture of Beersheba. The intention had been for the 53rd Division to make a frontal attack on the Kauwukah* System, while the 60th and 74th Divisions took the whole of the fortified area in flank and reverse. But, with the 53rd Division facing a strong enemy force in the hills, the 60th Division were ordered to attack the Kauwukah System, and the 74th had the job of taking the Turkish line in flank and reverse, when the time came.

During the night, General Mott received an order from the XXth Corps to advance as early as possible in the morning and gain touch with the mounted troops operating in the direction of Khuweilfeh (the 7th Mounted Brigade had established itself during the day on a hill two miles east of Ain Koleh). The 74th Division was to move to a position of assembly, in readiness to protect the left flank of the 53rd. One 60-pdr. battery, and one battalion of the Imperial Camel Corps were attached to the 53rd Division.

General Mott decided to advance in three columns. The 160th Brigade, which had been in reserve, was brought up from Muweileh to advance north up a valley lying to the east of the Abu Jerwal peak. The whole nature of the battlefield had changed, and the line of advance was over rocky, mountainous country. One battery of the 267th Field Artillery Brigade accompanied the 160th Brigade, and it was necessary to make wadi crossings, as the column advanced. The Gunners succeeded in hauling their guns up the head of the valley to a position within useful range of the Khuweilfeh Heights, but the track they used could not be described as passable for wheels.

The 265th Field Artillery Brigade accompanied the 159th Infantry Brigade, which formed the left column, advancing up the Kohleh track. The remainder of the Divisional Artillery moved east with the 5th Royal Welch Fusiliers, under Colonel Borthwick, to gain the better road clear of the main hills east of Lekiyeh Caves.

The 158th Infantry Brigade, less one battalion, remained in reserve, and sent all their animals back to Beersheba to water and feed.

To follow the progress of battalions step by step through this difficult country is impossible—no map shows the true configuration of the ground. The main Turkish position was in a mass of jumbled hills running down in many places to wadis with precipitous sides. There were, however, two main features; about the centre was a dominating hill, Khuweilfeh,

* Qawuqa—*R.G.S.*

the key to the whole position, and on the Turkish left a flat topped hill, the Tell, commanding a broad, fairly open valley, down which ran a track of sorts (more water course than track) to Beersheba. To the east of this valley was a north and south spur, culminating in the height of Ras el Nagb which was held by the 5th Mounted Brigade (afterwards relieved by the Imperial Camel Corps).

To add to the difficulties of operating in such a country there was an atmospheric obstacle—a true obstacle to movement—the Khamsin, which blew steadily and caused the postponement of the next stage of the major operation. The Khamsin had to be overcome by the determination of the Welshmen, but it caused much suffering.

"Hard days these. Very little water, never enough for a wash; bully beef and biscuits unvaried, no mails, officers' kits only 30 pounds and often miles behind, dust and heat. We wore 'tin hats,' and the intense heat of the sun on them made our heads feel like poached eggs. The battle of Khuweilfeh has been described in many narratives and despatches, but I have never seen mentioned the appalling shortage of water from which we suffered. We had about three pints for forty-eight hours, which included a long march up the stifling, winding ravines of the Judean foothills, followed by incessant fighting, the temperature, thanks to the Khamsin, which prevailed, being that of August. It was real hell. A lot of men went nearly mad with thirst."—(Le Fleming.)

But the 53rd Division advanced just the same, attacking in three columns.

The 160th Brigade Group had on its line of advance to make good the commanding heights of the range of hills rising to Khuweilfeh; the ground fell away to the left, where the 159th Brigade was operating, dropping to the great rolling plain. As the 160th pushed forward, the Turk, deprived of his commanding ground, made every use of the cover afforded by the steep, rocky ravines which scored the lower slopes opposite the 159th Brigade.

Brigadier-General Money says that "the great heat in the deep wadis made everyone suffer from thirst. The 4th and 5th Welch Regiment battalions suffered severely. The former made a most gallant attack on a rocky height, driving back the enemy, who were using bombs, and bayonetting them all. The 265th Artillery Brigade, under Lieut.-Colonel Walker, assisted me greatly, and the 7th Cheshires protected my left flank against largely superior forces of the enemy. Fighting continued until dark, the enemy at many points holding the opposite sides of deep

THE FLAT-TOPPED HILL AT KHUWEILFEH.

BURIAL GROUND AT KHUWEILFEH.

precipices and ravines, from 100 to 300 yards off. The majority of casualties were due to shell fire and machine gun fire from deep wadis in the low ground on our left flank. They amounted during the day to between 350 and 400 all ranks."

The hill taken by the 4th Welch was named by them " Stone High Hill." The country round this place was very broken and Lieut.-Colonel Hulton reported, after this exploit, that his battalion was much split up and scattered in the confusing and tumbled area. He, however, managed to advance and take another hill.

Slowly the Division pressed forward in the sweltering heat. By 12.30 the 5th Royal Welch Fusiliers, under Lieut.-Colonel Borthwick, had got up to the line held by the cavalry on the extreme right, and were in touch with the Turks on the lower eastern slopes of the Khuweilfeh position. The cavalry then withdrew to Beersheba, with the exception of those units holding Nagb.

In the centre, as the advance of the 160th Brigade continued northwards, the enemy resistance increased, and it became clear to General Mott that he had not to do with a rearguard, but that the Turks were holding this position in strength, and meant to retain it. Khuweilfeh appeared to be a series of knolls, with a spur running from the western flank to the plain. The ground between this simple looking position and that occupied by the 160th Brigade presented no particular difficulty to the eye, but on closer acquaintance proved to be formidable, and difficult to cross. The advance was continually held up by cleverly concealed machine guns and snipers. The Turks did not expose themselves in any numbers and were hard to locate. But, at the close of the day, Brigadier-General Pearson was within striking distance of the main line of defence.

The very intricacy of the country which impeded the advance offered opportunities for clever and stouthearted scouts. Just before sunset a patrol of the Sussex, with Major Scott, R.E., and an Interpreter as guide, succeeded in getting through the Turkish lines to the wells in rear, where it was fired on, but returned unscathed. This incident raised hopes that the Turks intended to evacuate their position during the night.

Under cover of darkness the Sussex occupied the lower slopes of the Tell,* the flat topped hill, and the 5th Royal Welch Fusiliers jumped some low hills on their front on the initiative of Lieut. Colonel Borthwick.

* The sketch map given is taken from the Map used at the time. The confusion of " The Tell " and " Khuweilfeh " arises from it. One cannot follow the actual engagement on it.

Amongst the day's casualties were two commanding officers, Lieut.-Colonels Wilkins (Queens) and Hulton (4th Welch), both wounded.

General Mott says that " the 160th Brigade had had an arduous day, having been on the move since 5.30 a.m., and completed twelve miles over very trying country, and the day had been unusually hot and close. I, therefore, ordered the 158th Brigade to march by night so as to rendezvous at the fork roads one mile north of Kh. el Ras by 3.30 a.m., it being my intention to attack the Khuweilfeh heights with a fresh brigade on the following day. My intention, however, did not please the 160th Brigade, and Brigadier-General Pearson requested that he might continue the attack on Khuweilfeh with his brigade at dawn the next day. I consented to his request, and ordered the 160th Brigade to complete the occupation of Khuweilfeh."

But dawn of the 4th November broke on a gloomy prospect. The convoys had again lost their way, and the men of the 160th Brigade were without food or water. The advance, however, commenced at 5 a.m., and the lower slopes of the hills were here and there occupied, and then the C.R.A. Brigadier-General J. W. Hope reported to General Mott that the ammunition which he had been ordered to get up the previous day had not arrived, and that he could not support a serious attack. General Mott promptly directed Brigadier-General Pearson not to press his attack, but to take up the best line he could.

A grizzly day! It was impossible to get food and water up to the 160th Brigade until nightfall.

When the general activity which had been stirred up amongst the Turks in the jumbled mass of hills died down, General Mott went forward with Brigadier-General Vernon to make a close reconnaissance of the enemy position. It was not done without protest from the enemy, whose snipers were numerous and vigilant. The Brigadier had previously reconnoitred the position and General Mott concurred with his views to attack from an east and south-east direction with the right of the attacking force on the flat-topped Tell, and the left on the Khuweilfeh hill, and in view of the many cleverly concealed machine guns, to do so before dawn. The Brigadier was ordered to work out all details, and the 4th Sussex and the 3rd Battalion Imperial Camel Corps were placed under his orders.

During the day sniping and shelling were active on the left, in front of the 159th Brigade, and two slight attacks were attempted by the Turks, but were broken. On the extreme right a strong attack was launched against the 5th Mounted Brigade, who still held the high ground at Ras el Nagb, but was beaten off. And, from the plain in the west, large bodies of Turks, estimated at two thousand at least, moved into the hills which faced the 53rd Division.

At seven o'clock in the evening orders were received from General Chetwode not to attack the Khuweilfeh heights without direct sanction from the XXth Corps.

But the lull in the great battle, which had been brought about by the Khamsin, was at an end. On the 5th November the XXth Corps issued orders for the general advance of the Corps on the 6th, and placed the 53rd Division under the orders of the Desert Mounted Corps.

. . . . .

THE GENERAL ACTION IS CONTINUED

It is of interest to consider the original forecast of the first phase in the battle, the attack on Beersheba. It was thought that the 60th Division would after the battle be on the conquered position, possibly with troops in Beersheba developing water, that the 74th would be between the Fara-Beersheba road and Kh. el Sufi, that the 53rd would be on the line Kh. el Sufi-Bir Imleih-el Girheir, with outposts covering the left of the 74th Division, and finally that the 10th Division would be at Shellal.

The situation was utterly different. Mounted troops had made no impression on the Turkish outposts on the Khuweilfeh position. The 53rd Division had been diverted and was heavily engaged in the Judean foothills, on the extreme right, and the 74th was on their left, the line was then carried on by the 60th and the 10th (about Abu Irgeig). The 53rd had been slipping to the right all the time, and some of the ground formerly occupied by them was taken up by the 74th. Behind the junction of these two divisions was the Yeomanry Mounted Division, ready to fill the gap which the diverging line of attack would cause.

So far as the 53rd Division was concerned, the Corps orders ran :—

" The G.O.C. XXth Corps intends to resume the attack on the 6th November with the object of securing the Sheria water supply and capturing the Kauwukah System. . . . The attack must be pressed with the utmost rapidity and determination, as the enemy must be given no respite until his resistance is broken down, and it is essential to secure the water at Sheria before nightfall. The Desert Mounted Corps, to which the 53rd Division will be attached temporarily from 0600 on the 6th November, is allotted the following task :

(a) to protect the right flank of the Corps;

(b) To take advantage of any retirement of the enemy to press forward and seize the Nejileh and Jemmame water supplies.

"The 53rd Division is about Ain Kohleh, and will extend its left so as to occupy the general line Khuweilfeh-Rijm el Dhib.* The Yeomanry Mounted Division of the Desert Mounted Corps is to be concentrated south-west of Ain Kohleh by 0700 on November the 6th, ready to close the gap between the 53rd and 74th Divisions, which attacks on the right of the XXth Corps, and to take advantage of any enemy retirement to push forward to the line Kh. Abu Rasheid-el Zubala, and thence to the right of the 74th Division."

This order placed the 53rd Division on the lower ground, and left the dominating heights of Khuweilfeh in the hands of the Turks, on the right flank of the Corps. That General Kressenstein was likely to commit the whole of his general reserve in that direction was not realised by the Higher Command.

General Mott writes of the situation as he saw it: "I felt an honest doubt as to my ability to carry out the operation ordered. A glance at the map shows the difficulties and risks that would be run.

"The 53rd Division, with two infantry brigades facing north and already in close grips with the Turkish position around Khuweilfeh, had orders to side-slip through the enemy's lines down to the lower slopes of the hills and occupy a line facing north-east from Khuweilfeh-Rijm el Dhib successively as the XXth Corps advanced on the Kauwukah system of trenches and Sheria.

"Khuweilfeh was the trump card for either side; if the Turks were defeated there it seemed clear that the XXth Corps advance would be protected, and it would free the 53rd Division from carrying out a very complicated operation of a nature only suitable against guerilla warfare.

"From the Turks' point of view the importance of the Khuweilfeh-Ras el Nagb position lay in the fact that if we got it he lost his alternative line of retreat to the Hebron road—as it was, although defeated after 24 hours of ding-dong fighting at Khuweilfeh, he succeeded in holding more than his own at Ras el Nagb, where the gallant Colonel Smith and the Imperial Camel Corps were so hard pressed that I gave them my last infantry battalion to reinforce them, and still the bulk of the Turks were able to get away on to the Hebron road.

"Khuweilfeh was also the dominating feature on the whole battle front, and therefore the best observation post for the direction of artillery fire on either side. It was the obvious place for von Kressenstein to assemble

* Rujm edh Dhib—*R.G.S.*

his general reserve if he meant to fight at all on his front; and if he were strong enough, what an opportunity to strike down on the flank and rear of the 53rd Division and XXth Corps provided he could hold it, with always a way back to the Hebron road if he were squeezed out of his retreat north. Such a blow might have been of a decisive nature if the 53rd Division left their present position on the high ground. Nor was von Kressenstein a general to be despised.

"It was a much simpler operation for the 53rd Division to take the initiative and knock the Turks off Khuweilfeh; moreover this plan freed the mounted troops for more important work.

"I therefore felt bound to go and put my views before XXth Corps. I was informed by Brigadier-General Bartholomew, General Staff XXth Corps, that mounted troops would deal with the Khuweilfeh position. I explained that the position was one of great strength, and it would be difficult for mounted troops to make any impression on it, and that nothing less than an infantry division would be able to tackle it; nor did I feel justified in abandoning the high ground under the assumption that mounted troops would take it. The terrain made it essentially an infantry operation, which required more artillery than the mounted troops possessed. My views were then put before the Corps Commander.

"Later in the day, Sir E. Allenby and General Chauvel, commanding the mounted troops, visited my headquarters, and I was able to show the Commander in Chief on the ground the Turkish position. In a few minutes the Commander in Chief approved of my proposal that the 53rd Division should attack the Khuweilfeh position, his only proviso being that the operation should be executed simultaneously with the advance of the XXth Corps—he wanted to avoid any possibility of the Turks retreating on their whole front before his general scheme was launched."

And so, during the night, the 265th Artillery Brigade, less one battery, was withdrawn from the left and brought round via Abu Jerwal to give additional support to the 158th Brigade. The whole of the artillery was placed under Colonel James Walker. This was the first of many extraordinary achievements by the gunners. Guns required not one, but two teams, and were manhandled as well; the move was not by batteries but by single guns! The country was not only difficult but unknown, with horses and men tired from incessant moving and fighting. Time did not permit reconnaissance or the selection of battery positions, or the usual registration. The guns were simply dragged up by the side of other batteries which had already registered, and opened fire on data supplied by them. After the battle, Brigadier-General Vernon asked that as many gunners as possible might be allowed to go on to the heights of Khuweilfeh and see what they had done—the Turks lay in heaps where the barrage had caught them.

The Imperial Camel Corps was ordered to attract the enemy's attention by a demonstration on the right of Ras el Nagb.

Brigadier-General Vernon had arranged to hold the 5th Royal Welch Fusiliers in reserve, and had detailed the Herefords to attack on the right, the 6th Royal Welch Fusiliers in the centre, and the 7th on the left, while the Sussex, attached to the Brigade, were to form a flank on the left.

The position was clearly marked. The 7th Fusiliers on the left had Khuweilfeh Hill, frequently referred to as the Tell; so also is the flat topped hill which was on the right commanding the valley between the ridges, and which the Herefords would envelop on the line of their advance. At all events there was no mistaking the shape of the hills. But the terrain was difficult, for although the two features were conspicuous the enemy's position was across a very grim and broken bit of country with steep minor hills and precipitous sided ravines. His machine guns were placed, some to fire down the wadis or ravines, others to sweep the crests of the lesser ridges.

After dark, the jumping off line was marked, by the aid of a compass, with sand bags, and the Intelligence Officers and scouts reconnoitred the ground and the approaches to it.

On the 6th November, at 4 a.m., in the light of approaching dawn, the artillery barrage opened and with it the sixteen guns of the 158th Machine Gun Company. From 4.20, all lifted 100 yards at a time and the advance of the infantry commenced.

KHUWEILFEH

The account of the opening of the battle given by the 7th Royal Welch Fusiliers is typical of all battalions. "The battalion formed up in column of route. Lewis gun ammunition was man-handled, the Lewis gun mules being used to carry spare ammunition and bombs. Arriving at the line of deployment, the battalion formed up on a four-platoon front in five lines at 25 yards distance, the fifth line being formed by Lewis gunners withdrawn from their platoons. The whole frontage of the battalion was 500 yards. Two water bottles were carried and 170 rounds of ammunition, also the unconsumed portion of the day's ration, one extra day's ration, and the iron ration. All ranks were clearly made to understand that on no account, without an order from the C.O., was any ammunition to be fired, and all work was to be done with the bayonet. At 4.23, three minutes behind scheduled time, the battalion moved off to attack the Tell (? Khuweilfeh Hill) under cover of the barrage, and gained its objective at 5.3 with apparently few casualties."

On the right, in the valley commanded by the flat-topped hill, there was a small hillock, and in the hillock a cave which was also a tomb, with a square door facing south. Here the Brigadier placed his headquarters, and had a good view of the fight. With two artillery brigades, the 265th and 267th, supporting them, the infantry advanced with confidence. " To us in the East it (*i.e.*, the artillery) was a revelation; judged by the standards of France it wasn't much. All the brigade's 16 machine guns joined in from the hillock on which we sat, and the din was terrific."

The whole attack went like clockwork, and all objectives were occupied just as dawn was breaking. The enemy, cowed by the creeping barrage, was bayonetted in large numbers. But the treacherous morning fog, which the 53rd Division had good cause to remember, visited them again, and robbed them of an important capture. The advance had been rapid and irresistible, and on the right Captain G. N. Berney, with a company of Herefords, came on a ravine and found nine Turkish field guns, limbered up, and about to move back. Captain Berney charged, bayonetted the personnel, and captured the guns. At that moment a thick mist came down. A certain amount of mixing of units and general confusion ensued, and the 7th Royal Welch Fusiliers, mistaking certain advance troops of the 6th and the Herefords, who had swept on over the captured guns, for Turks, called for artillery fire. The gallant Captain Berney was killed, but whether from our own artillery fire or not is uncertain, and a general retirement took place. The guns had to be abandoned.

But for this unhappy accident, the whole position would have been captured in one and a half hours, with insignificant casualties. Troops could not, in the mist, give each other support, and the Turkish machine gunners knew the ground and the direction in which they should fire. The Herefords on the right had over-run the flat topped hill, but found that they were so enfiladed by machine gun fire that the place was untenable, and so had to retire to the forward slope of the hill, but when the Brigadier received their report he put the hill under artillery fire and was able to deny it to the enemy.

The situation was uncertain and puzzling. After a while the Brigadier ordered all artillery to cease fire, and all troops to remain where they were until the fog lifted. When it was possible to see, about 7 a.m., the Sussex were found to be on their appointed objective, forming a flank to the Brigade, the 7th Royal Welch Fusiliers were in possession of Khuweilfeh Hill, the 6th Royal Welch Fusiliers were holding a spur running south-east from Khuweilfeh, the Herefords were on the forward slope of the flat-topped hill on the right, which was just short of their objective, and the 3rd battalion of the Camel Corps protected that flank.

The right of the line was, however, so swept by machine gun fire that it was deemed impossible in daylight to capture several minor features occupied by the enemy, which it would be necessary to hold before the line could be securely consolidated. A company of the 5th Royal Welch Fusiliers was moved up in support.

At nine o'clock the Turks started a series of counter-attacks by launching a strong force against the 7th Royal Welch Fusiliers on Khuweilfeh. They succeeded, by the weight of their attack, in driving the battalion off the hill, but prompt artillery support enabled the Fusiliers to advance again and retake the hill at the point of the bayonet. General Mott then sent up the Middlesex as an additional reserve, and the Brigadier ordered one company in close support.

During the day, the Turks made five separate attacks on the hill, but, with the exception of the first temporary success, spent themselves in vain. Similarly they tried repeatedly to re-establish themselves on the flat-topped hill, but the artillery and machine guns kept that place clear.

On the right, three troops of Westminster Dragoons performed useful work by keeping in touch with the Camel Corps.

And so the day passed, the Brigade holding what they had won in spite of galling enfilade fire from a few under features remaining in the hands of the Turks. At dusk, the Middlesex took over Khuweilfeh from the 7th Royal Welch Fusiliers, and also the Sussex position on the flank, the latter leaving one company in support; the 5th Royal Welch Fusiliers took over from the 6th and the Herefords. The casualties in the Brigade had been 36 officers and 584 other ranks.*

In other parts of the line there had been some excitement while the 158th Brigade was attacking. There was a rocky bluff, Hill 1250, between the 160th and 159th Brigades, which was held by the Turks. With this commanding feature in their hands they had worked forward in large numbers into a pocket. Brigadier-General Money had been ordered to advance on a bearing of 20°; but, with one battery only to support him, he was unable to make any headway, the 7th Cheshires, on his left, meeting a strong force of the enemy securely disposed on the far side of a precipitous ravine. General Mott's request to the Corps for a regiment of cavalry to take over less important parts of his line, and so release a battalion to

---

* Captain Fox Russell, R.A.M.C., attached to the 6th R.W.F., was awarded a posthumous V.C. for his gallantry in attending and rescuing wounded until he himself was killed.

attack the Bluff, was refused. Meanwhile the Turks, established in the pocket, wormed their way forward. It was only about four o'clock in the afternoon that Brigadier-General Money with his left still closely engaged, was able to release the 5th Welch, who arrived at divisional headquarters just in time—the Turks had got through between the 160th and 159th Brigades and were opposite General Mott's headquarters at a range of 1,300 yards. They retired, however, before the 5th Welch.

CAPTURE OF THE SHERIA POSITION

The 6th November was a day of far-reaching victory. While the 53rd Division was pinning down the Turkish General Reserves with their attack on Khuweilfeh and also protecting the right of the XXth Corps, the 74th, 60th, and 10th Divisions were moving against the Kauwukah System, with the water supply of Sheria as their main objective. All depended on the progress of the 74th Division on the right. The 74th attacked the enemy field-works east of the railway line, taking them in flank, but the works were strongly held and bristled with machine guns, and in addition the attack had to develop over open ground. This division had some heavy fighting but captured all objectives. The successful issue of the all-important flank attack—which had originally been allotted to two divisions—enabled the 60th and 10th Divisions to storm the Kauwukah Trenches. The 60th was then re-organised and advanced to battle for Sheria, which was finally occupied the following morning.

The part played in this hard fought but rapid and spectacular success by the 53rd Division was handsomely acknowledged by Sir E. Allenby. He realised quickly what had happened, and what they were doing. So early as half-past eleven in the morning he telegraphed to General Mott: "I congratulate you and your troops on admirable success of your efforts, and troops' gallant conduct. You have drawn enemy into very position required to facilitate success of main operations of XXth Corps. Your operations have given us most favourable prospects of success, which now depends on valour of 53rd Division."

At dawn on the 7th November, the 10th Division was launched against the Hureira Redoubt, a work of great natural strength well defended by artillery and machine guns, which they captured after a sharp fight.

The position on the morning of the 7th was that the enemy's centre was pierced, and a gap made for the cavalry. The Anzac Division rode through on the right of the 74th Division, which had long been out of touch with the 53rd, and the Australian Mounted Division (late Imperial

Division) sent a dismounted brigade to assist the 60th Division—who had found some difficulty in driving the Turks off the high ground overlooking the Wadi Sheria, and so widen the gap.

And while this was going on in the centre of the Army, General Bulfin discovered Gaza evacuated, and sent forward the Imperial Service Cavalry Brigade, and the 52nd Infantry Division.

On the morning of the 8th, the pursuit was taken up by the Anzac and the Australian Mounted Divisions and the 60th Division.

. . . . .

Meanwhile at 3.30 a.m., on the 7th November, a report was received by Brigadier-General Vernon that the enemy on his front was seen to be retiring. He could do nothing more than turn the artillery and machine guns on them. One large party north of Khuweilfeh Hill, sought to avoid the storm of bullets and shells by charging up the hill—the Middlesex drove them back with the bayonet into the zone of gun fire, where their losses were heavy.

The Division, now under the orders of General Barrow, as part of a force known as Barrowsdett, was ordered to stand fast and not attack the Bluff, which was still strongly held and a source of worry.

The 5th Royal Welch Fusiliers, armed with rifle grenades, bombarded and rushed a machine gun nest and party of snipers who had been causing much annoyance. The Middlesex repulsed a small attempt on the heights of Khuweilfeh. Away on the plain, the latter battalion could see large bodies of the enemy retiring in a north-easterly direction apparently making for the Hebron road, but Barrowsdett replied to General Mott that no cavalry was available for pursuit, all being required at Sheria, and the only thing that could be done was to turn the heavy artillery on the retiring enemy whenever possible.

With the fall of night the Turks continued their evacuation, a fact soon discovered by patrols who in the early morning brought in about 20 prisoners. One of these said that the Turkish troops had retired on Jerusalem.

The 159th Brigade went forward and took up an outpost position north of the wells—orders from Barrowsdett were that the Division should not advance further than was necessary to cover the Khuweilfeh Wells.

The Yeomanry Mounted Division was concentrated on the left and was engaged with Turkish rearguards; late in the afternoon on the 8th they were withdrawn to join the Desert Mounted Corps at Sheria. The 53rd Division reverted to the command of the XXth Corps. The Camel Brigade remained on the flank at Ras el Nagb.

On the 10th November, the Camel Brigade was relieved by the 160th Brigade, and this brought the operations, says General Mott, to a " sedentary period." The 159th and 160th Brigades remained in this area; the 158th moved to Sakaty* in order to relieve the supply difficulty.

* Sqāti—*R.G.S.*

GENERAL SITUATION
November-December, 1917.

Armistice discussions commenced between the Bolshevik Government and the Central Powers, 21st November.

German counter attacks at Cambrai, 30th November.

Permanent Allied Supreme War Council inaugurated, 1st December.

Suspension of hostilities between Russian and German Armies, 2nd December.

Hostilities between Roumania and Central Powers suspended, 6th December.

Cuba declares war on Austria Hungary, 16th December.

JERUSALEM

THE country which the big battle had opened to Sir E. Allenby ran from Beersheba to Dan ! The long Maritime Plain, broken by the incidental range of hills where it squeezes to a mere line of continuity round Mount Carmel to open on to the great Plain of Esdraelon ; the long mountainous backbone, broken again by the Plain of Esdraelon ; that unique watercourse, starting from the neighbourhood of Dan, sinking to the Sea of Galilee, sinking still further until it ends in the Dead Sea, 1,300 feet below the water level of the Mediterranean ; and then the gaunt, haggard mountains of Arabia !

Midway between Beersheba and the Plain of Esdraelon, on one side of the Central Range, near the edge of the weird ditch which is the Valley of Jordan, stands Jerusalem. Above Jerusalem, the Central Range falls directly on the Maritime Plain, but South of Jerusalem, the Judean Hills look on to a distinct and smaller range, of different lime stone, the Shephelah. The name means " Lowland."

Four main valleys, or passes, cut through the Shephelah into the Judean Hills. The first of these, from the south, is the Wadi el Alfranj, which provides a road through Beit Jibrin to Hebron ; there are several Roman roads, converging at Beit Jibrin. The second pass at Tell el Sufi, the Blanchgarde of the Crusaders, is the Wadi el Sunt, which leads to Bethlehem. The third pass is the Wadi es Surar, containing the railway line to Jerusalem. Finally the Valley of Ajalon, a broad, fertile plain, sloping up to the foot of the Central Range, where three gorges break through and run up past the two Beth-horons, and so to Jerusalem.

The great pursuit of the Turks streamed along the Maritime Plain ; and then one part of the defeated army turned east, into the Judean Hills, to defend Jerusalem, while the other stuck to the Plain and eventually formed a line slightly north of Jaffa.

The pursuit slowed down, and right up to the end of November there was some hard fighting to force the es Surar and Ajalon roads, the old line of advance taken by a long succession of ancient warriors in their attempts to capture Jerusalem—always from the west.

Former invasions of Judea had avoided the road from the south, probably because of the sixty miles of mountainous and barren country below Beersheba which have to be crossed, or skirted, before the level

Desert is reached. And yet the way from Beersheba is easy, a gentle ascent up the broad Wadi es Saba and Wadi Khulil to Hebron. The road is over moors, and in the spring time wheat is growing in the broader valleys—even in the narrower wadis wheat is grown on carefully arranged terraces, otherwise the slopes are mostly covered with scrub. There are olive groves near the villages, but elsewhere few trees.

The 53rd Division was near Dhaheriyah,* which is in the position of a border town. A little way off on the road to Hebron is Seil el Dilbeh, where there is water; the Ain Hegireh, with a shadoof for irrigation, on the north, and on the south the Ain Dilbeh, a square pool covered with weeds.

The 158th Brigade remained at Sakaty.

" There followed a period of waiting, of bad supplies, water shortage, a pest of flies, the latter in no small degree encouraged by the presence of innumerable dead horses and camels. All available transport was required for the XXIst Corps, on the other flank, so we had to go short. In this case hardship was cheerfully borne, for victory was in the air. They were great days, when each evening we would mark on a map fresh and thrilling limits to the advance. But the Judean wilderness offers few attractions except at sunrise and sunset—arid, rocky, treeless, a few autumn croci ! The inhabitants are Bedouin, untamed and unused to civilisation. They even used rifle stocks as firewood, so ignorant were they of the amenities of our modern existence. Agricultural life here is quite biblical. Any day one might see a young David minding the flocks. The septic sore scourge broke out with renewed vigour, and at least 50 per cent. of officers and men were incapacitated thereby."

THE WARNING TO ADVANCE OVER THE JUDEAN HILLS

But on the 24th November, while the XXIst Corps and Mounted Divisions were pushing through the Judean Hills to Jerusalem, from the west, General Mott, in splendid isolation on the south of Judea, received important instructions :—

" It is not desired to gain ground along the Hebron road at present, but to make all preparations to facilitate the despatch of a force to Bethlehem, and perhaps beyond, when the situation demands such movement. With this object in view, you should not increase the size of your advanced guard beyond what is necessary for security, and you should keep back, as far as possible, as much of your force as the

* Edh Dhahriye—*R.G.S.*

3RD

BATTLE OF GAZA

situation permits. With your troops thus disposed, you should do what you can gradually to accumulate supplies as far forward as the protection afforded by your advanced guard allows, making use of the transport of your rearmost troops for the purpose. You should also arrange that the whole of your force is in possession of one complete day's rations to be carried on the man in case a forward movement is ordered, in addition to the iron ration. It is possible that eventually a portion of your force may be required to march through to Bethlehem, to co-operate by action, either on the south-east or south-west of Jerusalem, with the XXth Corps operating on the west and north-west of Jerusalem. If this should be required that part of your force operating from Bethlehem would give up its present base altogether, and would have to maintain itself on the supplies carried, or previously placed on the Beersheba-Hebron road, until further supplies could be sent across from the Junction Station, Jerusalem railway, into Bethlehem from the west."

To this General Mott replied :—

" In accordance with your instructions, I propose to move my left brigade group (159th) at Burj el Beiyareh to vicinity of Dilbeh stream on 3rd December, followed by 160th Brigade on 4th December. This would bring the two brigade groups to a distance of sixteen miles from the present Turkish position covering the Jerusalem water supply.

" I do not anticipate rapid progress in this country, even two brigade groups would require a long road space when entirely confined to the road, and as the enemy is known to possess mountain guns with a long range it will be necessary to take the ordinary precautions with flanking detachments.

" I do not anticipate, therefore, being able to make any impression on the enemy till the early morning of the 7th. This is allowing for an eight mile advance per day from Dilbeh, and I consider to count on any increase in the distance covered would be inadvisable, as it is useless to try and fight in this country with exhausted infantry.

" My experience of the fighting in the hilly country at Khuweilfeh is that it is more than ever necessary to fight with small advance guards for information of the ground, enemy's dispositions of machine guns, and if possible draw his artillery fire before deciding on a plan of attack, and it is probable that if it is required to dislodge the enemy from his position covering the water, the earliest date on which an attack could be launched would be the morning of the 8th December.

"It is difficult to make calculations for advance in a strange country, but I would rather underestimate the rapidity of my advance than be late in co-operating with other troops.

"I attach scheme of supply for this division. On a mobile scale we should undoubtedly maintain more than two brigade groups for a short period north of Hebron, should operations demand it."

The question of supply depended, of course, on transport, with which Mott's isolated detachment was not too well provided. The infantry divisions not engaged in the pursuit had slipped away, first to Gaza, and then up the coast road, and with them went all but a minimum of transport. On receipt of the General Headquarters Instructions, General Mott, taking stock of his scattered dispositions, ordered all horses and wheels, not essential to units, and two field ambulances, to proceed to Karm. By sending animals to railhead, he thus saved the transport of forage. It also enabled him, by employing artillery teams in spare wagons, to form an additional train, and, with all camels pressed into service, to place daily at Beersheba two days' supplies for the division.

But there was not much time: the extemporary transport was organised on the 1st December, and by the evening of the 3rd would have six days' supplies in Beersheba. There was a previous accumulation of four days' supplies at Makruneh, and there was one day's reserve with units; in all, without the iron ration, eleven days' supplies.

Once on the move, however, only half a day's ration could be brought from Karm to Beersheba, and the dwindling dump would last for twenty-two days.

The scheme of supplies drawn up was for the rationing of two brigade groups only the third, the 158th, would be required in the vicinity of Beersheba and on the lengthening line of communications.

TURKISH DISPOSITIONS

On the 2nd December, General Mott, starting at 5.30 a.m., went to a Corps Conference at Latrun, and saw something of what was going on in the hills west of Jerusalem.

While the Anzac Division had pursued the right wing of the Turkish army to the far sides of the river Auja, the yeomanry had chased the left wing through the Vale of Ajalon. This mounted division did some wonderful hill fighting, and at one time penetrated as far as the village of Beitunia in an attempt to cut the Jerusalem-Nablus road.

THE HEBRON-JERUSALEM ROAD—A CORK-SCREW ROAD.
Note the distant Transport and two hairpin bends in the road.

HEBRON.

The 75th and 52nd Infantry Divisions, moving through the hills on their right had reached Neby Samwil.* And then the Turkish resistance had stiffened, and further advance came to a standstill. Towards the end of November, the XXth Corps commenced to take over the line, an operation of some difficulty as there was continuous and fierce fighting all the time; the relief was not completed until the 2nd December, and after that date there was a continual re-arranging of the line in preparation for the attack on Jerusalem. When General Mott arrived at Latrun the order of battle was complete, although units were side-slipping. The 60th were on the right, then the 74th, the 10th, and the Australian Mounted Division on the left.

The strength and dispositions of the enemy were believed to be—east of Bethlehem, the 7th Cavalry Regiment, 500 sabres; covering Bethlehem, and extending to the Jerusalem-Junction Station Railway, the 27th Division, 1,200 rifles; to the Latrun-Jerusalem road, the 53rd Division 2,000 rifles; to Neby Samwil, the 26th Division 1,800 rifles; to Beit Ur el Foqa, the 19th Division with 2/61st and 158th Regiments attached, 4,000 rifles; thence to the extreme left of the British XXth Corps, the 3rd Cavalry Division, 1,500 sabres; and in reserve at Bireh, the 54th Division, 2,700 rifles.

THE GENERAL INSTRUCTIONS

The result of the Conference was embodied in the following instructions which reached General Mott on the 4th :—

"The enemy are holding a line covering the Hebron-Jerusalem road, with works in the neighbourhood of Ras esh Sherifeh, behind which are the trenches near El Khudr, and round Bethlehem from about Kh. esh Shughrah, on the south-east, across the road to Kh. Kebah,† and thence northwards to about Square D4c.

"North of the railway the enemy have a series of trenches and redoubts from just west of Malhah to Neby Samwil.

"Facing the XXth Corps are believed to be anything from a minimum of 400 to a maximum of 1,200 on the Hebron road, and a maximum of 15,000 from the right of the 60th to the left of the 10th at Suffa, including reserves.

"The enemy defences are not deep, and once through them the troops have only difficulties of terrain, which make movement so difficult, to contend with. It is intended to extend the front now held by the 10th Division to include the Beit Dukka defences, the 74th

* Nabi Samweil—*R.G.S.*
† Error in map—Shaghrab and Kebar.

taking over from the 60th Division the front from Beit Izza, inclusive, to the Jerusalem Enab road. *This will give the attack two complete brigades of the 53rd, the whole of the 60th, and it is hoped two brigades of the 74th Division.*

"It is obvious that the form the attack will take will depend a good deal on the action of the enemy on the advance of the 53rd Division towards Jerusalem. The two brigades of this division reach a point to-night from which they are *two ten-mile marches* from the position north of Bethlehem which they will have to reach to co-operate with the remainder of the Corps.

"Should the enemy decide to strengthen his defences in front of the 53rd Division by pushing troops south of Jerusalem, the attack will take the form of the 60th and 74th Divisions driving straight in on the Jerusalem-Nablus road, the 60th throwing out a flank to the south-east, the objective of the move being the prevention of the escape of the enemy opposing the 53rd Division, either by the Nablus or the Jericho roads.

"Should, however (as is more probable), the enemy recognise the danger of such movement, and withdraw from the front of the 53rd Division, the attack will take the form of *a direct advance on the part of the 53rd Division on Jerusalem*, and a wheel by the 60th and 74th Divisions, pivotting on Beit Izza and Neby Samwil defences, designed to drive the enemy northwards, and with the following objectives:

"(*a*) A position covering the Jericho road to be occupied by a portion of the 53rd Division;

(*b*) The 60th and 74th Divisions to seize the general line Shafat-Neby Samwil, or if possible, point 2670 Kh. Ras el Tawil-Neby Samwil.

"In order to inflict a severe blow on the enemy before he has time to arrange to meet the attack it seems obvious that the advance of the 53rd Division must be as rapid as possible, once it moves from its present position, and the G.O.C. 53rd Division must endeavour to ensure, by careful reconnaissance of routes, that his brigades are on *the general line Sur Bahir-Sherafat by the early morning of Z day.*

"The date of Z day and, therefore, of the move of the 53rd Division, will depend on how soon ammunition can be accumulated, and how long it takes the 74th Division to hand over their present line to the 10th Division, to occupy their new line, and to conduct artillery and infantry reconnaissances. The shorter the time the better, consistent with the attack being thoroughly understood by those who take part in it.

"The two brigade groups 53rd Division, about Dilbeh, will be prepared to march on the 6th, but definite orders for the march will be sent before it takes place."

THE ADVANCE THROUGH HEBRON

Although, in the Spring of the year, a traveller from Beersheba will admire the refreshing green as he climbs to Hebron, the plateau which then lies before him has a different aspect. And December is the season of rain and cold.

Judea itself is no bigger than the county of Essex; the plateau from Hebron to Bethel is about 35 miles, and from the western edge of the hills to the east, where they drop into the desert, it is only from 14 to 17 miles wide. The greater part is moorland, with multitudes of boulders. In the hollows are stony fields and dry torrent beds. On the top of a low ridge there may be a native village of grey stone, looking like an outcrop of rock, but below the ridge there will be olive groves, fig trees, and a few terraces of vines. The prevailing picture is stones!—torrent beds of loose stones, paths that resemble the torrent beds, heaps of stones gathered from the fields, and the fields still covered with stones; on the moorland the stones become boulders.

For the rest there is little water, no big hills, no character. On the western side, the Mediterranean is visible; on the eastern side, the hills of Moab, with their shifting shades and shadows, lie beyond the crude blue of the Dead Sea.

Before receiving the above instructions, the move to cover Dilbeh had commenced, and General Mott wired to XXth Corps that in his opinion " we shall be doing well if we make vicinity of Bethlehem in two days from here, on the assumption that we are unopposed. Though the road is good, the gradients are punishing to gun teams and transport animals. Much the same country here as I saw yesterday near the 60th, so that it is impossible to estimate daily rate of advance as soon as I am opposed."

This opinion he repeated on the 4th. The roads had been blown up by the retreating Turks, and battalions were even then making good the damage. " Very pretty country," the General assured the Corps Commander, " but map distances give no idea of distance men have to march—sometimes two hairpin corners to get down a hill, and long ones at that. Suggest I should cover Hebron to-morrow with advanced Brigade group, so as to arrange my refilling point north of it, whence my camel train feeds me, and also so as to stop communication from Hebron to Bethlehem. Will Corps Commander approve?"

Permission was given, and at dawn on the 5th the 7th Cheshires moved north of Hebron and took up an outpost line covering the town.

A very good description of the road to Hebron—for it is the road which is of the greatest interest in this operation—is given by Colonel H. E. P. Pateshall, who rejoined the Division from Cairo on the 4th.

"4th December. Left in a car (from Beersheba) along the road to Hebron, which was made by the Turks. Views simply glorious. Huge gorges, and more green scrub and cultivation in terraces. The road had very many hairpin turns and twists, and had been barricaded by stones in several places. Our camp was in a lovely site (Dilbeh), plenty of running water in a gorge, with daisies, dwarf cyclemen, crocusses, buttercups, marigolds, mallows, radishes, turnips, and birdseye-perriwinkles; it was a real treat. Oranges, too, were on sale. On the evening of the 4th, Tuesday, Peter and I motored into Hebron, or the outskirts of it, to see it. It was really lovely to see the vine leaves turning a beautiful autumn colour, all in terraces, vines, figs, and olive trees. It was a little cloudy towards evening, and much colder. What struck me was the whiteness of the people, lots of Russian Jews about. We weren't allowed into the town at all, as the road passes just through the outskirts. Plenty of water in cisterns and wells. We got back just in time, as it rained a little during the night."

On the night of the 5/6th December, the advance guard complete was moved three miles north of Hebron, and one battalion of the 159th Brigade, 4th Welch, to the northern outskirts of the town. The remainder of the detachment was closed up to within road space intervals of these advanced troops, as it was certain that the distance to be covered was much in excess of that shown on the map owing to many bends in the road.

Lt.-Colonel Lawrence, in command of the advance guard, was given instructions that his advance along the road was not to be checked to allow of tactical reconnaissance on either side, but that he was to go full steam ahead until shot at. Unless this was done the detachment would never be up to time, for Zero day and hour was fixed at 5.15 a.m. on the 8th, and Mott's Detachment had been ordered to move on the 6th, and be in the Bethlehem-Beit Jala area on the 7th.

General Chetwode had made up his mind, from cavalry reconnaissance and other sources, that very little opposition would be found south of Bethlehem, and his orders took the form of a direct advance by the 53rd Division on Jerusalem, while the 60th and 74th pivotted on the Neby Samwil defences, in a wheel to the north (*see* Appendix).

General Mott, on the other hand, thought that he was more likely to be strongly opposed south of Bethlehem than further north. He had

MOTT'S DETACHMENT.

[*Sketch by Horsfield.*

in his mind that line of enemy trenches " covering the Hebron-Jerusalem road, with works in the neighbourhood of Ras esh Sherifeh, behind which are the trenches near El Khudr and round Bethlehem, from about Kh. esh Shugrah on the southeast, across the road to Kh. Kebah, and thence northward." ... True he had not far to go, but that long column, on a single road with twists and hairpin turns, gave him cause for grave anxiety.

Following Order 17 came a wire " Important you reach Sur Bahir-Sherafat by dawn the 8th to co-operate with 60th. Should enemy resistance prevent this, 60th Division will be instructed to detach troops to advance east from Ain Karim to Hebron-Jerusalem road to prevent escape of enemy on your front."

The order of march was as follows :—

" Mott's detachment will advance towards Bethlehem to-morrow, 6th December, in the following order of march : Heads of units of the main body (except where otherwise stated) will pass the starting point Hebron-Dura fork roads at times shown—

ADVANCE GUARD—to move from outpost line at 0600 :

Commander Lt.-Col. H. M. Lawrence
50 Mounted Cyclists.
7th Cheshires.
436th Field Company R.E.
1 Sect. Howr. Battery.
Detachment 2nd Welsh Field Ambulance.

Only technical and fighting transport will accompany the Advance Guard.

MAIN BODY—From Bivouac in Hebron :

Advanced Division H.Q.
H.Q. 159th Brigade.
0600 4th Welch.
From Starting Point—
0500 Westminster Dragoons (less transport).
0515 1 Battery Howrs. (less 1 section).
From Bivouac North of Hebron—
0615 1 Section 91st Heavy Battery.
From Starting Point—
0530 2 Bns. 159th Brigade.
0600 1 Battery Howrs.
0615 Wheeled transport 159th Brigade and Westminster Dragoons.

From Bivouac North of Hebron—
  0800 91st Heavy Battery (less 1 section).

From Starting Point—
  0715 1 Bde. R.F.A. (less Howr. Battery).
  0735 1 section 2nd Welsh Fld. Ambulance (less Detach.).
  0745 53rd Division H.Q.
  0748 53rd Division Cyclist Coy. (less Detach.).
  0800 53rd Division H.Q. Transport.
  0810 Camel Transport 159th Bde. and Westminster Dragoons.
  0930 160th Inf. Bde. Group (under Brigade arrangements).
  1100 1 Bde. R.A.F. (less Howr. Battery).
  1115 2 T.M. Batteries with Amm. Column.
  1130 Camel Transport 160th Bde.

2. Units will be warned not to bunch or close up their intervals when troops halt in front of them, unless ordered to do so, and will be careful to keep to the right side of the road."

The advance guard moved off as soon as it was light enough to see, and gained a strong position, without opposition 2½ miles north of the water of Wadi Arab by mid-day.

"Hebron," says Colonel Pateshall, "was looking lovely. We trekked at 6 a.m. to the hill country beyond. You could then see a glimpse of a place called Hulhul, where Jonah is supposed to have been buried. Past an old ruined square tower of Roman origin, with a Roman mile stone lying alongside the road called Beit Sur. Then passed a very interesting old place called Beit Ummar, and Beit Fejjar which was a very fine up-standing place perched on top of a hill with very long views. We came to running water in the valley below, and camped round it. The advanced guard could see Bethlehem and Jerusalem, and we went up and could plainly see it in glorious sunlight. Clouds came up, and then we caught a glimpse of it in sunlight while we were in clouds. We had a cosy little camp, in a side valley from the road. Towards night it grew much colder, and came on to rain—Scotch mist all night and very damp."

The natives at Beit Ummar stated that Turkish cavalry had been there the day before, and Arabs reported strong bodies of infantry moving south, along the Dead Sea road. They also stated that Bethlehem was strongly defended by machine guns, artillery, cavalry, and a few infantry. This news was communicated to Corps Headquarters, with the suggestion that, if it was true, Beni Naim and Yuttar should be held before any further advance was made. Corps replied that the original time table must be adhered to.

"I do not believe reports you have received, and even if they are true you must keep to time table allotted you in XXth Corps Order 17, and attached instructions G.22 of December 5th. None of your infantry or artillery that started with you is to be left behind, but you may use cavalry to clear up situation and, if absolutely necessary, to picquet road."

The advance guard took up their outpost position $2\frac{1}{2}$ miles to the north of the Wadi at mid-day, but the tail of the column did not reach the Wadi until 4 o'clock in the afternoon.

The report picked up at Beit Ummar was to some extent confirmed during the afternoon when from the outpost line, which ran through Kh. el Dilh, Beit Fejjar, Beit Suwir, enemy cavalry were seen on the high ground at Sherifeh and south of it. They were about $2\frac{1}{2}$ miles away, at a point where the main road bends due west towards a neck south of Sherifeh. General Mott decided that he must clear the neck and gain possession of the south of the ridge before his infantry advanced.

At dawn on the 7th December, the 7th Cheshires moved against the ridge. Batteries of the 265th and 266th Brigades had been playing leap frog on the flanks, covering the advance of the long column, and were in positions to support the Cheshires. The country was very broken, and movement was not fast, but the infantry made good the southern edge of the ridge soon after 7 a.m. without trouble.

The Turks were in a line of stone trenches further north along the ridge, and it looked as though a fight might develop, but when the guns began to register, the enemy evacuated the trenches, and the Cheshires were in them about 8 o'clock.

These heights dominated the whole of the surrounding country, and Bethlehem and Jerusalem could be seen plainly. The sun was shining, and attempts were made to get in communication with the XXth Corps by helio, but without success. Then clouds descended on the hills, it commenced to rain—a deluge of rain that was like a fog—and for the remainder of the day it was impossible to see more than 200 or 300 yards ahead.

The advance guard was ordered to push on and soon came in contact with the Turks on a ridge on the far side of Solomon's Pools (Burak).

THE RAIN

General Mott went down to the Pools to see if any further advance could be made, but found that the lower hills were covered with cloud, and that it was impossible to ascertain where the enemy fire was coming from, or to organise any attack that night. The column stretched many miles back along the single road, and the surface of it had become so sticky, that camels were unable to move—this, by the way, was a peculiarity appertaining to camels.

The nature of the downpour of rain and the effect it had on the operations is illustrated by one mishap, fortunately at the end of a descent. The road, cut out of the side of the hill, suddenly collapsed, and a gun and a team of the 265th F.A. Brigade rolled some fifteen feet down into the valley. The whole of the column in rear of that point was then held up until the Engineers had made a way for them.

Colonel Pateshall says: "I wore two woollies, a burberry, and a waterproof cape, and yet it wasn't warm. My horses had been sent on by mistake, so I walked for six miles to see our new place. The road was awful, slush and slippery mud, camels sliding everywhere and natives starved with cold. Scotch mist and driving rain alternatively. Found Headquarters overlooking Bethlehem, and caught a glimpse through breaks in the mist, which continued all day long. Pitched camp about dark in pouring wet. Dinner was cocoa and cold bully, and was most welcome. I found our camp was overlooking Burak or Solomon's Pools."

The men, however, had to endure the wet and cold with no more than a water proof sheet over their drill jackets and shorts.

The low hills covering Solomon's Pools were held that night (7th). It was evident that the advanced troops were close up against the main enemy positions defending Bethlehem, but as a result of the bad weather the enemy was hidden from view, and no guns could be got into position against him.

General Mott wired to XXth Corps that until the weather cleared he did not consider he would be able to move, but that he would, of course, attempt to do so at dawn. He reported that Australian troops had got in touch with his left.

General Chetwode replied that the plan would proceed as arranged, and that the 53rd Division would continue to advance regardless of the weather. The attack on Jerusalem was timed at 5.15 a.m.

It was a fight against the weather. General Mott gives the following account :—

"The situation on the evening of the 7th was as follows : we had pushed along the main road until the enemy held up our advance on the road with artillery and rifle fire. The hills in which we were advancing were enveloped in the clouds, and the rain was torrential at intervals. Covering positions were then seized beyond the Burak pools, our water supply for the night.

"From the reports of previous air reconnaissance it was certain our advanced troops must be quite close up to the system of Bethlehem defences, but the weather had denied us any glimpse of the terrain, or the position of the enemy trenches on which to base a plan of attack next morning. All we did know was that the terrain on either side of the road was very steep and rocky. It was clearly impossible to make any further advance until dawn next morning or until weather permitted our seeing the terrain in front of us.

"The 2/4th Queens and the 2/4th Royal West Kents of the 160th Brigade were brought up during the night, and also guns from the rear of the column ready to get into position so that there should be as little delay as possible the next day in launching the attack, as soon as the necessary reconnaissances were made. The 4th Cheshire Regiment, who had been ordered to protect the right flank, were quite ungetatable in the mist and rain that night. The Commanding Officer of this battalion managed to ride in and report where he thought he was, and informed the Brigadier that it was quite out of the question to attempt to get camels and pack animals to him that night. This battalion, especially, had a very rough time of it in the cold and rain.

"Soon after dawn (the 8th), the atmosphere cleared sufficiently to see the lie of the ground in the neighbourhood of Bethlehem-Beit Jala, but the periods of visibility were intermittent. Enemy guns in and round Bethlehem commenced an accurate shelling of the neck of the road which was behind the advanced troops, and over which the attacking troops would have to pass. Enemy 5.9's and several 77 m.m. plastered the road to some effect, and necessitated battalions dribbling their men forward. [The Queens lost 1 killed and 11 wounded while dribbling into a position of support.]

"At 0840 the above situation was reported to XXth Corps and repeated to 60th Division as follows : Hostile artillery in Bethlehem town, 5.9 in action east of Bethlehem. Must develop my right before I advance.

Country very difficult and advance will be slow. Can permission be given to engage guns in Bethlehem?

"The plan of action decided on was to develop the operation somewhat to the east side of the road, to prevent close observation by the enemy, because, unless this was done the neck and road would become impassable, at the same time to refuse Bethlehem and take the high ground west and south-west of Beit Jala.

"This attack was entrusted to Brigadier-General Pearson with the two battalions brought up the previous night, supported by the two battalions of the 159th Brigade, who were then holding the advanced positions. The Westminster Dragoons were ordered to operate from the south-west on the left of the attack.

"At 0922 a wire was received that the 60th Division line ran from B.36 to Y.25p, and at 9.53 the following wire was received: 'Report progress. It is most important that you push on as rapidly as possible. 60th and 74th both report objectives allotted to first stage captured by 0730.'

"At 1010 the following answer was sent 'Please see my wireless. Nothing further since.'

"At 1012 wire received from XXth Corps as follows: 'Report your position. Report situation on your front. Push your attack. 60th and 74th Divisions line B.36, Y.25, T.18, central at 0730.'

"At 1137 following wire sent to XXth Corps and 60th Division: 'Have ordered attack on high ground K.25 central and D.30a. It should develop about noon. From above high ground I shall dominate all terrain as far as Jerusalem west of Hebron road.'

"The attack had already been ordered on the Beir Jala heights when the above wires were received.

"The importance of pushing on had always been clear. But had those wires arrived earlier nothing more could have been done than had been done to expedite the operations in the circumstances in which we had been placed.

"It seemed clear that to push in a weak attack at dawn into the unknown would only result in failure and in increased delays, and an enemy success might jeopardise not only our own operations but those of the XXth Corps which at that time had not taken place.

"The news of the success of the 60th did not reach us till some time after our orders for attack were issued. As it was, in order to gain time, the attack arranged was weak compared to the strength of the detachment. Only the equivalent of an infantry brigade was assembled for the attack, and to save time two of these battalions were those holding my advanced position, notwithstanding they had been doing advanced guard on previous day, and had been in close contact with the enemy all night, during which the cold and rain was intense.

"By dint of night marching portions of the columns, and disregarding the ordinary measures for security by marching along the road till the column was shot at, we had succeeded in covering the distance from the Dilbeh area to the Burak Pools and attacking the Bethlehem defences a day sooner than the period asked for in our letter, marked B. attached, and had it not been for the bad weather on the 8th our attack would have gone in simultaneously with the 60th Division.

"It was hoped that the attack would get under weigh by noon, but the Beit Jala heights were some 3,000 yards north of the fork roads, the country was rough and steep, and, although every effort was made to accelerate its commencement, it was not till between 1400 and 1500 that the leading infantry battalions were approaching the enemy's position. In the meantime it was ascertained, from the Westminster Dragoons, who were operating on the left flank, that the enemy had been clearing from his positions, and that the southern portions of the high ground were clear of the enemy by 1400.

"At 1421 following wire was received from XXth Corps '60th Division right is held up, owing to pressure from western outskirts of Jerusalem. You must press on as rapidly as possible.'

"The following reply was sent, 'Have been doing my best.'

"After the enemy had lost this high ground north-west of Bethlehem, it was unlikely that he would remain in Bethlehem during the night, and small advanced guards were ordered to make good the high ground in front of the line as soon as possible during the night, and push into the outskirts of Bethlehem, so that there should be little delay next morning, in pushing through Bethlehem to Jerusalem. The following wire was sent to Corps at 1815 : 'Turks retired off high ground D30a as attacking infantry advanced about 1600. My line runs from M10a through M2a, D36d to D30a, 29 central to 28d, Infantry reported leaving Bethlehem late in afternoon, and enemy gun fire from east and north of Bethlehem ceased about mid-day. My advance should be quicker to-morrow as we have had intervals of good visibility. Should make K3 central about 0900 unless delayed by fog or enemy.'

" During the evening the following three wires were received : 'Advance of 60th Division is still held up and cannot continue until you progress further. Our cavalry now occupy Melhah, and 60th Division line to-night runs north from that point to Lifta. It is imperative that your advance should continue with the utmost energy, and that you report progress. R.F.C. say that enemy is gradually retiring northwards and eastwards from Jerusalem.'

(2) " ' If you find the enemy have retired hope you will quicken your advance by keeping as many of your troops as possible on the main road. On arriving line Sur Bahir-Beit Sufafa, you will carry out programme as ordered for to-day, namely, one brigade to move east of Jerusalem, and one brigade to the west of the town. On receipt of wire from you giving your position and hour at which you will commence your advance from Sur Bahir-Beit Sufafa line to clear country west of Jerusalem orders will be sent to 60th Division to advance simultaneously with you. There will be a gap between them and you, till you join hands west of Jerusalem. Please endeavour to give ample notice, so as to ensure co-operation 60th Division.'

(3) " ' It will very much assist me if you will send more frequent reports. I understand your difficulties from a communication point of view, but it is most difficult to co-ordinate movements of widely separated formations if one is not aware of what is going on. Chetwode.' "

. . . . .

PROGRESS OF THE MAIN ATTACK

But the weather, which had so seriously hampered the movements of the 53rd, affected the operations of the 74th and 60th Divisions. And they met with stout resistance from the Turks. The difficult country was admirably suited to defence, for as the defenders, under pressure, abandoned their field works they could always fall back on one of the boulder strewn terraces that scored each succeeding hill.

The first phase of the attack had provided for the advance of the 60th Division on the enemy works which lay between the railway and the main Enab road, while the 74th Division dealt with the strong position at Beit Iksa, and the line of the Wadi Abbeideh. The 60th experienced difficulties on both flanks. On their left, after the first line of defence was captured, troops were held up by a strong force in some houses on a ridge, which was only dislodged at the point of the bayonet at 4 p.m., and there were other difficult points round Deir Yesin. Had the 53rd been able to press forward, these points of resistance would, no doubt, have been overcome earlier in the day. The first phase over, there was to be a movement of artillery, but here the weather played its part. The first phase was completed in the afternoon, and when General Chetwode went to the 60th Divisional Headquarters to discuss the situation, he was faced with the impossibility of moving artillery over the sodden ground, and with the condition of troops, exhausted after marching and fighting in the rain since midnight. Further advance was, therefore, suspended.

Corps communication with the 53rd Division had been painfully slow. While reports on progress and situation came pouring in from the 74th and 60th Divisions no word was received from the 53rd, although several messages had been despatched up to mid-day. Also in his mental picture of the battle, General Chetwode had always seen the 53rd Division more forward than they were—somewhere about the Sur Bahir-Sherafat line at dawn on the 8th. General Mott, on the other hand, had been equally steadfast in his opinion that the advance of his two Brigade groups on a single road, and under the conditions that were imposed by precipitous gradients in that gaunt country, would be slow. And the moment he got in touch with the enemy on the 7th he had no alternative but to throw the 7th Cheshires out on the left of the road, and the 4th Cheshires on the right, all of which required time; it was not a simple business of marching along a country road. He had, from the first, envisaged the possibility of the enemy forcing him to deploy, but neither he, nor anyone else, had foreseen the weather conditions which robbed him of vision in face of the enemy.

The point of the delay is not, however, one of peril, but of an open road for the escape of the retreating Turks; and escape they undoubtedly did.

In the evening of the 8th, the Queens and Middlesex had occupied the high ground to the northwest of Bethlehem, from which the Turks had retired, and the line was carried on to the right by the 7th Cheshires, 4th Welch, and 4th Cheshires.

The general advance was ordered on the 9th according to plan.

THE 5TH WELCH ENTER JERUSALEM

At 5.30, half an hour before dawn, the 5th Welch passed through the outpost line, followed by the 4th Welch, 4th Cheshires, and 7th

Cheshires. The road was blown up in four places between the starting point and Bethlehem. At Bethlehem a few prisoners were taken, but there was no opposition—and away to the west the 60th and 74th found no Turks in front of them. The 5th Welch were at Mar Elias at 8 o'clock and at the walls of Jerusalem at 8.45, a few minutes after the Mayor, who had left from the western side of the city, had met the outposts of the 180th Brigade, 60th Division, and surrendered the keys of the city. Led by a troop of the Westminster Dragoons, the 5th Welch marched through Jerusalem, but not within the old walls.

"The inhabitants appeared to be very excited and pleased on our troops passing," is the only comment of the 5th Welch. "We had hardly got through the city when we came under machine gun and rifle fire. The two troops of Westminster Dragoons took up a position on the east side of the walls of Old Jerusalem, and the 5th Welch halted just under the walls on the north side. Observation was obtained from the cemetery just on the north side of the Jerusalem-Jericho road."

. . . . .

The body of Mott's Detachment stretched out along the Hebron road. "Sunday, 9th December," writes Colonel Pateshall, "will be a day to store up in my memory because I came through Bethlehem and entered Jerusalem! We went through the outskirts of Bethlehem, where, being a Christian town, everyone was out to welcome us, sisters, nuns, and the very picturesque Bethlehem women in their high white headgear and Magyar blouses and skirts beautifully worked. Priests of all Christian sects welcomed us. I rode on with troops to the monastery of Mar Elias, where I went on to the roof, where the signals and staff were given white wine and pork brawn by the monks. Very fine, lovely day, but cold wind. Glorious view looking back at Bethlehem, and you could see the Dead Sea and overlook Jerusalem to a certain extent. Got into touch with the other forces coming by up helio, which gave one a very happy feeling that at last the fruit of our labour was within our grasp.

"I was ordered on with the A.P.M. and police to the head of the column, close outside the station at Jerusalem; then was sent out to the Jaffa Gate. Past the Jaffa Gate and on to the Turkish Post Office, where our first troops had met the first troops of the other Divisions. It was a glorious feeling having at last joined up again. That night guards were mounted on all the Gates by the 7th Cheshires, guided by the Turkish police, who had surrendered. I was then sent to the Governor of Jerusalem, Borton Pasha, as a staff officer."

THE FIRST GUARD ON THE JAFFA GATE, JERUSALEM, 9TH DECEMBER, 1917:
NO. 11 PLATOON, C COMPANY, 5TH WELCH REGIMENT—LIEUT. W. A. WOODS
IN COMMAND.

A guard was mounted by the 5th Welch over the Jaffa Gate. One wishes that a busy pen had written down impressions, hot from a wondering mind, on this historic occasion. Captain le Fleming was not present, being on a course in Cairo, but he arrived a few days later, when the excitement of the people had died down, and entered by the Jaffa Gate—' or rather by the breach in the wall made by the blasphemous entry of the German Emperor. On the one side is Mount Sion, crowned by the massive keep of the 'Citadel of David,' on the other, surmounting the old mediæval gate, is a hideous and incongruous clock-tower. The broad road and pavement soon end in the dark, stone-paved passages of the market. On either side are little cave-like booths, the fruit shops piled high with golden oranges, great red radishes, cauliflowers, dried figs and green artichokes—strange to say these are not the Jerusalem variety—and meat shops, whence issue weird, and to western nostrils, noisome odours—on the counters skewered lumps of cooked meat, within the sizzling pots and bright pans; the shoe-makers' shops, a blaze of yellow and scarlet; and many more, each adding a splash of colour to the scene. In those narrow alley-ways jostles, pushes, and bustles the most varied throng imaginable; tall, dark Bedouins from beyond the Jordan, proud of bearing and picturesque in flowing robes and head-dress, patriarchal Arabs from the villages in camel-hair cloaks and sheepskins, some wearing the green turban of the Hadji, grey uniformed Gendarmerie, greasy, furtive looking Jews in their round black hats and black coats, curley ringlets dangling in front of their ears, yashmaked Mohammedan women, unveiled Christians, women of Bethlehem in their beautiful white head-dress, embroidered with red and gold crosses, Greek priests, Coptic priests, Abyssinian priests, Armenian priests, monks of every sect and order, a sprinkling of Turks and Europeans dressed in western style, the female element in Paris fashions of ten years ago.

"The gutteral expostulations of the men, increasing in intensity and apparent fury as a bargain is being clinched, are mingled with the querulous tones of the women and the screaming of the children. Sharply we turn into a deserted stone-stepped passage, and pass between high, barren, and ugly walls, here and there relieved by some old Saracenic archway, here and there by a dark door or latticed window. Suddenly we emerge into a flood of sunlight, and find ourselves in the little court in front of the Church of the Holy Sepulchre."

But, on this day, under the walls of the city, the 5th Welch were under machine gun fire!

. . . . .

THE MOUNT OF OLIVES

From the cemetery a considerable number of the enemy were seen on the Mount of Olives. It was necessary to get more elbow room.

The main body of Mott's force was, at this time, in the neighbourhood of Mar Elias, when General Mott received the order from XXth Corps to cover Jerusalem from the east and north-east with one Brigade group, and to push his cavalry at least six miles down the Jericho road. He, therefore, ordered the 159th Brigade to continue the advance along the Jericho road.

The situation, however, did not seem too good to Brigadier General Money. Soon after one o'clock, he directed the 5th Welch to advance if possible, but "do not take undue risks, as you will not have artillery support until clear of the town. Am sending 4th Welch to outflank the enemy on your right."

But when the 4th Welch, who were the next battalion on the line of march, moved east of the Hebron road, they were faced with a precipitous wadi, of such a nature that it effectively barred their passage, and prevented them helping the 5th Welch who were definitely held up by the enemy, with a number of machine guns, on the Mount of Olives.

There was great reluctance on the part of the Higher Command to shell the neighbourhood of Jerusalem, but the military necessity was strong. General Mott asked for, and obtained permission to shell the Mount of Olives. All preparations were made for an attack at four o'clock, but it was postponed and an outpost position was occupied for the night.

Just before dawn the following morning, the 5th Welch advanced and occupied the crest of the Mount without opposition, but found the enemy in force on the eastern side of it.

Meanwhile the 4th Welch had to march round the deep wadi, via Jerusalem, and came into action on the right of the 5th, and on the left of the 4th Cheshires, who had been able to go forward from their position on the Hebron Road.

The country was extremely difficult. The 265th and 266th Artillery Brigades gave energetic support, but even so the conformation of the ground favoured the Turks, who contested every inch of the road. Progress was slow and patchy. An officers' patrol of the 5th Welch seized a white house giving good observation over Aziriyeh, and during the afternoon the battalion made good a commanding hill northwest of that place. The 4th Cheshires pushed on to some high ground on the right.

BRISK ENTERPRISE ON THE JERICHO ROAD

Early in the morning of the 11th, the 159th Brigade advanced again, the 4th Cheshires occupying Abu Dis, and the 4th Welch Aziriyeh. A few prisoners were taken by the Cheshires.

On this day, Mott's Detachment ceased to exist. The battalions, however, remained in their positions, contending with what were called " good Turks," hard fighters, winning their way slowly forward, hill by hill, ravine by ravine, over a wide front. The kind of warfare that was being carried on is exemplified in the following reports :—

Lt.-Colonel Pemberton reports that two platoons of the 4th Welch advanced at 0415 hours on the 12th, " from the northeast corner of the garden of the Greek Monastery, situated about 500 yards east of Aziriyeh, with a view to clearing a ridge about 800 yards east thereof of a party of snipers. The platoon advanced in line and completely surprised the enemy, strength unknown. About six rifle shots were fired by the enemy, whereupon our men rushed the post with the bayonet, and dispersed the enemy. The two Lewis guns belonging to these platoons were immediately hastened up, and No. 17 Platoon remained at the place where the enemy picquet had been dispersed. No. 5 Platoon moved about 200 yards to the north. The ground being too rocky to dig in, stone sangars were constructed, and the position maintained. . . . The men's boots were muffled with sandbags, which materially aided the element of surprise."

On the same night, Lt.-Colonel Bowen reports that one company of the 5th Welch advanced on the battalion front. " No. 7 Platoon ran into what was, presumably, an enemy listening post, killing one and capturing four. . . . On proceeding over the crest of the hill the enemy about 50 strong was encountered. Nos. 7 and 8 immediately charged with the bayonet, scattering the enemy. These two platoons were withdrawn about 20 yards (from the crest) to dig in. Enemy about 20 strong was holding out behind the forward slope on rocks, being supported by machine guns. They were eventually cleared out with bombs."

The 7th Cheshires, who had been garrison troops in Jerusalem, finding guards on all gates, etc., had moved into the line, and of the night 13/14th December, Captain Flunder reports : " Owing to lack of opportunity to make a reconnaissance, very little was known of the nature of the ground to be covered. The formation adopted was sections in echelon from the left, covered by a screen of scouts. Time of start from 5th Welch outposts, 0130 hours.

"On approaching, route was found intercepted by four deep wadis, the slopes of which, in places, were far too steep to scale. This made it difficult for platoons to keep in touch.

"On leaving the outpost line we immediately came under rifle fire from the enemy's advanced snipers, and as we continued to advance on to the ridge of the next hill the enemy vacated this position and retired to the next ridge, where sniping fire was resumed with increased volume. This ridge was taken with well directed rifle grenades, the enemy retiring to the third ridge, which was taken in the same way. Here the company was reorganised and the advance resumed.

"The ridge beyond this was our final objective, and the scouts reported difficult ground in front and on the left so that two platoons changed direction half-left, while the right platoon continued straight on. Heavy rifle and machine gun fire was encountered, and the two platoons on the left had to clear the isolated hill which stands in front of the left of the ridge, and a portion of my left platoon reached the final objective. The two right platoons had to descend into a deep ravine which was enfiladed by machine gun fire from the left. The upward slope was found too difficult to climb in the face of heavy rifle and machine gun fire, and a continuous shower of bombs from the caves on top. This caused the two platoons to retire a little to a position where they, with the machine guns, could best support the left platoons until their part of the objective was taken.

"It was then decided that the position would be untenable if taken, owing to its being commanded by higher hills on the right and left. We, therefore, withdrew to the third ridge, which overlooks the original objective and consolidated."

Another side of the picture is seen when Lt.-Colonel Swindells reports that at 11 a.m. on the 14th, a post held by the 4th Cheshires was attacked by the Turks. "No. 15 Platoon was being relieved by No. 14 at this post. The hill on which the post is situated is very steep all round. There were three observation posts, two of one N.C.O. and three men each, and one of a Lewis gun and two men. At about 11.10 sniping grew very brisk, and opened on the post from the right. Two of the sentries were hit, and the sniping caused the remainder to keep low. While this was going on a party of Turks crept up under cover of a steep slope, and reached the top unobserved. One of the Lewis gun team was hit, and the gun was temporarily out of action owing to a damaged drum. For a short time a small panic and confusion reigned, but 2/Lieut. Green, commanding No. 14 Platoon, rallied his men and reoccupied the crest within five minutes of the Turks appearing. There were between 20 and 30 Turks.

While the platoon was consolidating again they were fired on by our own shells (but not from C/266 Battery) which caused them to abandon the hill temporarily until the battery was stopped, when they went out again and re-occupied it. I consider that 2/Lieut. Green did extremely good work... in a very sudden and unexpected attack.... I regret to say that one Lewis gun was captured...."

The casualties during this period were: 1 Officer and 8 other ranks killed; 5 Officers and 69 other ranks wounded.

THE SUPPLY TRAIN

Although "Mott's Force," as a separate entity, had ceased to exist, the 53rd Division was "on its own" with regard to supplies. The Division was fed by the Hebron road. An extraordinary degree of freedom and discretion was conceded to individual officers of the Royal Army Service Corps. It was the proud boast of the 53rd Divisional Train that the men and animals of their division were the best fed in the whole Egyptian Expeditionary Force.

The advance of the main force along the coast was followed by the railway, but the railhead on which the 53rd Division depended never got beyond Karm. All supplies, including bread baked at Port Said, came from Qantara, the railhead on the Suez Canal, to Karm; they were then conveyed by caterpillar tractors over a sandy and broken country to Irgeig; thence on the old Turkish narrow gauge railway (the trucks being drawn by mules) to Beersheba, where G.S. Wagons of the Divisional Train and their mules took the supplies a stage further north; then motor lorries conveyed them to a dump three miles north of Hebron, where they were loaded on to camels and taken to the forward Divisional dump, either at Solomon's Pools, or Bethlehem, or Jerusalem, or ten miles north of Jerusalem, as the advance extended; and so the first line transport of the units took them to the line.

As the advance progressed the length of each stage from Beersheba onwards had to be stretched, until it almost reached breaking point. Many of the native camel drivers had come from Upper Egypt, and had never seen rain or felt cold, and they were called upon to march 30 miles a day in wind, rain and cold, along a single track over a mountainous country; their endurance was wonderful, but many fell by the wayside. And so did the camels. The foot of the camel is adapted to march over sand and is not suited to give a grip on wet and slippery soil; the poor beasts fell and injured themselves. The cold and wet took a heavy toll, and the record tells of 45 camels dying on one wet night at Solomon's Pools.

But troops seldom went short of food, and the horses and animals had a good ration of grain, even if hay was sometimes short in quantity and poor in quality.

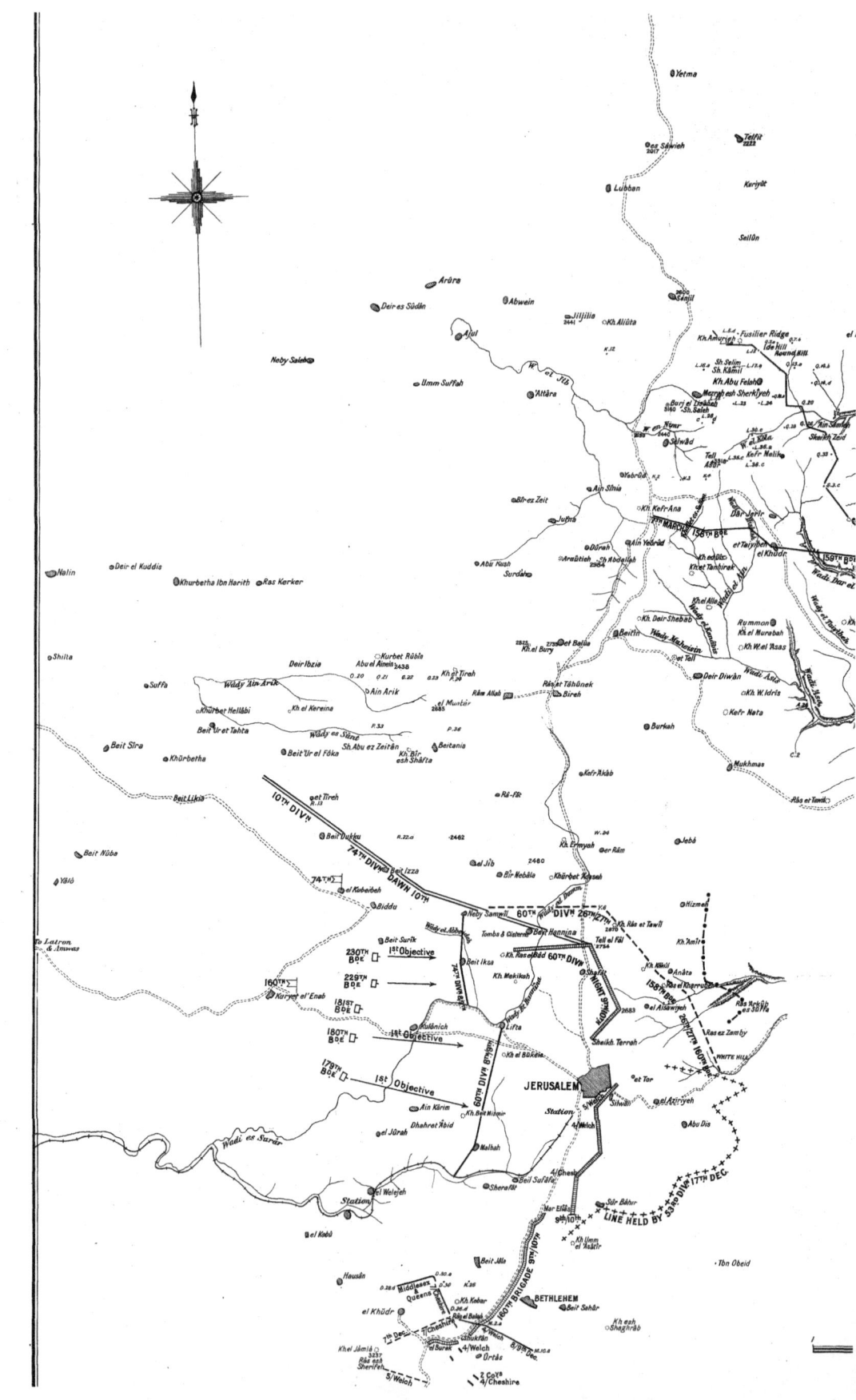

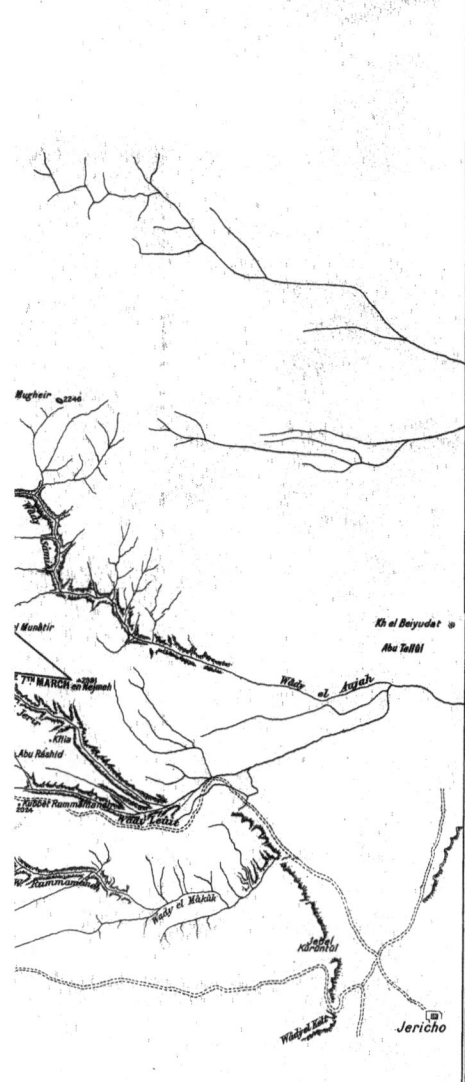

THE TURKISH COUNTER ATTACK

GENERAL SITUATION

16th December, 1917—1st January, 1918.

Battle of Jaffa, 21st December.

Peace negotiations between Bolsheviks, Central Powers, Bulgaria and Turkey open at Brest-Litovsk, 22nd December.

THE TURKISH COUNTER ATTACK

IT was said that an Arab Prophet had foretold the ejection of the Turk from Jerusalem, when the Nile flowed into Palestine and a leader, Ali Nebi, advanced from the west; the mispronunciation of the Commander-in-Chief's name, and the Pipe Line from the sweet water canal, seemed to justify the Arab, and account for the Turkish retreat. But the Turks made one desperate attempt to stay the irresistible march of Fate.

Sir E. Allenby made his official entry into Jerusalem on the 11th December, the 53rd Division being represented by detachments from all Units.

The British front then ran in a diagonal line from north of Jaffa to Jerusalem, and curled round the east of the city. The 159th Brigade were in touch with the 60th Division, opposite Ras ez Zamby; the 160th Brigade were on the right.

THE AFFAIR AT ZAMBY

With the object of improving the position held by the Division—still two brigade groups, but the 158th had been ordered to concentrate in the Jerusleam area by the 21st December—two minor operations were undertaken.

On the 17th, the 160th Brigade seized the commanding ridges east of Abu Dis. The attack was made in two columns; three companies of the Sussex, supported by the 266th Field Artillery Brigade on the right, had first to clear a knoll before they could reach their final objectives, known as Scrag Hill and Sussex Ridge, and had quite a stiff little fight, losing two officers and seven other ranks killed, and 19 other ranks wounded; but the knoll once cleared, the ridge was occupied without opposition. On the left, three companies of West Kents, supported by the 265th Field Artillery Brigade, gained their objective without difficulty. Five Turkish officers and 121 men were captured.

When the success of the 160th Brigade was seen, the 7th Cheshires attempted to seize the conical hill of Ras ez Zamby, but were held by enfilade fire from a curious feature called " the Wall." The enemy line, covering the Jericho road, ran from Ras Arkub es Suffa—Ras ez Zamby—White Hill. Between Zamby and White Hill was a natural outcrop of stone which formed a perfect wall. It was decided that Zamby and White Hill must be taken.

Brigadier-General Pearson staged a full battle on the 21st. The position was subjected to a bombardment, and the infantry advanced under lifting barrages from the 265th and 266th Field Artillery Brigades, and from one section 189th Heavy Battery. The objectives were— (1) Ras ez Zamby, (2) the stony outcrop, "the Wall," (3) White Hill: and the task of assault was allotted to three companies of the Queens, with two companies of the Middlesex in reserve, the whole under Lt.-Colonel S. D. Roper of the Queens.

The orders were for the leading company of the Queens to advance on Zamby from the position of assembly, make good Zamby and clear the ground for a distance of about 100 yards on the forward slope; the second company to follow the first to Zamby, make good the Wall, and continue to advance and seize White Hill; the third company was to make for the Wall, and remain there in support.

Before daylight, the fourth company of the Queens, who were holding Flunder's Post, pushed forward to an intervening ridge, Cheshire Ridge, and cleared it of a party of the enemy who had occupied it during the night. The three attacking companies assembled in some hollow ground between Flunder's Post and Cheshire Ridge.

The Field Artillery barrage opened at 5.15 a.m., and lifted at 5.40. The leading company advanced.

When Cheshire Ridge had first been cleared the Turks immediately counter-attacked, and regained the crest. It was, however, reported that the crest had been again cleared with bombs and grenades, but it would seem that some of the enemy had remained on the reverse slope. At all events the attacking company attempted several times to cross the right shoulder of the ridge, but was met with such heavy rifle and machine gun fire that it was unable to do so. There was also a considerable amount of fire from Ras ez Suffa, and from the right flank.

The advance being definitely held up, the artillery plan was re-arranged, and from 7.20 to 7.40 all 18 pdrs. concentrated on Ez Zamby and the Wall.

One company of the Middlesex, led by Captain McIvor, was then ordered to advance, and passed through the Queens, crept forward close behind a lifting barrage, and assaulted Zamby immediately the guns ceased fire.

The second company of the Middlesex and one company of the Queens pressed forward meanwhile, parallel with the Wall and seized White Hill.

From mid-day until dark the Turks made repeated attempts to regain Zamby and White Hill, and some close hand to hand fighting ensued, but the positions were held, and so far as the enemy's fire permitted consolidation was carried out.

It was a stiff little battle, fought in the rain. The Queens lost four officers and 32 other ranks killed, five officers and 76 other ranks wounded; the Middlesex lost six other ranks killed, two officers and 23 other ranks wounded. Two Turkish officers and 33 men, and three machine guns were captured.

Captain McIvor was specially mentioned by Brigadier-General Pearson in his report of the operation.

The gunners, too, had a strenuous time. The expenditure of ammunition was heavy and supplies came each night from a dump at Enab, the road there being very hilly and difficult. Added to this the fodder ration was reduced to 6lbs. per horse and many of them died under the hard conditions.

But while all this was going on preparations were being made for another big " push."

. . . . .

FURTHER OPERATIONS

On the 14th December General Mott had received a Corps letter on future operations, of which the following are the salient points.

" The Corps Commander, who has now seen the ground from Shafat, Kubeibeh, and Khurbet Hellabi (Tahta), submits the following sketch of future operations to Divisional Commanders, and would be obliged if they would send in any criticisms, suggestions, or objections to the proposed plan; after which a conference will be held, probably at Enab, to decide the final plan.

GENERAL PLAN.—The general plan will be to squeeze the salient now held by the enemy by a combined movement northwards from Jerusalem, and eastwards from Beit ur et Tahta.

" The advance will be undertaken by the 53rd Division, less one brigade group, and the 60th Division; one brigade group of the 53rd Division being used to hold the Jerusalem-Jericho road and possibly to picquet a certain portion of the Jerusalem-Nablus road against the enemy to the east.

"The centre will be lightly held by one brigade of the 74th Division, from Beit Izza (inclusive) to el Tireh (R.13).

"The extreme left attack will be undertaken by the 10th Division. It is proposed that the 53rd and 60th Divisions should begin operations by making a preliminary advance overnight to a position to be selected by Divisional Commanders about the line Kefr Akab (W.11)-Rafat, behind which the artillery could get into position before the morning.

"At dawn on the following morning the 10th Division will capture the line el Kereina-Deir Ibzia, making every effort to move guns forward as far as possible.

"As soon as the Division has secured the above line, two brigades of the 74th Division, assisted by cross fire from the 60th Division on the right, and from the 10th Division on the left, will assault and capture Beitania-Zeitan ridge.

"This will conclude the first day's operations.

"On the morning of the second day, a simultaneous advance will will be made by the 53rd and 60th Divisions to their final objective, and by the 10th Division to the line Ain Arik-Abu el Ainein (Pt. 2438), if not already captured. On this day the 74th Division will not move without Corps orders, but will push forward strong reconnaissances into the gap between the left of the 60th and the right of the 10th Division, to ascertain the best line of advance should it be necessary to employ a part of the Division towards Kh el Tireh.

"In preparation for the above operations the following movements will take place as soon as possible. The remaining brigade of the 53rd Division, now on the Hebron road, will join its division at Jerusalem. The two mountain batteries now with the 60th Division will be transformed to the 10th Division.

"On the arrival of the 158th Brigade of the 53rd Division, now on the Hebron road, the 60th Division will take over the line from the 74th Division as far west as Neby Samwil (inclusive)."

General Mott's comments on the above were confined to his position on the flank of the Army. Roughly, Jerusalem lies on a parallel with the head of the Dead Sea. Although that sheet of water and the gaunt, haggard escarpment of the Jordan Valley offered difficulties, this latter weird feature was not an insuperable obstacle on which to rest a flank. He therefore replied that :—

"(a) The Turk has three roads of approach westwards from Jericho :—(1) a northern track leading on Mukhmas; (2) the main Jericho road; (3) a southern track leading to Bethlehem (now being reconnoitred by the Westminster Dragoons). Yesterday's aeroplane intelligence located Turkish troops on all three tracks, but only a few cavalry at present on the southern track.

"(b) The Turks have three divisions based on Jericho, somewhere on this front, estimated at 8,000 rifles in all.

"(c) Very large accumulations of supplies were reported at Jericho, and in addition the Turks will obtain the weekly supplies that regularly come to Jerusalem.

"(d) All the country between the Dead Sea and the Hebron-Jerusalem road is hostile, and will be a dubious factor until adequately protected by British troops.

"(e) The Tribe of Teamera, occuping the high plateau, Bukeia, east of Bethlehem, is in communication with Muhammed Ali, the chief of the Dead Sea tribe, which is friendly to and armed by the Turks, and it is a question whether this tribe could not be bought over to our side if we pushed troops out east of Bethlehem.

"(f) As the matter now stands the whole of the strip of country between the Hebron-Jerusalem road and the Dead Sea will be cleared of all British troops by the 21st December.

"(g) It is clearly advisable that Bethlehem should be adequately protected.

"Taking these factors into consideration, it is suggested that more elbow room is required to the east before an extensive advance northwards is undertaken. I am reconnoitring to L.24 (Ibn Obeid) which is a very commanding hill, and possibly it may be advisable to hold this as an additional advanced flank to my present one, and as a jumping off place for the Westminster Dragoons; such action would facilitate the purchase of the tribe on the Bukeia over to our side. In addition, if an advance was made on the Jericho road, the flank of the XXth Corps would be in a better position for the advance of the 60th Division northwards.

"It is also recommended that a small garrison be placed at Yatta, Naim, and Hebron, at any rate until this unvisited country settles down. One garrison battalion should be sufficient for the three posts, if one flank is brought up to L.24.

"The Turks on the Jericho road are good Turks, who have fought for every inch of ground from the walls of Jerusalem. They probably formed the Turkish rear guards west of Jerusalem, and at Bethlehem, and, although there should be no danger of them making any impression on us towards Jerusalem, it appears to me equally necessary that they should not be allowed to stir up the country east of Bethlehem and north of Hebron, whether the Division draws its supplies from Jerusalem or Beersheba; but whilst the latter is the case it is imperative that my communications should not be molested even by small parties of camel men.

"I also beg to bring to your notice that by moving up the 158th Brigade complete the Administrator of Hebron is depleted of any escort, and I do not consider that he should remain at his post without one.

"May I be informed whether this division is still responsible for the protection of the Lines of Communication to Beersheba, or whether they will be taken over by the G.O.C., L. of C., Palestine, till it is closed permanently?"

To this, the Corps replied that a battalion of Gwalior Infantry would shortly be at General Chetwode's disposal, and that 100 men would be placed at Hebron, and 200 at Bethlehem, the latter only to be under General Mott's command. "The Corps Cavalry Regiment, which is at your disposal, will remain in the neighbourhood of Bethlehem to patrol the approaches to that place from the east, and also the Bethlehem-Hebron road. You are empowered to send assistance from the Corps Cavalry Regiment to the O.C. Detachment, Gwalior Infantry at Hebron in an emergency, and to ensure rapid communication with you the telegraphic office at Hebron will be kept open."

The Corps Commander further stated that he was responsible for the provisions of troops to protect the Lines of Communication, but he did not consider he could afford to allot any troops to Yatta and Naim.

The following are the notes on the Corps Conference which followed the first outline of the scheme :—

"At the Corps Conference, held on December 20th at Enab, it was decided that 'immediately after the objectives allotted for the forthcoming operation have been attained, the Corps Commander intends to withdraw the 60th Division and 74th Division to reserve areas, which will relieve the supply situation, enable men and animals to receive full rations, and ensure that the present strain on the animals of the Divisional Train is relieved. The distribution he will aim at is the following :—

The line will be held in two groups.

Right Group. Bireh-Ain Arik area to be held by one division (53rd); reserve (60th Division).

Left Group. Ain Arik-Nalin area to be held by one division (10th); reserve (74th Division).

"The following are the general lines on which it is proposed to construct defensive systems to cover Jerusalem and the Corps front from the north.

(i) Shafat-Neby Samwil-Beit Ur el Foka-Suffa-Shilta.
(ii) Shafat-Beitania-Sh. Abu ez Zeitan-Kereina-Suffa-Shilta.
(iii) An additional line on the front about to be attacked, and a fourth on the final line taken up by the Corps, work beginning on the most forward lines.

"These lines will be so designed that they can be held by the minimum number of men, and no attempt will be made to hold a continuous line. The defences will consist of a series of fortified localities, so sited that they can serve as pivots for counter attack in case the enemy penetrates the line at any point.

"For a defence of this character it is absolutely necessary to provide good supply roads perpendicular to the front, and good lateral communications behind the various lines so that the reserves can be transferred rapidly from one portion of the front to another.

"The two roads on which it is imperative to concentrate work at first are the Jerusalem-Nablus road, from which troops so far west as Ain Arik will be supplied, the Latron-Beit Sira-Beit Ur et Tahta road, and possibly a third road from Ramleh towards Suffa. . . .

"The Corps Commander is very anxious to avoid any useless work, and he wishes Division Commanders carefully to consider the best alignment for all branch roads from the main supply road, and for lateral communications before the construction of any road is commenced."

The line across the Jericho road was still held by the 53rd Division, with a slight extension to the left. On the right, General Mott sent a Company (Middlesex) of the 160th Brigade to garrison Deir Ibn Obeid (L.23) about two and half miles south of his flank; they were accompanied by a squadron of the Westminster Dragoons.

The major operation ordered by the Corps was based on the outline communicated to General Mott (see Appendix), the 10th and 74th Divisions attacking in an easterly direction, and the 53rd and 60th Divisions in a northerly direction. The date selected was the 27th December. But on the 24th reliable information was received that the Turkish IIIrd Army was to make an attack to recover Jerusalem, and that it would take place either on the 25th or 26th.

Christmas Day passed without disturbance, and on the 26th a further warning was issued by XXth Corps that the Turks would attack Tel el Ful and Ras Tawik, giving great importance to the latter, and deliver a holding attack along the Jericho road.

On this information the Corps issued an after-Order to No. 19 (*see*

ON THE LINES OF COMMUNICATION

Of the doings of the 158th Brigade, Captain Peter Ashton's diary gives an attractive account.

"As the Division moved up the road (to Jerusalem), General Mott's headquarters got further and further away, till by the beginning of December the Brigade was practically detached and on its own. We had attached to us a section of the 11th Light Armoured Car Battery, under one Goldsack, with two armoured cars and three tenders with which to patrol the road. As the Division got further away, and our sphere of road mending enlarged, we had to send—first, detachments, and then whole battalions after them. By 6th December, the 5th R.W.F. had moved up to a little spring called Ain el Unkur, and the 6th to the neighbourhood of Dahariyeh, the 7th, machine gunners and camels, to Sakati, leaving Brigade headquarters with the Herefords and various oddments at Beersheba. . . . Going up the road in a Rolls tender to inspect work, and incidentally to see life, was a great amusement. On the 8th I went with Francis, commanding our Field Company R.E., to Hebron, where we called on Divisional Headquarters. It was a magnificently engineered road, all hairpin bends and corkscrew curves, through most wild and picturesque country. Hebron proved to be most beautiful, a city of gardens, with the square tomb of Abraham in the middle. On the 10th we went up to see Bethlehem, where the Division was installed in the Mar Elias Convent. We got our first view of Jerusalem, a mile or two further on, and saw heavy fighting going on on the Mount of Olives. . . . As the Brigade was now very much strung out, with headquarters at one end of the line, the Brigadier moved headquarters to Hebron on 14th December, where we opened up in a hideously cold stone house in the main street, that had, I understood, been somebody's harem. . . . On the 16th we were ordered to concentrate the whole Brigade forward at a place called the Wadi el Arab, about half-way to Bethlehem, by the 19th. The Herefords, R.A.M.C., and sundries, were still in Beersheba, and had 39 miles to go, so we got them as far as Makruneh the first evening. . . On the 18th, we moved Brigade Headquarters forward to the Wadi el Arab, sitting down in a big, bare Russian hospice on the top of a hill. By the night of the 19th, the whole Brigade was concentrated there, less one company of the Herefords, temporarily dropped in Hebron for the Military Governor, till some Indian troops should arrive. . . . After a day's rest we moved on again to join the Division, through Bethlehem, and finally bivouacked in the north-west quarter of Jerusalem, troops in the Valley of Jehosaphat, and Brigade Headquarters at St. George's School, opposite the Church of England cathedral.

"We were not destined to spend long in idleness. The other two brigades had borne all the burden during the last six weeks, fighting over intensely difficult country in intensely atrocious weather, so on the 22nd we despatched the 5th R.W.F. to take over part of the front line, and come under the orders of Brigadier-General Money, 159th Brigade. The 159th and 160th Brigades were holding an outpost line round the east and north-east sides of the city. The valley of Jehosaphat, starting at the north-west corner of the city, passes across its northern face; then, getting deeper and broader, down its eastern face, till it finally turns east itself, a little way south of the city. To the north of the town the ground is practically flat, rising to a ridge about $1\frac{1}{2}$ miles out. This ridge runs east and then south, forming the far side of the Valley of Jehosaphat; and at the point opposite the turn, *i.e.*, east of it, becomes the Mount of Olives. The Garden of Gethsemane is half-way up the western face of the Mount, facing across the Temple area.

"The only road for wheels, at that time, ran north to the ridge, and then east and south to the Russian Hospice at the end, whence it fell down, at a precipitous angle, to the Jerusalem-Jericho road. This ridge formed the line of defence, with the actual outpost line pushed well down the far slope, which was rocky, rough, and very steep.

"Both Brigades had their headquarters in the palatial Kaiserin Augusta Viktoria Hospice, on the Mount of Olives. It was a magnificent building, luxuriously furnished, with a German housekeeper and cooks, with a chapel, banqueting hall, and all the rest, ornamented with statues, frescoes, and paintings—chiefly of the Kaiser—and with wonderful views all round.

"The relief by the 5th Royal Welch Fusiliers was very steep and difficult, and was not completed till next morning.

"Christmas Day dawned in the usual torrents of rain, and the Valley of Jehosaphat, in which the Brigade was bivouacked, became a rushing torrent. It was, of course, a most ridiculous place to put troops in anyway, and to our annoyance we couldn't get any help from the Q Staff at the Division, beyond a grudging permission to make what arrangements we could. There were in our area various large monasteries, which we tackled. . . . We got the whole brigade under cover by nightfall.

"In the evening, the General and I and a good many more from the Division, dined with the American Mission, at their big common living house, run by Mr. Vesper and his wife. The whole Mission lived together in this large house, as far as I remember six families, and two or three old ladies. The men each plied a trade. The Vespers kept a shop, where we bought carpets, amber, wonderfully coloured photographs, etc., and all put their profits in a common pool—communists in the finest sense. The ladies ran a school for childern of any and every religion, and also taught the native women needlework and housekeeping. They were really very charming and simple folk, living the lives of real saints.

" We had a large, solid, Christmas dinner, and then an entertainment, at which the children danced and sang, and the ladies, too, and no one smoked, and the whole evening was, of course, severely teetotal—a sore trial to some of us.

" The brigade did not have long to enjoy its billets (unwillingly given), for the next day we were ordered to take over from the 159th Brigade entirely, which we did after dark. The 6th Royal Welch Fusiliers and Herefords took over the right and left sections of the line, with the 5th in reserve at the Russian Hospice (south of the German Hospice), and the 7th in reserve at Sir John Grey Hill's house (north of the German Hospice). Brigade headquarters joined the 159th and the 160th Brigade headquarters at the German Hospice itself."

THE TURKISH ATTACK.

The whole Division was now assembled, with the exception of one half company of the Herefords. On the left the Division was in touch with the 60th Division at Ras el Kharrubeh, the 60th line running through Tell el Fal, across the Jerusalem-Nablus road to Neby Samwil; thence the 74th Division carried it through Beit Izza, Beit Dukku, and el Tireh, where they joined with the 10th Division through Tahta to Suffa, which marked the extreme left of the Corps. Suffa was on the right of the Australian Mounted Division, also under the orders of the XXth Corps; and then came the XXIst Corps to the sea, north of Jaffa.

The ultimate objective of the next advance was Deir Ibn Obeid, which was in the neighbourhood of the high point mentioned by General Mott, $2\frac{1}{2}$ miles south of his right, Ras el Zamby-Anata-Hizmeh-Jeba-Burkah-Beitin-el Balua-Kh el Burj-Deir Ibzia-to Shilta.* The left of the line would probably be extended to Nalin in the later operation.

On the assumption that the general advance would take place on the night 24/25th the 180th Brigade, 60th Division, sought to improve their line by the occupation of the high ground at Khurbet Adaseh at dawn on the 23rd. This they were unable to do, owing to heavy enfilade fire on their flanks. The 181st Brigade, however, made a slight advance.

* Burj—map error, Bury.

All was ready for the general action on the 24th, but the weather had for some days been wet and cold, and the troops had suffered much hardship. Heavy rain, accompanied by a gale of wind, continued all Christmas Day, and the whole country became water-logged, and the roads half a foot deep in mud. The date of attack was postponed, until the weather improved.

The rain ceased on the night 26/27th, and at 11.30 p.m. the Turks launched their great attack to recapture Jerusalem. They drove in the outpost line of the 60th Division about Ras el Tawil.

As soon as General Chetwode realised that the Turks were committed to an attack on Jerusalem, he ordered the 10th and 74th Divisions to carry on with the offensive previously ordered at dawn.

Dawn on the 27th December broke to find the weather fine but misty. The night attack on the 60th Division had spread to the 53rd Division front, and White Hill and Zamby were submitted to a furious bombardment.

The whole of the Turkish flank attack was delivered on this portion of the front held by the 160th Brigade, and repeated assaults were made on White Hill and Zamby which were held by the Queens.

When the Middlesex and Queens had first taken White Hill, the Wall and Zamby, enemy fire from Suffa, and from positions on either flank, had seriously hampered proper consolidation, and the trenches they succeeded in digging had a very limited field of fire; they were barely on the crest and mostly on the reverse slope.

The Turks, who came on with great bravery, succeeded in reaching bombing distance on several occasions. Casualties were severe, and a company of the Middlesex was sent up to reinforce the garrison of Zamby.

But the awkward position of the Queens on White Hill, with their limited field of fire, was taken full advantage of by the Turks. The forward slope of the hill was cut by several wadis, and in them the Turks could assemble untouched, and work their way round to the flanks. Soon the Queens found the enemy on three sides of them, but the Wall was still open, and under its protection they withdrew to Zamby, except one small post, which held out on the reverse slope of the hill.

White Hill then became No Man's Land, for the artillery denied the crest of it to the enemy.

The Middlesex had, meanwhile, moved two more companies into Zamby, who started to retake White Hill, but met a furious attack by the Turks on Zamby, and had to turn aside to beat it off.

The fight continued all day, but the Turks never succeeded in reaching the line held in front of Zamby, or in occupying the crest of White Hill.

The West Kents, on the right of the Brigade, were not molested, but the detached post, at Deir Ibn Obeid, consisting of the fourth company of the Middlesex under Captain J. C. Downie, was attacked by a force estimated at 700, with mountain guns. Under cover of the guns the Turks worked up to within 100 yards of the Monastery Wall, but were held there by rifle, Lewis gun and machine gun fire. The garrison was entirely surrounded, and at six o'clock in the evening the Turks brought two guns close up and endeavoured to breach the monastery wall from the east, but were unsuccessful. About 400 shells were fired into this post, which had the support of one section of A/266 Battery, firing at the limit of range from a position to the northwest. The Turks withdrew in the morning, on the approach of the Sussex.

Meanwhile, after a lull, the enemy made an attack of unexpected suddenness at 12.55 p.m. against the whole front of the 60th Division and succeeded in reaching certain portions of the front line, but a counter attack restored the line and the Turks were driven off. The nett gain, after delivering about 13 costly attacks was that the Turks had captured Ras et Tawil and some quarries (Y.6.)

At Corps Headquarters the situation gave rise to no anxiety. At 9.45 in the morning, General Bartholomew telephoned to General Mott that the Corps Commander was not concerned as to how near Bethlehem the enemy reached. The Left Attack, as arranged, was launched at 6 a.m.

This Left Attack (10th and 74th Divisions) was organised in right, centre, and left groups. The advance commenced with the right group and considerable opposition was experienced at Deir Ibzia, but once this was taken the objective was reached with little trouble. At 7 a.m., the centre group moved and reached its objective. At 7.50 a.m., the left group started from its position of deployment, and by 9 o'clock had secured the west end of the Sh. Abu ez Zeitan ridge. But again opposition was encountered and the ridge was only cleared after dark.

At the end of the day the situation was that the great Turkish effort to recapture Jerusalem had been held by the 53rd and 60th Divisions, and the 10th and 74th had carried out the pre-arranged plan and were, generally speaking, in possession of their objectives.

The 158th Brigade, on the left of the Divisional front, had scarcely been touched that day. All the fighting had been against the 160th Brigade, on their right, and the 60th Division, on their left. The Brigade

THE STAFF.

Battle Headquarters had been established in a summer house at the bottom of the German Hospice garden. " It was a most extra-ordinary situation," says Captain Ashton, " from the garden the ground fell away very quickly into the east, and from our summer house we got a sort of aeroplane view of the whole battle area below ; with glasses one could see practically every man and what he was doing except for the extreme left of the Herefords. The 160th Brigade and the Gunners had their headquarters in the same place, while we had the Major-General and a good proportion of Division Headquarters most of the day—a perfect galaxy of talent ! Waiters brought down sandwiches and drinks on silver trays at lunch time, and it was more like a field day than ever ! And though they shelled the road on both sides of the hospice the Turks never shelled us once ! We could only assume that being Hun the Hospice was sacrosanct."

A feeble advance against the 6th Royal Welch Fusiliers was easily checked ; and the Herefords captured a patrol of ten men. Towards evening the 158th Brigade was ordered to take over all that part of the 160th Brigade line which lay north of the Jericho road. This meant the recapture of White Hill, and Colonel Harker, 7th Royal Welch Fusiliers, was ordered to reconnoitre the position before it was dark.

The Fusiliers took over at dusk, and under a barrage occupied White Hill at 1 a.m. The Turks counter-attacked but were easily beaten off.

THE 53RD ADVANCE ON THE RIGHT FLANK

A warning had been issued by General Chetwode when the success of the day's operations was assured. " In order to prepare for a further advance at the earliest possible moment, the line to be occupied by the XXth Corps westwards of Kh. Ras el Tawil, as soon as possible, will be Kh. Ras el Tawil-Bir Nebala-el Jib-Kh. el Jufier-eastern end of Kh. Bir es Shafa-Zeitan ridge-P.33 central-P.13 central. To carry out this movement the 60th Division, pivotting on Kh. Ras el Tawil, will swing forward its left to include Bir Nebala and el Jib as soon as the situation permits. The gap from el Jib (exclusive) to the junction with the right of the Left Attack on the Kh. Bir es Shafa-Zeitan ridge will be filled by the reserve brigade under General Girdwood. A preliminary movement by this brigade to the approximate line Kh. Neda (R.29c)-junction with the right of the Left Attack will be made to-night, touch being kept with the left of the 60th Division. As soon as the new line has been occupied, the Corps Commander, who is anxious to assume the offensive all along the line as soon as possible, will decide whether to drive the enemy east and northeast, across the Nablus road, or to advance the 60th and 53rd Divisions northwards according to his original plan."

This was followed by a telegram during the early hours of the 28th December: " Advance north by the 60th Division will be resumed to-day as soon as possible. 53rd Division will co-operate to protect the right flank of 60th Division in the manner prescribed by Corps Order No. 19. G.O.C. 53rd Division will arrange co-operation in close consultation with G.O.C. 60th Division."

As a preliminary to the protection of the 60th Division in their advance, the 158th Brigade was ordered to capture Ras Arkub es Suffa, and the high ground beyond Anata village. General Mott went down to the German Hospice and talked over the attack with Brigadier-General Vernon. It was then about 11 in the morning, and the advance was to be made as soon as preparations were completed.

At 3.45 p.m. the advance commenced. It consisted of three distinct operations. The Herefords, assembled behind the hill of Kharrubeh, advanced in two waves round the sides of it and made straight for the village. Well supported by the artillery, they passed through the village, leaving parties to bomb the cellars, and on to the high ground beyond.

The 6th Royal Welch Fusiliers, led by Captain Emrys Evans, took their objective, a hill called " Grey Hill," on the right of the Herefords.

But the attack on Suffa, by the 7th Royal Welch Fusiliers, failed at first, owing to heavy machine gun fire on the flanks. Suffa was joined to White Hill by a saddle, about a mile long. Colonel Harker directed the attack along the length of the saddle, and the Turks held the low ground on either side with machine guns: the men on the skyline above provided an easy target. " From the summer house," Captain Ashton says, " we watched the attack getting slower and slower till at 4.50 p.m. it stopped altogether, and reported itself unable to get on." Only $1\frac{1}{2}$ companies had been used, but it was decided to wait for darkness before pressing the advance. Zamby and White Hill, held by the 7th Royal Welch Fusiliers, with the responsibility of the Jericho road, was taken over by two companies of the 5th Royal Welch Fusiliers; the artillery opened short bursts of fire on Suffa during the night, and at midnight the 7th Royal Welch Fusiliers assaulted and captured the hill.

Two hours later the Herefords occupied a hill near Khirbet Amit.

Meanwhile, the 159th Brigade had, on the 28th, been put in on the left of the 158th, and as the 60th Division advanced the 4th Welch occupied Ras ez Tawil, and the 7th Cheshires a ridge further north. By 5.25 p.m. the 60th Division was on the Er Ram-Rafat line, and were ordered to continue the advance to the final objective at 8 o'clock the next morning (29th).

The 53rd Division Artillery was then grouped: 265th Bde. R.F.A. in support of 159th Inf. Bde; 267th Bde. R.F.A., in support of 158th Inf. Bde.; and 266th R.F.A. in support of 160th Inf. Bde.

The 74th and 10th Divisions had advanced to the line Rafat-el Muntar-Kefr Skiyan-Abu el Ainein-Kh Rubin. These operations were carried out over extremely difficult country intersected by deep ravines. The enemy had numerous machine guns hidden amongst the rocks.

The next morning the 159th Brigade found that opposition had died away, and Hizmeh, Jeba, and the high ridges to the north-west were occupied in succession.

The 60th Division also found little opposition until within effective range of Bireh and Ras el Tahunek, when a check was experienced. But soon after nine that night the final objective Beitin-el Balua-Kh. el Burj was occupied.

By that time the 74th Division was in touch with the 60th and their line ran north of Ram Allah to Kh. et Tireh. The 10th Division were on the Kh. et Tireh ridge.

All organised resistance had ceased, and at daybreak on the 30th only a few snipers remained.

During the three days' fighting the XXth Corps captured 39 officers, 711 other ranks, 17 machine guns, 3 automatic rifles, and 1,006 enemy dead were counted. Of the latter number 271 dead were buried on the front of the 53rd Division.

.   .   .   .   .

A rearrangement of the front had been foreshadowed, and on the 31st, Brigadier-General Vernon accompanied by his Brigade Major reconnoitred the area round Beitin. "The country was like that we had come through, south of Jerusalem—very steep and precipitous, planted where there was enough soil to plant anything, with here and there terraced hill sides to save the precious soil all being washed to the bottom in the rains. As soon as one got off the Jerusalem-Nablus road the country was impossible for wheeled transport. The natives don't use wheels, using donkeys or camels in single file; their tracks are merely narrow lanes, about three feet wide, with stone walls on either side. A further trouble lay in the fact that the only map was one made by Lord Kitchener, in 1878, and it was rather sketchy."—(Ashton.)

GENERAL SITUATION
January, 1918.

Arab forces begin actions for et Tafile, 1st January.

President Wilson delivers a message to Congress, laying down the Fourteen Points, 8th January.

Trebizond retaken by Turks, 24th February.

JERICHO

THE CAPTURE OF JERICHO

ON the 4th January, 1918, the 53rd Division took over the line, the 158th Brigade on the right, in the Kh. Mukatir-Burj-Beitin-Kh. Deir Shebab area, and the 159th Brigade on the left, in touch with the 10th Division on the Wadi Nakib.

On the right, just behind the line, and running in a southerly direction, was a deep wadi, and the 158th Brigade had to find many tiring fatigues constructing a road in and out of it. Indeed, road making was the principal occupation of all troops for some months, and as, at that time, the winter rains had not ceased, it was far from a pleasant one.

From the top of Kh. Nisieh a fine view was obtained to the east, the ground falling away, with bare hills and wooded valleys alternating, until it reached the arid jumble which marks the abrupt descent into the Jordan Valley. On the left of the 158th Brigade front was Sh. Abdalla, which was brought within the line by the 160th Brigade on the 18th January, and another hill, Arnutieh, which the 158th Brigade secured on the 29th.

The enemy had no settled front line, occupying a succession of positions, sangars, rocks, edges of villages, and so on.

The left sector was much the same, a wild, incredible succession of hills, and precipitous wadis. Here again there was the Wadi Hamis, running west from Ram Allah, which had to be provided with entrance and exit roads.

Although, towards the end of January, the wild flowers which abound in Judea commenced to bloom in the sheltered valleys, all ranks had a hard and depressing time with road making in drenching rain, especially as there was a great scarcity of fuel.

The brigade in Divisional Reserve bivouacked behind Bireh.

Any further advance north was out of the question. Not being a country for wheels the old Roman roads had been allowed to deteriorate into mere bridle paths, and the question of supplies was a difficult one, rendered still more so by the frequent spells of wet weather. Also the right flank of the army still rested on the hills between Jerusalem and the Jordan, which were not an insuperable barrier.

The Valley of the Jordan can be seen from all the important heights of Judea as a great rent in the surface of the earth. " The depth, the haggard desert through which the land sinks into it, the singularity of the gulf and its prisoned sea, and the higher barrier beyond, conspire to produce on the inhabitants of Judea a moral effect such as, I suppose, is created by no other frontier in the world " (George Adam Smith). General Mott had studied this amazing country and was aware of its dangers and the difficulties which might serve him.

Sir E. Allenby had intended to make a simultaneous advance north and east of the Jordan, but it was obvious that if he carried out this idea he would have to wait until he had accumulated supplies, and perfected his communications, in fact some considerable time. He, therefore, decided to advance east as a separate operation as far as the Jordan, with a rectification of his line to the north up to the river Aujah. The possession of the crossings over the Jordan would prevent the enemy raiding the country west of that river, and give him the control of the Dead Sea. He had in his mind, too, the basis for further operations eastward, to cut the Turkish line of communication with the Hedjaz.

On the 9th February, General Mott informed his Brigadiers that further operations were contemplated :

(*a*) To advance on the Jericho road, and drive the enemy east of the Jordan, inflicting as much loss on him as possible ;

(*b*) To destroy, or remove, stores near the beach and the enemy motor and sailing boats on the Dead Sea, so as to prevent a renewal of the grain trade ;

(*c*) To obtain information as to the country west of the Jordan.

The warning order points out that it was impossible to fix a date for the operations owing to the bad state of the weather, but " Z-1 day will probably be the fourth fine day after the present spell of bad weather ends."

The first stage of the operations was forecasted by " Corps " as taking place on Z-2/Z-1 night, when the 60th Division would occupy Mukhmas to provide a starting off place for reconnaissance of Ras et Tawil, and as a preliminary to the concentration of the brigade in that area.

On the same night the 53rd Division would advance their line to include Deir Diwan and Green Hill (N.28c.).

On Z day the 60th Division would advance to a line through El Muntar and Arak Ibrahim, and the 53rd Division would take Ras et Tawil and the high ground between the Wadi el Ain and the Taiyibeh-Jericho road, if possible occupying Rummon in order to be in a position to keep the road under fire.

On Z-1 day, or as soon as possible after the completion of stage 1, the second stage would be put into operation. The 60th Division would advance in three columns; the right column on Jebel Ektief; the centre column on Talet el Dumm; the left column along the Ras et Tawil-Jebel Kuruntul* track.

The 53rd Division would advance their line, if possible, to the Taiyibeh-Jericho road, and so command all approaches from the north between the Wadi Dar el Jerir and the Wadi el Asa.

In this second stage, one, and possibly two, cavalry brigades would move from the neighbourhood of Muntar, with the object of cutting off any of the enemy about Jericho, and afterwards occupying a line of picquets to cover the el Goranieh Bridge over the Jordan, and to block the crossings over the Wadi Aujah.

The advance eastwards of the three columns of the 60th Division would be limited by the line of cliffs from Kh. Kakum through Jebel Kuruntul to Um Sireh, unless the cavalry required assistance to clear Jericho.

By a re-arrangement of the Bireh front on the 11th February (held by two brigades), the right brigade sector was divided into two brigade sections, the 159th and 160th. The operation contemplated was an extension of the right flank eastwards, with the high ground about and to the north of Rummon village, the high ground on the left bank of the Wadi Asa, as far south as A.26, as the Divisional objective.

The objectives on the 60th Division front were so widely dispersed that co-operation was impossible between the three brigades. The first move of the left brigade (181) was Mukhmas and Tel es Suwan, on the 14th February; from which places a reconnaissance could be made in the direction of Splash Hill (C.2. central). But, before this took place, the 160th Brigade occupied Deir Diwan, and the 159th Brigade a hill named Green Hill on the night 13/14th without opposition. A post was also established in the Wadi Asis. The 181st Brigade then moved forward and captured their allotted position.

Three days were spent in reconnaissance, and at dawn on the 19th February the 60th Division attacked all along their front. Once more the 53rd Division moved ahead of the 60th; the West Kents advanced

* Qruntul—*R.G.S.*

their line during the night to Kefr Nata, while the Middlesex and Sussex battalions commenced a difficult advance with the object of occupying a position which would enable them to rush the high ground and the village of Rummon at dawn.

At 5.30 a.m., the West Kents had occupied the spurs overlooking the Wadi Asa, and were in touch with the 181st Brigade at Splash Hill. Meanwhile the Sussex and Middlesex had found no opposition to their advance on the high ground, but one company of the latter battalion found some difficulty in clearing the village of Rummon, which was not finally captured until 8.30 a.m.

The flank of the 60th Division was now secured.

Frequent officer patrols failed to discover any movement of the enemy on the Taiyibeh-Jericho road.

While these moves of the 53rd Division were being completed, the 2/23rd London Regiment, opposed by some 300 Turks, captured Splash Hill at 6 a.m. The 2/24th London found that Ras Tawil had been abandoned.

The 53rd had nothing further to do than watch the road. The 60th Division pushed on, through the most appalling country, until they were in a position to attack Jebel Ekteif and Talat Dumm the next morning. On their right the Anzac Division was concentrated at El Muntar by 7 p.m.

After some fearful climbing, marching, and fighting, the 181st Brigade captured Talat Dumm at 2.15 p.m.; while on their right the 179th Brigade reached Jebel Ekteif.

Before dawn on the 20th, the 181st Brigade commenced to advance against Kuruntul, but were held up by enemy rearguards, skilfully handled in a country especially suited to rearguard actions. Orders were issued that it was unnecessary to incur heavy losses by a rapid advance, and the Brigade, therefore, did not press the attack.

On the right the Anzac Division was held up by Turkish infantry at Neby Musa, and the 2/14th London and 10th Mountain Battery marched towards that place and cleared it at 6 a.m. on the 21st.

A general advance then took place and the final objectives were captured.

The Australian Mounted Brigade, advancing across the plain, entered Jericho at 8.20 a.m., the Turks having withdrawn during the night, and patrolled as far as the Wadi Aujah, to the north, and to the el Ghoraniyeh

Bridge. The enemy was found to be holding the high ground to the north of the Aujah, and also a bridgehead covering the el Ghoraniyeh Bridge with guns on the left flank. As a direct attack on the bridgehead would have involved heavy losses, without compensating advantages, it was not attempted.

On no other occasion had such difficulties of ground been encountered; as an instance of this a Field Artillery Battery took 36 hours to reach Neby Musa, the distance covered, measured on the map, being only eight miles. The 53rd Division were to have many such experiences.

GENERAL SITUATION
March, 1918.

Peace signed between the Bolsheviks and Central Powers, 3rd March.

Preliminary treaty of Peace between Rumania and Central Powers, 5th March.

Peace signed between Roumania and Bolsheviks, 9th March.

Erzerum retaken by Turks, 12th March.

TELL ASUR
" GOREU ARF, CALON DDEWR "

THE operation which resulted in the capture of Jericho and driving the enemy across the Jordan had secured the right flank of the army; but the base obtained was not sufficiently broad to permit of further operations to the east of the Jordan. Sir E. Allenby considered that the first essential to his plan was to cross the Wadi Aujah and secure the high ground on the north bank covering the approaches to the Jordan Valley by the Beisan-Jericho road, and, secondly, by advancing northwards on either side of the Jerusalem-Nablus road deny to the enemy all tracks and roads leading to the lower Jordan Valley. The Turks would then have to make a considerable detour if they wished to transfer troops from the west to the east bank of the Jordan.

With the above object in view, the XXth Corps was ordered to secure Kh. el Beiyudat and Abu Tellul, in the Jordon Valley north of Wadi el Aujah; and further to the west the line Kefr Malik-Kh. Abu Felah, the high ground south of Sinjil, and the ridge north of the Wadi el Jib running through Kh. Aliuta-Jiljilia-Abwein-Arura thence to Deir es Sudan and Neby Saleh.*

The general advance was to be over a front of twenty-six miles to a depth of seven miles. The order of battle would be 60th Division on the right, then 53rd, 74th, and 10th; the XXIst Corps would conform to the advance of the XXth Corps.

THE POSITION OF THE 53RD

The position of the 53rd Division must be observed. From the watershed, two miles east of the Nablus road, the fall to the Jordan Valley is short and sharp and the beds of the wadis are deep and their sides precipitous. The intricacies of this " haggard desert " country presented many and grave difficulties to large bodies of troops. The objectives of the 60th Division were down in the Jordan Valley, and a gap would exist between their left and the right of the 53rd Division which, in spite of the difficulties of the country, was of such a distance that the 53rd must still be considered the flank of the main army.

The line of advance on the eastern side of the watershed which lay before the 53rd Division was sufficiently forbidding. The physical

* Alyata, Jiljliya, En Nabi Salih—*R.G.S.*

effort required to move forward was tremendous. The succession of high, rocky ridges and deep valleys contained many places where men must hoist themselves up, or lower themselves down, and, as was afterwards discovered, the conformation of the ground frequently confined troops to one ledge on which the enemy could concentrate his fire. Roads had to be made in feverish haste for the artillery so that the infantry might not move beyond the support of their fire; and also to bring up food and water for the troops. Added to all this there was the constant danger of losing direction, for the Palestine Exploration Fund one inch map was not of much use to a company commander; it was, therefore, wise to point out objectives to officers and men on the ground—which was not always done.

ORDERS FOR ATTACK

General Mott decided that the 158th Brigade should deliver the main attack from the Wadi Hishish. Brigadier-General Vernon was to advance on a two-battalion front to the high ground in L.36.c and L.35.c if possible by dawn. The line of advance was west of the Wadi Dar el Jerir until it became necessary to cross it in order to climb the high ground in L.36.c.

The first objectives for the Division were, hill in L.30.c.-Tell Asur-enemy guns, if any.

Simultaneously, with the advance of the 158th Brigade, the 159th Brigade on their right were to advance on a two-battalion front on the other side of the Wadi Dar el Jerir: the right battalion from the neighbourhood of Nejmeh, to the high ground in S.16a (Munitar); and the left battalion on the village of Dar Jerir, from the neighbourhood of El Khudr. As soon as the right of the 158th Brigade had sufficiently advanced the latter battalion was to work towards Kefr Malik, if necessary.

One battalion of the 160th Brigade was to hold the gap between the left of the 158th Brigade and the right of the 74th Division, conforming to the advance of the 158th Brigade. The remainder of the 160th Brigade was to be employed in making roads. (*See* Appendix.)

Four composite Artillery Brigades would support the attack of the 53rd Division, and General Mott proposed to detail two to each Infantry Brigade, but he provided that the fire of three Artillery Brigades should, if necessary, be concentrated to support the main attack of the 158th Brigade. The 10th Mountain Battery were to support the attack of the right battalion of the 159th Brigade.

The General also had at his disposal the 1st Australian Light Horse Brigade, which he proposed to hold back at Beitin, using one Regiment, when the time was ripe, towards Nejmeh to enable the right battalion of the 159th Brigade to advance with freedom instead of diminishing their strength by picquetting the ground.

Supply was a grave problem, and all available men were set to work navvying in the rain so as to get the roads well forward before zero day.

It will be seen that this plan presumed a jumping off position which was not as yet in the hands of the Division, the line Nejmeh-Taiyibeh-N. 18.a-N.16 central-Kefr Ana (exclusive). It was the more desirable to move forward as the enemy was, roughly, five miles away, and the General wanted what he called " more elbow room," and also better opportunity for detailed reconnaissance.

This preliminary operation was carried out on the night 6/7th March, the most difficult portion of it being successfully accomplished by units of the 159th Brigade.

NO MAN'S LAND

The situation in the belt of country separating the 53rd Division from the Turks is illustrated by the report of one of the many patrols sent out at the end of February.

At 4 a.m., 28th February, a patrol consisting of three officers and sixteen men of the 7th Cheshires, left Rummamaneh, and moved in a direct line across country with the object of reaching Kilia ridge and examining, in daylight, the Wadi Jerir. They crossed the Wadi Taiyibeh and followed a little used mud track to Abu Raschid, where they found a well with a plentiful supply of water. Pressing forward in a north-easterly direction, across stony ground and some meagre cultivation, they reached the highest point of the Kilia ridge at about 6 a.m. Here they found a series of sangars but no sign of a Turk. Up to this point, the gradients had been fairly easy, but the north-east side of Kilia was found to be very steep, and the side of Nejmeh appeared precipitous. They moved south-east along the ridge to the ruin of a large square house and a solid tower. Here they found about 30 shell boxes, some containing live shells of 77 c.m. calibre. From the tower a fine view was obtained of Nejmeh with a Mosque just below the summit of the hill, and of the wooded crest of Munatir. Nejmeh dominated all the country towards the Jordan, and the patrol found that on the Mosque side the gradients were easier. Only one Turk was seen here, but on the top of Munatir, some distance away, several bivouacs were observed. Altogether, over a wide expanse of the enemy front only a dozen Turks were seen. The patrol then withdrew.

The ground having been thoroughly well reconnoitred, the 7th Cheshires, supported by the 4th, moved out from Rummamaneh on the night 6/7th March. The Wadi Jerir was reached without incident—the transport going as far as Abu Rashid—and two companies, under Captain Stott, made straight for Nejmeh along a tributary wadi which fell into the Jerir, while the other two companies, under Captain Flunder, moved to a position on the left between Nejmeh and Munatir. A few small parties of the enemy occupying the heights were completely surprised, and fled, leaving their arms and equipment. Some sniping was, however, carried on during the day at Captain Flunder's force.

It was no small achievement to cross that roadless country in the dark; Nejmeh was in the hands of the 7th Cheshires by five o'clock in the morning.

PREPARATION FOR THE ATTACK

Meanwhile the 5th Welch, on the left, had marched, under Lieut.-Colonel Bowen, on Taiyibeh and occupied it with little opposition. Behind them the 4th Welch, under Major Pemberton, and the West Kents, had every available man at work rushing through the construction of a road from Rummon to Taiyibeh, which was completed and ready for wheeled transport and guns by the evening of 7th March. At the same time the 159th Pioneer Company had made a path for mules up and down the steep sides of the Wadi Dar el Jerir. The other three battalions of the 160th Brigade were employed on the Beitin-Tell Asur road.

The left of the new position selected by General Mott was occupied by the 158th Brigade without opposition.

All was now ready for the moving up of guns, which commenced at once, one Brigade being in position south of Taiyibeh, and another east of the road by Ain Yebrud on the night 7/8th. The 53rd Divisional Artillery had, on the 7th, been reinforced by the 301st Field Artillery Brigade and B/302 Battery (60th Division), the 10th Mountain Battery, and D/69 (Howr.) Battery (7th Indian Division).

The 74th Division on the left made a similar preliminary advance; Welsh battalions of that Division—the 24th Welch Regiment and 24th Royal Welch Fusiliers—occupying Kh. Kefr Ana and the west of Sinia.

Nothing occurred on the Corps front on the 8th; a certain number of the enemy were seen, a movement of troops which indicated that the Turks were on the alert; on the 53rd Divisional front most of the movement was about Dar Jerir.

THE BATTLE

The battle opened in the early morning of the 9th March.

The objectives of the 60th Division were Kh. Beiyudat and Abu Tellul, down in the Valley of the Jordan, and the 181st Brigade, entrusted with this task, had great difficulty in crossing the Aujah in the dark; also they met with stout resistance. Success eventually crowned their efforts about three o'clock in the afternoon, but, not being in touch, the movements of the 60th Division had no immediate effect on the 53rd Division.

The objectives of the 53rd Division, given by the XXth Corps, were Abu Felah-Mezrah esh Sherkiyeh (exclusive); those of the 74th Division Mezrah esh Sherkiyeh-high ground in K.12; those of the 10th Division Neby Saleh-high ground in D.7 and 8.

General Mott gave as the first objectives of his Division the line Munatir-S.3.c-L.30.c and Tell Asur, with instructions that these objectives must be reached by dawn (*see* Appendix).

Following the events from the right of the line, the 159th Brigade had on their front the complication of the steep sided Wadi Jerir, and so worked in two columns. The 4th Cheshires, supported by the 7th Cheshires, were given by Brigadier-General Money, as first objective, Munatir ridge and S.3.c or Pear Hill, as it was called, and then to " push on " to Q.33 and Kafr Malik; the 4th Welch, supported by the 5th Welch, was given Dar Jerir, and then to " push on " to L.36.c or Drage's Hill.

As there was every likelihood that communication might be difficult, Major Moir, 7th Cheshires, was directed to take command of both battalions of the right column if visual signalling with Brigade Headquarters was interrupted.

THE CHESHIRES

The Cheshire battalions started from Nejmeh and Kilia, supported by the 265th Brigade Field Artillery, and the 10th Mountain battery. Considerable fire came from the wooded crest of Munatir, but the 4th Cheshires cleared the position by 4.30 a.m. They then faced Pear Hill (S.3.c) a strong position, which could only be approached over a bare open ridge a mile long. The Turks poured a heavy rifle and machine gun fire across the ridge, and the 265th Field Brigade had to be called on for a special bombardment. Under cover of the guns the 4th Cheshires advanced and occupied the crest of the hill, some 400 Turks being seen retiring by the Forward Observation Officer who turned every available gun on them and inflicted heavy casualties.

The next step was Q.33, a hill covered with ruins, stone walls, and trees, aptly named Rock Park. The enemy had concentrated at this favourable place in force, and thrown out machine guns on their flanks to enfilade the 4th Cheshires, who found themselves unable to advance from Pear Hill. While they were re-organising, the 7th Cheshires, leaving a post to hold Munatir, moved up in close support.

The Wadi Dar Jerir, being now clear in the neighbourhood of Taiyibeh, Brigadier-General Money ordered the 1st Australian Light Horse to escort the 10th Mountain Battery to a position behind the 7th Cheshires. The 1st A.L.H. then released the Cyclist Company, who had been holding Nejmeh, and sent out patrols to try and gain touch with the mounted patrols of the 60th Division along the Wadi Aujah.

Meanwhile the 265th Field Artillery Brigade bombarded Rock Park, commencing at 4.15 p.m., while the 4th Cheshires worked their way forward. When Brigadier-General Money, from his Battle Headquarters, saw the infantry approaching the position, he gave orders for intensive artillery fire, and by 5 p.m., the whole of the forward slopes of Rock Park were taken.

The sustained effort of the two Cheshire battalions through the long day, during which they had suffered from continual shelling from the east, was now spent, and no further advance could be made.

THE 4TH WELCH

The left column had started off at 4 a.m., and the 4th Welch had met with stout resistance in the village of Dar Jerir, but in half an hour the place was cleared, some prisoners being taken and a number of the enemy bayonetted. By 5 a.m. this battalion was on the upper slopes of L.36.a. Drage Hill, where they were severely punished by fire from L.30c or Chipp Hill. Several attempts were made to advance on Kafr Malik, but without result, the enemy, drawn up on Chipp Hill and on a ridge running south-east of it, checking them each time.

THE 158TH BRIGADE

The Herefords, on the right, made an attempt to take Chipp Hill, but failed, and a bombardment and combined attack was arranged, but had to be postponed owing to the situation on Tell Asur.

The operations of the 158th Brigade, round about Tell Asur, were of vast importance. This commanding hill, the highest in Judea, was a position which the enemy would cling to tenaciously. Brigadier-General Vernon had the 266th, 267th, and 301st Field Artillery Brigades to assist him in his advance, and his handling of his battalions reveals some interesting manœuvres.

The task of the 158th Brigade, as set forth in Divisional Orders, was to advance to the high ground in L.30.c and L.35.c. on a two-battalion front, keeping west of the Wadi Dar el Jerir, and east of a north and south line through the Cairn in L.35.c. Tell Asur to be occupied by the 158th Brigade as soon as possible after arrival on this line, and communication established with the right brigade of the 74th Division.

The preliminary advance of the 158th Brigade on the night of the 6/7th had brought them west of Taiyibeh, where they formed up, the Herefords on a hill on the right, and the 5th Royal Welch Fusiliers on a hill on the left. The Herefords were given Drage Hill (L.36.a) and then Chipp Hill (L.30.c); the 5th Royal Welch Fusiliers, Cairn Hill (L.35.c). Tell Asur was to be taken from the east.

The description of these hills given by Captain Ashton is that Cairn Hill was a kind of hump between Drage Hill and Tell Asur; Chipp Hill was a hill in succession to Drage Hill to the north-east. " Tell Asur we could see as a high, steep, rocky hill going straight up out of the valley at its foot, and we somehow assumed that the country would fall on the other side in the same way; most hills do. Actually Tell Asur was the edge of a high plateau."

At 2 a.m. the leading battalions started to advance, the 7th Royal Welch Fusiliers were in support to the Herefords, and the 6th R.W.F. to the 5th; but they were some way in rear. Although a considerable space still separated the point of assembly for attack from the objectives, the Turks held no intermediary ground; the artillery was, therefore, silent. Nevertheless, the advance across that rough country in the dark was difficult and, of necessity, slow. The factor of physical fatigue must always arise in any prolonged battle, but in this country it presented itself with insistence in the grim, terraced, and rock-buttressed hills which had to be scaled. A start at 2 a.m. with a day measured by light before them, called for a strenuous physical effort on the part of all troops.

But, in the early morning, the 158th Brigade was hampered by a fog as well. The 159th Brigade had found communication by visual signalling extremely hard to maintain owing to clouds, and the conditions on their left were decidedly worse.

At first, the visibility was such that when the 5th R.W.F. approached Cairn Hill, the Turks opened fire on them from their immediate front and also from Tell Asur. Lieut.-Colonel Borthwick promptly deployed his battalion, which, up to the last moment moved, for greater speed and effective control, in close formation, and assaulted Cairn Hill, advancing up the slope into the fog. The battalion swarmed up the hill but became scattered, and although the enemy retired before them, much time had to be spent in re-organising and regaining control.

Meanwhile the Herefords reached Drage Hill (which was also in a fog), at 6 a.m. on the upper slopes of which the 4th Welch were established, and faced Chipp Hill and the ridge lined with enemy riflemen and machine guns.

CHIPP HILL

It was now that the pause by the 5th Royal Welch Fusiliers engulfed in the fog on the left gave rise to rumours and false reports. At 6 a.m., Brigadier-General Vernon was informed that Tell Asur had been captured, and passed on that news to Division, at the same time ordering the 6th and 7th Royal Welch Fusiliers to move up in close support. Soon after he received further and more accurate information, and halted the support battalions in dead ground. The Herefords were then directed to take Chipp Hill.

The fighting on Chipp Hill was severe. The Herefords reached the summit and held it for a couple of hours, when they were driven off by a strong counter-attack. By this time, Lieutenant Colonel Borthwick had reorganised the 5th Royal Welch Fusiliers and, under artillery support, attacked and captured Tell Asur, just about the time that the Herefords were driven from Chipp Hill—9.30 a.m.

Then followed a long pause. At 7.30 a.m. the Brigadier had ordered the 7th R.W.F. to move up behind Drage Hill, and the 6th behind Cairn Hill. He now ordered the 7th to relieve the companies of Herefords on Drage Hill, and the 6th to relieve the 5th, where they stood on Tell Asur. This relief was not completed until 11.30 a.m.

Meanwhile, on the left, the 10th Shropshire Light Infantry (74th Division) had secured Selwad early in the morning, but this brigade, the 231st, found itself with both flanks in the air, neither the 158th on their right nor the 230th on their left being able to advance; they, therefore, had to stand fast.

The 6th and 7th Royal Welch Fusiliers had no sooner completed their relief than they were attacked by the Turks. The enemy was active and persistent, and succeeded in regaining the top of Tell Asur which they held for a time. A counter charge by the 6th R.W.F. eventually drove them off again.

It was a report of the above proceedings which reached Brigadier-General Money and delayed the combined attack of the 4th Welch and Herefords on Chipp Hill and the ridge north-east of Drage Hill. The attack did, however, take place at 3.30 p.m., and, although the 4th Welch succeeded in taking the ridge, the Herefords failed to take Chipp Hill.

THE FIGHT THROUGH THE NIGHT

Just before 5 o'clock that evening, General Mott received a wire from General Girdwood, commanding 74th Division, to say that he was not continuing his advance in daylight, but would attack at 6.15 p.m. To conform with the 74th General Mott, therefore, ordered the 158th Brigade to clear Chipp Hill and to push north of Tell Asur to L.28.c and d. and, if the 231st Brigade crossed the Wadi Nimr, to advance their left still further. A company of the Middlesex was sent to fill a gap between the 6th R.W.F. and the 231st Brigade, and a second company was held in support behind Tell Asur.

In accordance with these instructions Brigadier-General Vernon ordered Colonel Drage to attack Chipp Hill after dark, without artillery preparation. This was done at 6.30 p.m. by two companies of the Herefords under Lieutenant Parker, and a position won about the crest; the two companies were immediately relieved by the 7th R.W.F.

This last relief was not completed until 10 o'clock. Twenty minutes later the Turks counter-attacked, but were repulsed, although the line seems to have shifted a little.

The orders were for a general advance when Chipp Hill was taken, but the Herefords, on relief, went back to Drage Hill, where rations and bombs were distributed. Soon after, about 3 a.m., they took over the position again from the 7th R.W.F. who were ordered to advance north from Chipp Hill to L.23.b. and L.24.c. A start was made at 4 a.m., but before the battalion had advanced very far they bumped into a large force of advancing Turks who immediately spread out and opened fire. The 7th R.W.F., however, stood their ground, although they had to report their inability to advance. They were still on the slopes of Chipp Hill.

Meanwhile the 6th Royal Welch Fusiliers, on Tell Asur, who since taking over the position early in the day, had been attacked five times, were relieved by the 5th and ordered to conform with the advance of the 74th at 6.30 p.m. They had three companies on Tell Asur and one on Cairn Hill. The plateau on Tell Asur fell slightly before the position they were holding, but was covered with great boulders. The conformation of the ground was not known to Brigade headquarters who seem to have expected the Fusiliers to stream down the opposite side of the hill to drive the Turks from further hills. The enemy had only retired a short distance along the plateau to take up a fresh position amongst the boulders. The three companies of the 6th failed to advance and were driven back to their original line.

This failure coincided with the partial success of the Herefords on Chipp Hill. In his report, Brigadier-General Vernon states: " Since the battalions on my flanks could not move I decided that my best course was to drive one battalion as a wedge through the centre, and ordered the 6th Royal Welch Fusiliers to push on from Cairn Hill and take up a line in the vicinity of L.24a, L.23 central, L.22 central. By this means I hoped to get behind the Turks on the forward slopes of Tell Asur and Cairn Hill. This battalion should have reached its objective long before midnight, but owing to the slowness of its advance, which it did without opposition, it did not get there till about 0900, 10/3/18."

The order for this operation was not received till ten o'clock, and Lieut.-Colonel Mills was then instructed to leave one company facing west to deal with the enemy on Tell Asur, but a later order directed that this duty should be fulfilled by the 5th R.W.F. The latter took over the position about 4 a.m. The 6th advanced at 4.5 a.m., or about the time that the 7th advanced from Chipp Hill. The check of the 7th was thought to be a retirement from Chipp Hill, and no doubt the unexpected meeting with the Turks was disconcerting, and Lieut.-Colonel Mills ordered his battalion to stand fast while he waited for fresh orders. On receipt of these, two companies went forward across the Wadi Kola, found the enemy had retired, and occupied the ridge L.22.b to L.23 central by 9 a.m.

At mid-day, the situation of the 158th Brigade was: 6th R.W.F. on hill L.23 central; 7th R.W.F. on Chipp Hill; 5th R.W.F. and Herefords in support at Cairn Hill and Drage Hill. Two companies of the Middlesex were holding the gap between the 158th Brigade and 74th Division.

THE 159TH BRIGADE

On the right the 159th Brigade had also been closely engaged. Late in the afternoon the 7th Cheshires, less one company on Munatir ridge and one company on Pear Hill, were in close support to the 4th Cheshires on Rock Park; the 5th Welch were on the slopes of Drage Hill in support

VIEW FROM ROCK PARK.

VIEW FROM TINTO, NORTH OF TELL ASUR.

to the 4th Welch, who held the ridge northeast from Chipp Hill. At 7.30 p.m. the Australian Light Horse took over Munatir ridge and Pear Hill and the released companies rejoined their Battalion.

At 4.30 a.m. on the 10th—much the same hour of advance as that of the 158th Brigade—advance guards from the 7th Cheshires and 5th Welch marched on L.30.b and Q.25 central, and towards Kefr Malik; the 4th Cheshires were ordered to support the 7th, but to leave an adequate force to hold Rock Park (Q.33 central); the 4th Welch were in Brigade Reserve.

The 5th Welch, leaving their ridge, became heavily engaged with the enemy still on the forward slopes of Chipp Hill, and were not able to move until 8.45 a.m. when, on the initiative of Lieut-Colonel H. R. Bowen, the companies were side-tracked to the lower ground in the direction of Kefr Malik, where they found and attacked the enemy at Q.25 central, cleared the surrounding wadis and broken ground, and relieved the situation on Chipp Hill.

On the right, the 7th Cheshires found the ridge Q.26 strongly held, but under cover of a heavy and well directed bombardment, they advanced and secured the position.

The two battalions then sent forward patrols which entered Kefr Malik about 2 p.m. on the 10th. The 5th Welch pushed on to Hill Q.19.a and put out outposts on Q.19 and 20; the 7th Cheshires held an outpost line from Kefr Malik to Rock Park.

No further advance was attempted by the Division during the remaining hours of daylight, but General Mott issued orders to resume at midnight, with the objectives Q.14.b and d-Abu Felah-L.12 central-L.11.a.

THE 160TH BRIGADE

The 160th Brigade then came into line, taking over the left of the 158th Brigade front. This Brigade had been in Divisional Reserve making roads. The two companies of the Middlesex, filling the gap between the 158th and 231st Brigades, had remained on Tell Asur, and on the 10th the Sussex had moved up to connect the 158th and 231st. The Sussex now took over the ground held by the 6th Royal Welch Fusiliers, with the 5th on their right and, next to them, the 7th, on Chipp Hill. The Middlesex moved to the left of the 160th Brigade front.

At the same time the artillery brigades succeeded in moving forward to N. 2, 3, and 4.

On the 11th a slight advance to more favourable positions was unopposed and completed by 9 a.m., but a patrol of the 5th Royal Welch Fusiliers which attempted to enter Abu Felah drew machine gun and rifle fire and retired.

The 158th Brigade then went into Reserve.

ACTION ON THE 12TH MARCH

On the 12th, the task allotted to the 159th and 160th Brigades was the line Q.13.a and b-Kh Abu Felah-L.12.a Kh. Amurieh. Moving before daylight all the positions were gained—(the 4th Welch took some prisoners in Abu Felah)—without opposition, except Kh. Amurieh. The capture of this village fell to the Middlesex, and the company detailed for the assault of the hill—all the villages were on the crests of hills—was greatly hampered in its movements by a thick mist, and had, in addition, to move over ground it had neither reconnoitred nor seen, with nothing but the small scale and inaccurate Palestine Exploration Fund map to help. The advance was slow and detected by the enemy, who allowed the troops to climb almost to the top of the hill, before pouring in a murderous fire, in which machine guns posted on a neighbouring hill joined. The company suffered 42 casualties, and was obliged to retire.

The battle, which had been sustained for four days and nights then petered out. Actually the losses in the Division were not severe: five officers killed, 35 wounded, and two missing; 62 other ranks killed, 337 wounded, and 53 missing; but the physical effort expended by all who took part in this advance was tremendous. The men were tired.

"The country was very bad, very precipitous and trackless. We had very little transport and for over a week nothing except what we carried on our backs. Fortunately, we had a dry spell then."—(F. S. Harries.)

Throughout the four days the artillery supported the infantry nobly. They got their guns and their supply of ammunition over incredible obstacles. Major Colville, who commanded the Mountain Battery (10th), was entirely successful on the right flank of the 159th Brigade, and with the accurate shooting of his battery, and his invincible determination that his guns should move, gave winning support.

The 53rd Division had, as was their custom in this campaign, built up a long flank from Nejmeh to Amurieh; the 74th were on the heights overlooking Sinjil, and the low lying country to the north-east; the 10th Division carried on to Neby Saleh; while, further to the left, the right of the XXIst Corps registered a considerable advance.

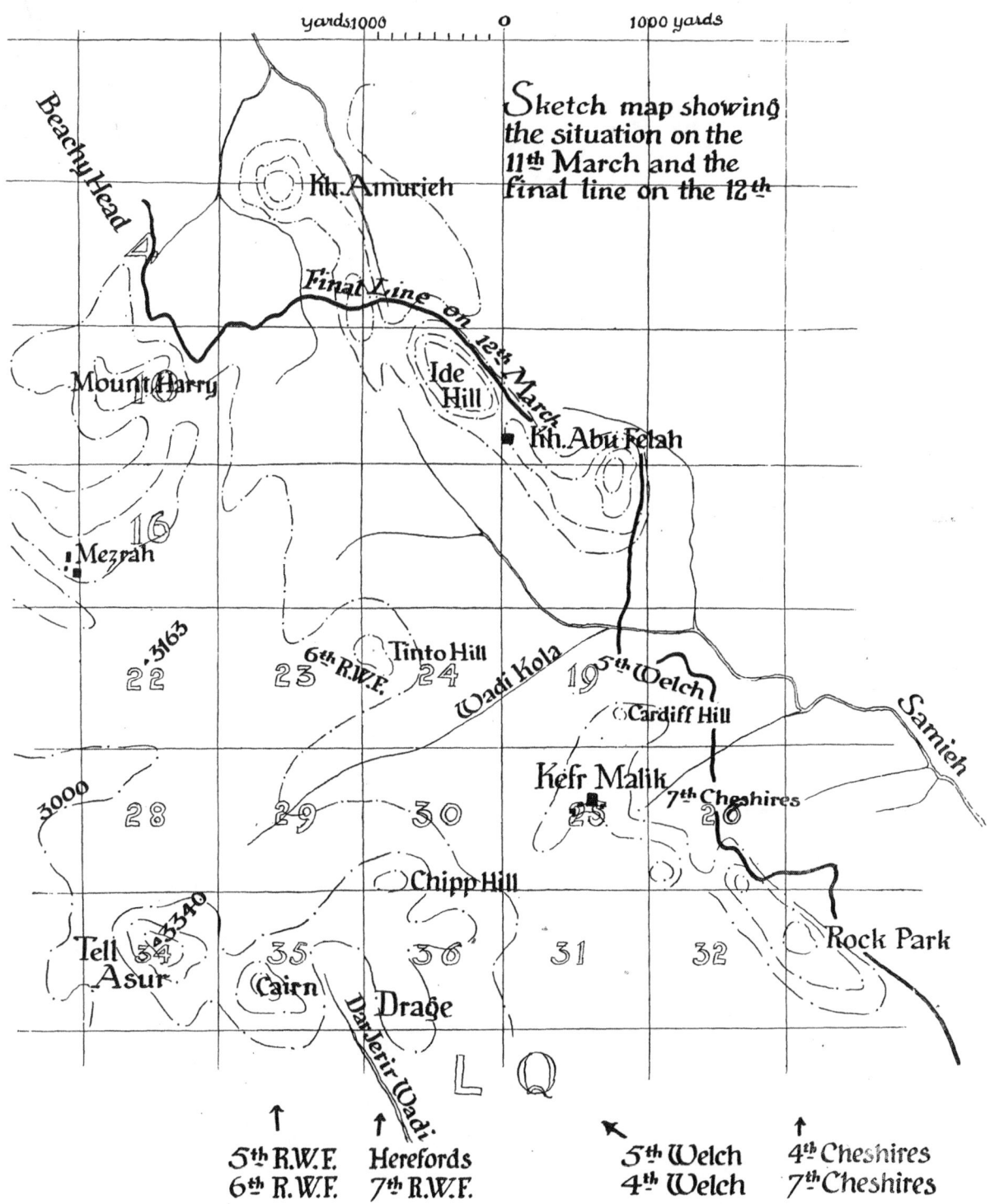

THE VALLEY OF THE JORDAN

GENERAL SITUATION

March—September, 1918.

Great German offensive started on the Western front, 21st March.

Sir Douglas Haig issues " Backs to the Wall " Order of the Day to troops in France, 12th April.

General Foch appointed Commander-in-Chief of Allied Armies in France, 14th April.

THE VALLEY OF THE JORDAN
AND THE XXIst CORPS OFFENSIVE

SIR E. ALLENBY could now think of his designs against the Turkish communications with the Hedjaz, and of operations in conjunction with the Arab forces of Sherif Feisal. He contemplated no more than a raid on Amman with the object of destroying a railway viaduct and tunnel.

Amman is thirty miles from Jericho. The intervening country was described by Sir E. Allenby from a military point of view: " From the banks of the Jordan to the clay ridge, a mile east of the river, the ground is flat and afterwards becomes marshy. Beyond the ridges the country is covered with scrub and is intersected by numerous wadis. For the first five miles the total rise is only 500 feet. In the next twelve miles the ground rises some 3,500 feet, till the edge of the plateau of Moab is reached. The hills are rugged and steep. The main wadis descend from the plateau to the Jordan in deep valleys. The plateau itself is undulating, the lower part of it marshy after rain. The hills which rise from it are rocky and covered with scrub. They are isolated features and only form continuous ridges immediately west of Amman, which lies in a cultivated plain, extending some twelve miles west and four miles north-west of the town. The plain, which is the site of many ruins, is intersected by numerous deep wadis difficult to cross—especially the Wadi Amman, which runs from south to north, leaving the town of Amman on its right."

The 60th Division, Australian Mounted Division, Imperial Camel Brigade, a Mountain Artillery Brigade, the Light Armoured Car Brigade, and a Heavy Battery were to advance in this country to carry out the raid. The 60th Division was, of course, still holding the line in the Valley of the Jordan.

On the 13th March, orders were received for the relief of the 53rd Division by the 74th. The 158th Brigade had already replaced the 160th on the left, and the latter, under Lieut.-Colonel Lawrence, who was acting for Brigadier-General Pearson, on short leave to Egypt, moved back to Bireh. With them went the 265th Field Artillery Brigade, and C/266th Battery, No. 3 Section D.A.C., the 439th Field Company R.E. and the 1st Welsh Field Ambulance. Thus a whole Brigade Group lay around Bireh, and was ordered on the 14th to proceed to Jerusalem, to be held in reserve to the 60th Division.

The 53rd Division imagined that they would, according to routine programme, go into Corps reserve at Ludd,* and enjoy a well-earned rest, but the exigencies of war decreed otherwise, and only the 159th got as far as that doubtful haven. ("When we came out of the line we had a really shocking bit of weather. The sight of native drivers and camels dying by the roadside was awful. Some of the natives were so affected by the rain and cold that they simply made up their minds to end it."—F. S. Harries.)

THE 160TH BRIGADE

The operations in the Jordan Valley started on the night 21/22nd March. On the 17th, the 160th Brigade marched from Jerusalem to Talaat ed Dumm, along a mountain road congested with traffic. The next day to the Wadi Nueimeh, via Jericho—a trying night march—and on the 19th to the Wadi Aujah, where they relieved the 181st Brigade in the line : Middlesex on the right, Sussex in the centre, Queens on the left, and West Kents in reserve.

After the rain in the Judean Hills the Jordan Valley was found to have compensations. "After two days soaking rain on the Mount of Olives, we marched down the winding road to Jericho," writes Captain le Fleming. " In the pitch dark the roar of water in the Kidron gorge and the grim beetling rocks seemed quite eerie, but when we emerged on the plain and entered Jericho it was quite a different scene. Trees and hedges loomed faintly on either side of the road and the sweet scent of orange blossoms filled the night air. Fine and warm, after the rain swept heights above, the valley seemed quite a little paradise. Near Jericho run several little streams which make their way into the Jordan, so water was plentiful and good. While the 60th Division raided Amman we took their place in the line among the foothills. The dry watercourses were full of white and yellow daisies and scarlet poppies. There were a large number of partridges just beginning to nest, and storks so tame that one could ride up to within a few yards of them. . . ."

" This is a most wonderful country for light and shade. We are in the foot hills on the west of a big valley ; across the other side are steep mountains. The shadow effects on the mountains are wonderful. We are nearly always in sunshine. The mountains behind us show up black and gloomy, and those in front all patched with sunlight and shade. Yesterday there was a great cloud bank half way down the eastern mountains. The country is already less green and is drying up, but, as the newspaper described it, we were marching on slippery grey soap a few weeks back."

* Lydda—*R.G.S.*

Life in the front line of the Jordan Valley was not one of complete ease and freedom from war. On the 26th the Sussex made a raid on an enemy post with one company under Captain J. C. Pesket, and with artillery preparation. Nine dead Turks were found. On the 29th, one company of the Middlesex, one company of the West Kents, and one company of the Queens went out together for the purpose of locating the enemy posts and capturing prisoners. They came across a few Turks who beat a hasty retreat after discharging their rifles.

THE 158TH BRIGADE

The 158th Brigade also moved down from Jerusalem while the Amman raid was being carried out. Two battalions, the 6th and 7th Royal Welch Fusiliers, moved first and marched to Talaat ed Dumm. "We had a very hot and tiring march, stiflingly dusty, as there was a lot of traffic both ways, and very unsavoury, as there were quantities of dead camels no one had buried. Talaat showed the ruins of another Crusader Castle, a famous stronghold, and also the remains of a building said to be the Inn to which the Good Samaritan took the wounded unfortunate who fell amongst thieves. Apart from these the area was very bare and dusty, the heat considerable, and the sense of hope deferred continued to jaundice our outlook on life. Next morning, the Brigadier and I rode to General Shea's headquarters, and were told to march on to Kh. Kakua, on the very edge of the high ground where the hills fall, in many places, sheer to the floor of the valley, and where the road makes a final drop at an angle of about one in three, with a rocky surface at that. . . . Our new area was a perfect farce, consisting of a few square yards on either side of the road, all stone and without a flat spot in it. We even had to dig a terrace to put our little Brigade H.Q. mess tent on. On the north side of the road, and parallel to it there was a most remarkable ravine, the Wadi Kelt, which runs down into the valley. Very deep, and in some places so steep that the sun only strikes the bottom for a very short time each day; the stream never dries up. The Brigadier and I went exploring, and found, right down at the bottom, a beautiful little bridge leading to a lovely but deserted and sadly damaged little monastery, all littered with broken glass, torn books, and smashed furniture, the usual legacy of the retreating Turk. . . .

"After we had all reconnoitred the route to Pearsons (160th) we had a ride round the ruins of old Jericho. There is nothing much left except mounds, but some old pieces of masonry and a long rectangular pool were rather beautiful, while the tropical foliage, with bananas and such like growing, was lovely. The modern Jericho is a dusty ramshackle little hole, remarkable for nothing. . . .

"The heat was now intense and dust storms followed by rain storms were the usual order. Much as we disliked the whole thing we seemed fated to be drawn deeper and deeper into it, for on Good Friday, 29th March, the 7th (R.W.F.) was sent forward to a position beyond the Ghoraniyeh Bridge of the Jordan, while at the same time the rest of the Brigade, together with the 266th Brigade R.F.A., was started off down the road from Jerusalem.

"On the 1st April, we were informed that the operation was over, and that Shea's force was returning. Now, at last, we thought, for Ludd and the rest camp. In fine 1st April spirit, however, Corps sent a later wire that the 158th Brigade would be returning to Ram Allah shortly—probably in two days' time, exactly where we had come from. This really was the crushing blow, and a lot of hard things were said about Corps. As a matter of fact, the big bad news from France, the March break through, was in, and the 52nd and 74th Divisions were for France very soon."

Still another point of view is contained in a note in the 160th Brigade diary for the 31st March, reviewing the month: "On the whole, the health of the Brigade had been good. The genial temperature of the Jordan Valley has proved extremely beneficial." And, on the 5th April: "Arrived in the Jerusalem area to find the sky overcast, a cold wind blowing from the south-west and light rain falling. An unpleasant change from the Jordan Valley."

THE 159TH BRIGADE

AN ABORTIVE ATTACK BY THE XXIst CORPS

The 159th Brigade had not enjoyed the amenities of Ludd for long. The Brigade Group arrived at Latron on the 19th; the camping ground was too wet for them to move in on the 20th, so they completed the march to Ludd on the 21st and bivouacked in the neighbourhood of Haditheh. On the 7th April, the Brigade Group commenced to move to Rentis; and on the 8th a secret letter B.M.O./D/e was issued setting forth the G.O.C.'s intentions during forthcoming operations in conjunction with the XXIst Corps. (*See* Appendix.)

This interesting document sketches a major operation for which full preparation had been made. The XXIst Corps, with the 75th Division

A Pontoon Bridge over the Jordan at El Ghoraniyeh.

The Mount of Temptation (Kuruntul), showing the Monastery on the Hill-side.

on the right, the 54th in the centre, and the 7th (Indian) Division on the left, was to attack distant objectives, with a cavalry division in readiness to ride through and cut off the enemy's retreat.

The intention was to win positions covering Nablus and Tulkeram, and to establish a line about Tubas, Arrabeh, and Caesaria. The enemy's centre was to be broken between Azzam and Kalkilieh, and a turning of the inner flanks thus formed would follow.

The plan was that the left of the Corps should first move forward some 2,000 yards to enable the artillery to bombard Jiljulieh, Sir Adar, and the Tabsor system. Then, six days before zero, the 75th Division would advance their right flank to Kh. Surieh, Sh. Subieh and Arara, at the same time driving out the enemy who threatened from Berukin and El Kefr. The main attack on zero day would be delivered by the right and right-centre of the Corps, and a gap was to be made in the enemy's line about Jiljulieh and Kalkilieh, through which the cavalry division would advance. All this was to follow the Jordan Valley operations.

The 159th Brigade would assist in these operations by protecting the right flank of the 75th Division.

The 75th duly attacked on the 9th April, and secured Berukin, Kefr, and Rafat.

On the 10th, the 4th and 5th Welch were marching to relieve the 2/4th Somersets on what was known as Tin Hat Hill, and the 5th Devons in Berukin, when the enemy counter attacked and broke the 75th line north of Kefr. The relieving battalions and the 159th Brigade were ordered to stand fast and were placed under the orders of the 232nd Brigade, while the 7th Cheshires were placed under the 233rd Brigade. Late that night, the 75th having restored their line, the 4th Welch took over the left of the 232nd Brigade front line; the 7th Cheshires, Mughair ridge; the 5th Welch were in Brigade reserve. The next day the 4th Cheshires relieved the Somersets on Tin Hat Hill, and the 5th Welch the Devons at Berukin. The whole of the 232nd Brigade being now relieved, Brigadier-General Money assumed command of the sector with his Headquarters at Sh. Kawash.

The 159th remained in the Berukin-Kefr sector until the 17th, without incident, when they were relieved by the 232nd Brigade and marched back to Haditheh. On the 20th the Brigade moved to Beit Sira on their way to rejoin the 53rd Division.

The attack of the XXIst Corps was cancelled.

The opening of the attack had been a failure, and had met unexpected opposition; also the influence of the stirring events in France had reached Palestine, and the War Cabinet had already wired to Sir E. Allenby that a substitution of Indian for certain English Divisions would take place—every man he could spare would be useful, he was informed.

REORGANISATION

GENERAL SITUATION

April—July, 1918.

Guatemala declares war on Germany, 23rd April, 1918.
Nicaragua declares war on Germany, 8th May.
Costa Rica declares war on Germany, 23rd May.
German forces reach the Marne, 31st May.
Death of Mohammed V of Turkey, 3rd July.
Haiti declares war on Germany, 12th July.
Ex-Tsar, ex-Tsaritsa and family murdered, 16th July.
Honduras declares war on Germany, 19th July.
German forces retire across the Marne, 20th July.

REORGANISATION

THE 74th and 52nd Divisions were put under orders for France. On the 3rd April, orders were issued for the relief of the 74th by the 53rd. The 158th Brigade accordingly marched to Jerusalem on the 4th, Ram Allah on the 5th, and came into the 74th Division area and under the orders of that Division on the 6th; the 160th arrived at Ram Allah on that date.

The next day the 158th Brigade relieved the 230th in the left sub-sector, while the 74th Artillery Group was relieved by the 266th Field Artillery Brigade.

On the 9th, the right sub-sector was relieved by the 160th Brigade, and 267th Field Artillery Brigade. Divisional Headquarters opened at Ain Sinia.

The left sub-sector is described by Captain Ashton as very strong, " though not so strong as the right, where we were to go later. On our right we were on the Tell Asur plateau, the northern end of which was a prominent height called Mount Harry which sloped down and onwards to a final feature known as Beachy Head, which, like its namesake, stuck out like a cape into a flat green valley to the north, which formed No Man's Land. Up the west side of the cape ran the main road, and so down into the green valley, a mile or so wide, and disappeared into the hills beyond on its way to Nablus. Just across the valley were the ruins of Shiloh.

" Immediately west of the road, and about level with the end of Beachy Head, there arose, running east and west, a ridge which took its name from the village of Sinjil on its northern slope. Behind this ridge was a little open valley with a funny little sugar-loaf Tell in the middle. Further along the Sinjil ridge we joined hands with the 10th Division. Behind the line there were numerous hills of various size which were made into defended localities.

" Trenches were practically impossible, as the rock cropped through everywhere; breast works and sangars were the usual order of things, defended with barbed wire and held only at night; by day the garrisons retired behind Beachy Head or the crest of Sinjil ridge, as necessary."

Of the right sub-sector he says : " Far down on the right was Nejmeh as a detached locality under Divisional Command. Then after a gap of

4,000 yards along the Wadi Samieh, Rock Park, Round Hill, and Ide Hill, all in a line.

"The position faced north-east and, at the left end of it, nearly north, and was really the far end of the Tell Asur plateau. On the right our line ran on the near side of the Wadi Samieh, a tremendous ravine with steep sides; in the centre the ground was more open and the main positions were beyond the Wadi. On the high ground of the plateau we had all the guns, and the most wonderful observation imaginable."

Captain le Fleming adds to this picture. "From Nejmeh, our most easterly post, we used to look down an almost sheer drop of 4,000 feet at the valley below. It lay as though in miniature panorama. Away to the south was the weird stillness of the Dead Sea, the great mountains of Moab reflected on its motionless surface, its southern end wrapped in haze. A great white patch of desert, studded with nobbly bumps of salt and sand marks the site of Sodom and Gomorrah; Jericho, a little green gem, lies huddled at the foot of the great square-topped Kuruntul, the Mount of Temptation. Perched perilously on a ledge half-way up this sheer mountain is a small white monastery, while at the foot are numerous caves, once, no doubt, the homes of cenobite monks. Across the valley lie the mountains of Moab, sometimes green, sometimes misty blue, sometimes patched with shade, in a way reminiscent of Gallipoli heights. The track from Nejmeh ran through a deep wadi with huge beetling rocks on either hand, a rotten, barren and bare ride until one emerged just below the village of el Taniyibeh, with its little Christian church, a sad scene of desolation within, for it had been desecrated by the Turks."

And Captain F. S. Harries :—

"Just imagine yourself like me, on a hillside 2,800 feet high, on a sunny, warm, peaceful day, looking towards Jerusalem. On the left the mountains of Moab in the haze, formidable and massive. Below lies the plain of the Jordan, crossed by a snakelike white road which leads to Jericho, though the town is too far below the intervening hills for me to see it. Just above a low crest of the hills I see a glimpse of the Jordan, and further down the Dead Sea appears. Its setting is very impressive, as any sheet of water must be that is, as it were, overwhelmed by hills and mountains on three sides. In front of me stretches range upon range of precipitous hills, some barren and dark, some with fresh green grass to illuminate them. They get higher near Jerusalem, and as usual the German Hospice stands out insolently on the Mount of Olives. Parts of Jerusalem are just visible, too, while away to the right the hills rise higher, topped in many cases with villages. The only destructive feature is Johnnie's

R.W.F. NABLUS ROAD, SOUTH OF SINJIL. [*War Museum.*

VIEW FROM OUR LINE AT SINJIL

contemptible efforts to shell us, and his pipsqueaks rumble along at intervals and burst on my hill.

"I wish, too, you could see the flowers. A scarlet anemone blazes everywhere, while small flowers abound. If it were not too poetical, it would be literally true to say some favoured spots are carpeted with them."

The 160th Brigade, had no sooner taken over this right sector when, on the night of the 11/12th, the Turks tried to raid Round Hill, held by the West Kents. Three Turks were captured, the rest fled.

Days passed uneventfully, broken by the ordinary routine of reliefs.

On the 23rd April the 159th Brigade arrived at Tell Asur area.

On the 26th April a more determined effort was made by the Turks against the Queens, in the right sector. The inhabitants of the village of Abu Felah, on the crest of the hill, had been evacuated a few days before the attack; it was a place only held at night. The enemy made a strong and obstinate attempt to regain it. They launched three separate attacks at different times, which merged into one on a front from Ide Hill to Fusilier Ridge. Commencing at the favourable hour of 3 a.m., about the time when troops withdrew from the forward positions, they were, however, held on Fusilier Ridge; but the garrison of Abu Felah had withdrawn to their bivouac area on the south slopes of the hill when they heard, to their dismay, that the Turks were in the village, and also on Ide Hill. The whole battalion of the Queens Regiment had to be used before the enemy was ejected, and as he was hotly supported by his artillery, casualties were heavy: 19 other ranks killed; 4 officers and 41 other ranks wounded. But the situation was not fully restored until, at one o'clock next morning, the Middlesex swept the ground in front of the original line clear of small parties.

Nothing more was done by the enemy, and nothing much by the 53rd Division, which was soon rent by the internal convulsions of reorganisation. On the 22nd May, a warning order came from G.H.Q. that the Division would shortly be reorganised on a mixed British and Indian basis. This meant the loss of the Herefords, 4th and 7th Cheshires, 4th Sussex, and 2/4th Queens.

INDIAN BATTALIONS

The first Indian battalion to arrive was the 21st Punjabis, on the 28th May, who relieved the Sussex. At the same time, the 4th Wiltshires relieved the Queens; the 2/18th and 2/19th London Regiments (from the 180th Brigade, 60th Division) relieved the 4th and 7th Cheshires;

and the 2/22nd Battalion London Regiment relieved the Herefords. These hardened and war-wise battalions prepared for their journey to France.

In the early part of June other Indian battalions arrived; on the 4th, the 3/152nd Indian Infantry Battalion; on the 5th, the 4/11th Gurkha Rifles and the 2/152nd Indian Infantry Battalion; on the 10th, the 3/153rd Indian Infantry Battalion; and on the 28th, the 1/110th Mahratta Light Infantry Battalion. Meanwhile the five lost battalions were on their way to Qantara, and so to France.

At the end of June, the three Infantry Brigades stood as follows:—

158th Brigade
- 5th Royal Welch Fusiliers.
- 6th Royal Welch Fusiliers.
- 4/11th Gurkha Rifles.
- 3/153rd Indian Infantry Batt.

159th Brigade
- 4th Welch Regiment.
- 5th Welch Regiment.
- 2/153rd Indian Infantry Batt.
- 3/152nd Indian Infantry Batt.

160th Brigade
- 2/4th Royal West Kent Regiment.
- 2/10th Middlesex Regiment.
- 7th Royal Welch Fusiliers.
- 21st Punjabis.
- 110th Mahratta Light Infantry.

One other change must be noted: Lieut.-Colonel A. E. M. Sinclair Thomson, who had so long and successfully filled the position of G.S.O.1., also left the division on the 15th June, and his place was filled on the 22nd by Lieut.-Colonel W. C. Garsia.

The feast of Ramadam commenced on the 10th June, and special night activity by patrols and artillery was ordered. A raid was carried out on Bidston Hill by Captain D. E. F. Morgan, 6th Royal Welch Fusiliers, on the 11th. The objective, as was generally the case in Palestine, was at some distance, but was assaulted with complete success. Seven Turks were killed, and two prisoners captured; the 6th had three slight casualties. The raid was so swift and silent that the garrison was surprised, and took to their heels after a few wild shots; they were estimated as between 50 and 60.

The following night the 4th Welch swept over Forfar Hill, but found no enemy. But on the night 16/17th a party of the 2/153rd Indian Infantry lay out in the Wadi Samieh and ambushed a Turkish patrol, killed two and captured five.

Small affairs of this kind were carried out from time to time until on the 21st July the Division was relieved in the line by the 60th Division and went back to rest billets. "Water is our great problem. The men get a decent wash once every nine days or so. Isn't it appalling? Better dirty than thirsty, I suppose, but it is abhorent to the men themselves."

On the 1st August further changes took place. The 5th and 6th Royal Welch Fusiliers were amalgamated, and became known as the 5/6th, under Lieut.-Colonel Borthwick; also the 4th and 5th Welch Regiment, who became the 4/5th under Lieut.-Colonel Hohler; and the 2/10th Middlesex and 2/4th Royal West Kents were disbanded. Also one of the Indian battalions, the 116th Mahrattas, left the Division.

When the 53rd Division went back to the line on the 21st August, it was as follows :—

5/6th Royal Welch Fusiliers (Borthwick)
4/11th Gurkha Rifles (W. L. Dundas)
3/153rd Indian Infantry (G. B. Kidd)
3/154th Indian Infantry posted 4th Aug.,
    (Dawson)
} 158th Brigade.

4/5th Welch Regiment (Hohler)
153rd Indian Infantry posted 2nd Aug.
    (C. M. J. Withers)
2/153rd Indian Infantry (C. A. James)
3/152nd Indian Infantry (H. J. Doveton)
} 159th Brigade.

7th Royal Welch Fusiliers (T. H. Harker)
21st Punjabis (W. G. R. Murray)
17th Indian Infantry posted 6th Aug.
    (B. J. Fagan)
1/1st Batt. Cape Corps posted 19th Aug.
    (C. N. Hoy)
} 160th Brigade.

All through the heat of summer preparations were being busily and quietly pushed forward for the last great battle. Life was made as pleasant as circumstances permitted for officers and men.

"Had you walked into our officers' tent last night after dinner you would have been surprised. You would have seen a Padre, the Battalion Water

Officer, the Signal Officer, O.C. A Coy. (*i.e.*, myself), and another, passing a book of selections of poetry round choosing extracts for one another to read. I believe the row rather disturbed the Major.

"We had a really great game of hockey in the afternoon against an Indian Battalion. Most of us hadn't played for years and the ball at times got partially buried in the dust; but everybody thoroughly enjoyed it. We just lost a very hard game. One or two sepoys were first rate.

"A local variety party gave us a couple of performances last week The " girl " has improved immensely during the past few months, and really doesn't dance half badly.

"We have quite a good Band, now-a-days. Our new Colonel brought it with him and takes a great interest in it. Guard mounting is an imposing performance. The men are spotless. The band marches up and down, and all within six miles of ' Johnnie.'

"Everyone is frightfully pleased with the news from France."

(12/8/18.)

"Some of our old friends who left this country for France have had a bad knock. Numerous officers we knew as well as we know our own fellows have been killed or wounded. We all thank our lucky stars we weren't selected to go. Unheroic and mean? Well, perhaps so, but the zeal to get out that one had in 1914 and 1915 has vanished. Everybody is fed up in much the same way that one gets fed up at the theatre when a play goes on scene after scene and one thinks it is time for the curtain! No one, of course, dreams of making peace except on our own terms.

"The weather continues very hot and the nights are close.

"The Indian soldier is a great trial in camp. He won't act as cook or sanitary man, so special men have to be employed, and his ideas on domestic arrangements generally are not hygienic. Still he is, like all of us, ready to put aside many of his convictions because it is wartime."—(9/9/18.)

"An old Arab with two little girls, about 15 and 8 respectively, accompanied by two women came into one of my sentry groups. Such visitors are unwelcome because Brigade and Division want to keep the natives away, but once they reached my post I had to send them through, as they had seen our dispositions. So I went to talk with them. Imagine my surprise to find one of the women spoke German fluently and well. We had a long talk, and she gave some information that I believe may prove useful. She had had a curious career. Her German she had learnt in a German school out here. She had been to Cairo and Alexandria, and had been a teacher of Arabic in France. Yet here she was without shoes or stockings, very thinly clad, looking more like a gipsy."—(F. S. Harries.)

GENERAL SITUATION

September—October, 1918.

Battles of the Hindenburg Line begin, 12th September.

Battle of the Canal du Nord begins, 27th September.

Battle of Ypres begins, 28th September.

Armistice between Bulgaria and Entente Powers signed, 30th September.

German and Austrian Governments send Notes to President Wilson proposing an Armistice, 4th October.

Turkish Note to President Wilson proposing an Armistice delivered 14th October.

Ostend, Lille and Douai retaken by Allied forces, 17th October.

Austrian Government ask Italy for an Armistice, 27th October.

Armistice between Turkey and Entente Powers signed, 30th October.

Battle of Valenciennes begins, 1st November.

Battle of the Sambre, 4th November.

Revolution breaks out in Berlin, 9th November.

Mons retaken by British Forces (Canadian), and

Armistice concluded between Allied and Associated Powers and Germany, 11th November.

THE BATTLES OF MEGIDDO

SIR E. ALLENBY opened his last despatch by pointing out that "the latter part of the period covered by my despatch of September 18th, 1918, had been spent in the reorganisation of my force. The last Indian battalions to arrive had been incorporated in divisions early in August. Some of these battalions had only been formed a few months, and I should have liked to have given them further opportunities to accustom themselves to the conditions prevailing on this front before calling on them to play a part in arduous operations on a large scale. The rains, however, usually commence at the end of October, rendering the plains of Sharon and Esdraelon impassable for transport, except along the few existing roads. Consequently operations could not be postponed beyond the middle of September."

At the beginning of September the total Turkish strength opposed to Sir E. Allenby's army was estimated at 4,000 sabres, 32,000 rifles, and 400 guns, representing a ration strength, south of the line, Rayat-Beirut of 104,000.

Astride the Jerusalem-Nablus road was the VIIth army, extended on a front of some twenty miles, estimated at 7,000 rifles and 111 guns.

The general reserve was given as 3,000 rifles and 30 guns only.

With the exception of this small reserve the whole of the Turkish force west of the Jordan (VIIth and VIIIth Armies) was enclosed in a rectangle, 45 miles in width and 12 miles in depth. "The northern edge of this rectangle was a line from Jisr ed Damieh, on the Jordan, through Nablus and Tul Keram to the sea. All the enemy's communications to Damascus ran northwards from the eastern half of this line, converging on El Afule and Beisan some twenty five miles to the north. Thence, with the exception of the roads leading from El Afule along the western shore of the Sea of Galilee, his communications ran eastwards, up the Valley of the Yarmuk to Deraa, the junction of the Palestine and Hedjaz railways. Thus El Afule, Beisan, and Deraa were the vital points on his communications. If they could be seized the enemy's retreat would be cut off. Deraa was beyond my reach, but not beyond that of mobile detachments of the Arab army. It was not to be expected that these detachments could hold the railway junction, but it was within their power to dislocate all traffic.

"El Afule, in the Plain of Esdraelon, and Beisan, in the Valley of Jezreel, were within reach of my cavalry, provided the infantry could break through the enemy's defensive systems, and create a gap for the cavalry to pass through. It was essential that this gap should be made at the commencement of operations, so that the cavalry might reach their destinations, 45 and 60 miles distant, before the enemy could make his escape."

Experience, gained by the 53rd Division, had shown that an advance, astride the watershed of the Judean Hills, could not be expected, in the face of determined opposition, to show more than five miles in the day, and a great deal more than that was necessary for success on the scale contemplated by Sir E. Allenby. On the other hand, the Maritime Plain, on the XXIst Corps front, was barred by the Hills of Samaria, which shoot out from the main Judean highlands to Mount Carmel on the coast, and form a barrier to the Plain of Esdraelon. The Hills of Samaria, however, are not a series of piled up ranges like the Judean Hills, but run to a point. It was decided that the break should be made on the coast.

"I entrusted the attack on the enemy's defences in the coastal plain to Lieut.-General Sir Edward Bulfin, K.C.B., C.V.O., commanding the XXIst Corps. In addition to the 3rd (Lahore), 7th (Meerut), 54th and 75th Divisions, which already formed part of the XXIst Corps, I placed at his disposal the 60th Division, the French Detachment, the 5th Australian Light Horse Brigade, two brigades of Mountain Artillery, and eighteen batteries of Heavy and Siege Artillery.

"I ordered him to break through the enemy's defences between the railway and the sea, to open a way for the cavalry, and at the same time to seize the foothills southeast of Jiljulieh. The XXIst Corps was then to swing to the right, on the line Hableh-Tul Keram, and then advance in a north-easterly direction through the hills, converging on Samaria and Attara, so as to drive the enemy up the Messudie-Jenin road into the arms of the cavalry at El Afule.

"I ordered Lieut.-General Sir Harry Chauvel, K.C.B., K.C.M.G. commanding the Desert Mounted Corps, less the Australian and New Zealand Mounted Division, to advance along the coast, directly the infantry had broken through, and to secure the crossings over the Nahr Falik. On reaching the line Jelameh-Hudeira, he was to turn northeast, cross the hills of Samaria, and enter the plain of Esdraelon at El Lejjun and Abu Shusheh. Riding along the plain the Desert Mounted Corps was to seize El Afule, sending a detachment to Nazareth, the site of the Yilderim General Headquarters. Sufficient troops were to be left at El Afule to intercept the Turkish retreat there. The remainder of the Corps was to ride down the Valley of Jezreel and seize Beisan.

"I ordered Lieut.-General Sir Philip Chetwode, Bart., K.C.B., K.C.M.G., D.S.O., commanding the XXth Corps, to advance his line east of the Bireh-Nablus road on the night preceding the main attack, so as to place the 53rd Division, on his right flank, which was somewhat drawn back, in a more favourable position to advance and block the exits to the lower valley of the Jordan.

"I ordered him to prepare to carry out a further advance with both the 53rd and 10th Divisions, on the evening of the day on which the attack in the coastal plain took place, or later, as circumstances demanded.

"The main difficulty lay in concealing the withdrawal of two cavalry divisions from the Jordan Valley, and in concentrating secretly a large force in the coastal plain.

"To prevent the decrease in strength in the Jordan Valley being discovered by the enemy, I ordered Major-General Sir Edward Chaytor, K.C.M.G., C.B., A.D.C., to carry out, with the Australian and New Zealand Mounted Division, the 20th (Indian) Infantry Brigade, the 38th and 39th Batts. Royal Fusiliers, and the 1st and 2nd Battalions British West Indies Regiment, a series of demonstrations with the object of inducing the enemy to believe that an attack east of the Jordan was intended, either in the direction of Madeba or Amman. The enemy was thought to be anticipating an attack in these directions, and every possible step was taken to strengthen his suspicions.

"At this time a mobile column of the Arab Army accompanied by British armoured cars and a French Mountain battery, was assembled at Kasr el Azrac, fifty miles east of Amman. The real objective of this column was the railway north, south and west of Deraa. There was always the possibility, however, that this concentration might be observed. Should this occur it was hoped that the demonstration by Chaytor's force would strengthen the enemy's belief that a concerted attack on Amman was intended."

GENERAL CHETWODE'S APPRECIATION OF THE SITUATION

This plan left General Chetwode with two divisions only in his Corps—the 10th and 53rd. In considering the action of his Corps, General Chetwode assumed that the Turks anticipated an attack during the month of September, but that they were ignorant of its scope and direction, and were making arrangements for a general advance all along the line. Also that their general plan was to fall back through the hills fighting a delaying action, hoping to collect their whole force together at Nablus where they would stand, or at any rate gain sufficient time to withdraw in good order.

A withdrawal of this nature was always possible, as the radius of action of the attacking force must be limited by considerations of supply.

Arguing from the Turkish point of view he imagined that they might say, " The mistake we made in the Gaza-Beersheba operations was in not taking advantage of the pause after the first British attack to get our troops away in time. This time we will get away as soon as the first British attack is delivered, and before they have time to reorganise and follow it up. Our repulse of the two British attacks on Amman, and of their offensive in April in the foothills east of the railway, has shown us that we can delay a superior force for a long time in the hills."

If this forecast was correct, it was obvious that the VIIth army, astride the Nablus road, having a shorter distance to go than the VIIIth Army would move later, becoming the pivot of the Turkish retirement. It would, therefore, be of importance that the VIIth army should hold their positions astride the Nablus road for some time.

The VIIth Army had three main centres of resistance from its right to left—the defences at its junction with the VIIIth Army; the defences from Amurieh to Abu el Auf, directly covering the Nablus road; and the Valley View-Hindhead position covering the main watershed which runs north.

A rapid move along this watershed would turn all the Turkish defences to the west, and it was really the key to the whole of the VIIth Army positions. But the enemy seemed to have devoted less attention to this part of his line than to that which immediately covered the Nablus road. The Turks probably thought that the difficulties of the ground and the distance of the British right flank from the Valley View positions would prevent any rapid advance in that direction. At all events they were devoting much labour to strengthening their defences covering the Nablus road.

The attack of the 53rd Division might, therefore, take them by surprise, and would probably cause them much anxiety, as they would see the pivot of their whole retirement threatened.

The Corps Commander, therefore, concluded that the Turks might be expected to re-act strongly against the attack of the 53rd Division.

They would, however, be loath to move troops from the vicinity of the Nablus Road, unless they discovered the British dispositions, and so counter-attacks might be expected from the east rather than from the west.

ENEMY STRENGTH

As to the probable strength of these counter attacks, the Staff had placed the Turkish forces as follows (from the British right to left); Part of the Turkish 53rd Division, 26th Division, 11th Division, 1st Division, part of the 16th Division. The average strength of these divisions was about 1,400 rifles, with the exception of the 16th, which was nearly twice as strong as any of the others. The average number of machine guns with each division was taken at between 50 and 60; but it was believed that the 26th Division had 78, the full number to which all divisions would be raised.

The Turkish 26th and 53rd Divisions, opposite the right of the XXth Corps, yielded the greatest number of deserters, and were considered bad and low in morale; the 11th Division, in the centre, was also not considered a good division; but the 1st Division was considered better, and the 16th the best of all those likely to be encountered—it had, for a long time, had a stiffening of Germans and might still have a German detachment with it.

On the immediate front of the 53rd (Welsh) Division, there were, between Turmus Aya and Valley View, four Turkish regiments—one of the 53rd and three of the 26th Divisions. Their strength was estimated at 400 rifles each and from 20 to 25 machine guns—total, 1,600 rifles and 80 to 100 machine guns. Excluding Turmus Aya and Kh. Amurieh, which would be outside the front to be actually attacked by the 53rd (Welsh) Division, the Staff believed that there were only seven battalions, or under 1,000 rifles. But the five excluded battalions (there was one east of Wadi Bakr) would have to be reckoned as available, within a few hours, as first reinforcements. Other Turkish reinforcements available would be the reserve battalion of the 53rd Division (400 rifles) believed to be located at Aain Fusail, about three quarters of an hour's march from Domah, and at least an hour and a half from the time it moved until it could come into action about Square Hill; the attack companies of the 26th and 53rd Divisions from about Julad and Mejdel Beni Fadl—both these divisions were believed to have attack companies of picked men—strength about 100 rifles per company; but they, also, would take about an hour and a half to reach the scene of action; the Regiment of the 53rd Division which held the position in the valley opposite Chaytor's

Force on the right (Bakr Ridge, etc.), which at the very earliest would be two hours before it could come into action against the 53rd (Welsh) Division.

The next, or later, possible reinforcements the Turks could bring up were—(a) the reserves of the 11th Division, astride the Nablus road, probably one battalion from each of three regiments, total not more than 500 rifles. It was believed, however, that the Turks would move these with reluctance, and not until they were certain of the British plan, and that they would hardly need to be taken into account on Z day. (b) Troops from the 24th Division, astride the Jordan; but these could not be expected to get into action during the first twenty-four hours of the battle.

Finally, the Staff expected that the preliminary operations of the 53rd (Welsh) Division might be opposed by about 1,000 rifles and 50 to 60 machine guns; by a further 1,500 to 2,000 rifles during the early hours of the next day, and that there was no likelihood of an increase of force before the next night.

The 10th Division would encounter an estimated force of 2,000 rifles and 60 to 80 machine guns, but the question of Turkish reinforcements was complicated by the action of the XXIst Corps, on the left, where Sir E. Allenby had concentrated 35,000 rifles against 8,000, and 383 guns against 130, and, in addition, two cavalry and one Australian Mounted Divisions.

On the XXth Corps front the number of Turkish guns was estimated at fifty-six 77 m.m. guns, twelve 15 c.m. guns, twenty-four 4.2in. guns, and two 24 c.m. mortars.

Viewing his line from En Nejmeh to Kefr Ain, General Chetwode decided that his attack should take the form of a converging movement from both flanks towards the general line Akrabeh-Jemmain; and that the enemy positions opposite the centre of the XXth Corps should not be attacked at all.

THE POSITION OF THE 53RD.

The positions held on the right were much the same as described by Captain Ashton (who by the way had gone to England on leave, but Colonel Garsia, G.S.O.I., steps into the breach with an account). Standing on Nejmeh, the extreme right of the line, was, says Colonel Garsia, like being on a roof of a gigantic sky scraper, with the Jordan Valley below as a street, and the hillocks and ridges which covered it appearing as cobble stones, an intricate and confusing pattern. The course of the river

Jordan, even at that time of year, is marked by a narrow strip of green, running down the centre of the valley; joining it from the west is another slim line of green, which is the Aujah, called at its source the Samieh.

The Samieh is a perennial stream which gushes from the rocks at the bottom of a vast amphitheatre; this is the Samieh Basin, and Nejmeh is the most southerly point overlooking it. It is $4\frac{1}{2}$ miles from north to south, by $3\frac{1}{2}$ miles, and sinks down from the surrounding hills about 2,000 feet. "In the afternoon, when the slanting rays of the sun strike on the spurs and wadis on the other side of the basin, on the wide stretch of the Jordan Valley, rounded off by the Dead Sea, and on the Moabite Mountains beyond, there is a range of colour and shade that beggars description. Added to a family of browns, chocolates, and yellows, always present, there are other families of purples, mauves, and violets, and of all imaginable shades of grey, salmon, pink, and blue."

The Turkish defences lay along the northern edge of the Samieh Basin—on the tops of spurs separating numerous wadis, tributaries to the Samieh, which runs through a narrow gorge to the east, becomes the Aujah, and so flows on to the Jordan.

The 53rd Division were on the southern side of the Basin. Facing them, behind the Turks, ran the watershed of the main range of hills, straight away to the town of Nablus—a narrow plateau broken by rocky limestone hills from 500 to 600 feet in height. On their right was the escarpment along the edge of the Jordan Valley, on their left the main Jerusalem-Nablus road.

The Corps Commander's plan of attack took the 53rd Division along this watershed, after it had crossed the Samieh Basin, with no further deep wadis or other obstacles to cross, while the 10th Division would cross the spurs on the other side of the watershed.

THE SKELETON CENTRE

With only two divisions, and the full strength of each required for the attack, it was obvious that a wide gap would exist in the centre of the Corps front. It was decided to employ the Corps Cavalry Regiment, the two Pioneer Battalions of the 53rd and 10th Divisions (which would be required to repair the main Nablus Road as soon as it was opened), and to form a temporary detachment from the five per cent. reinforcements sent by battalions to the Corps Reinforcement Camp, to fill the gap and prevent the enemy noticing any change in the Corps dispositions. This force was called Watson's Force.

During the nights 15/16th and 16/17th September, the centre of the Corps front, from Highgate Ridge (inclusive) to Arura (exclusive) was taken over by Lieut.-Colonel Watson (2/155th Pioneers) and his composite force, thus enabling the 10th and 53rd Divisions to concentrate on either flank.

WORK OF THE ROYAL ENGINEERS

But before this was done there was much preliminary work, especially by the Royal Engineers. This silent and gallant Corps had to construct a wagon road through Kefr Malik to the outpost line at the Wadi el Kola, just south of Round Hill, improve the metalling of the main Nablus road to the outpost line near Sinjil; construct a wagon road from Neby Saleh down the Wadi Rima, complete a lateral road between the two Corps from Deir en Nidham to Abud, and a connecting road from near Beit Rima to Ain es Zerka; construct poled signal lines up to the nearest outpost lines; lay a waterpipe line from Tell Asur along the Wadi Kola to south of Round Hill, and arrange for water storage amounting to about 200,000 gallons near Kefr Malik.

MOUNT EPHRAIM

All this work was done, and the day approached for the last advance over country which had seen sieges and massacres through countless ages; for the last ten miles of the Judean Plateau, with its steep gorges, on the one side to the Jordan, on the other to Ajalon, were in ancient times the debatable land across which was traced an ever shifting frontier line. The old name for this section of the central range of Palestine was Mount Ephraim, and of the table land south of it Mount Judah. From a distance, from the Mediterranean, all those hills of Samaria, except Mount Carmel, seem to merge together into one mountain mass. There are entrances, but it is compact, and from the sea there is but one conspicuous pass shown on the skyline, that in which the town of Nablus lies, between the hills of Ebal and Gerizim. Nablus is on the divide, some of its springs flowing to the Jordan, others to the Mediterranean.

Beyond Nablus, Mount Ephraim commences to fall to the great Plain of Esdraelon—not hurriedly, and most sharply in the centre—to Jenin, which lies, as it were, at the head of a gulf with two headlands stretching on either side: on the left Mount Carmel, on the right Mount Gilboa, where the plain itself drops gently through the Valley of Jezreel to the Valley of the Jordan. Beisan lies down in the Valley of Jezreel (the furthest point of the great cavalry ride from the coast), and to the right of the 53rd Division front; while Afule lies like an outpost island in the mouth of the gulf, between Mount Gilboa and Mount Carmel. Nazareth is further north on the hills bordering the plain.

MOVEMENT AND CONCEALMENT

The rôle given the XXth Corps by Sir E. Allenby was to block the exits into the Jordan Valley, a task which would fall entirely on the 53rd Division. As the Division stood, the flank which they formed was not only drawn back, but had the considerable obstacle of the Samieh Basin before it. The success of the Corps plan depended on a rapid advance, and the Corps Commander asked permission to move forward to the north side of the Basin at the end of August, but it was decided by General Headquarters that no operation should take place until just before the main one.

The pains taken to conceal the real objective were stupendous. All concentrations were carried out at night, and full use was made of the many olive groves round Ramleh, Ludd and Jaffa to conceal troops by day. And there was a lot of movement.

On the XXth Corps front, on the night 2/3rd September, an 18 pdr. Battery of the 10th Division was sent to the Jericho Valley to join Chaytor's force in exchange for the 39th Mountain Battery; and at the same time two Howr. Batteries of the 53rd Division which had been attached to the Desert Mounted Corps returned from the Jordan Valley. The Corps Cavalry, (the Worcester Yeomanry Regiment) which had also been attached to the Desert Mounted Corps returned during the first week of September.

On the night 10/11th September, the 96th Brigade R.G.A., consisting of the 91st Heavy Battery, the 378th, 383rd, and 440th Siege Batteries, and also the 422nd Siege Battery of the 97th Brigade R.G.A., started to join the XXIst Corps, moving by Khurbetha Ibn Harith, Latron and Surafend.

On the night 13/14th, the 60th Division commenced to march from the Corps area, via Ain Arik, Latron, and Surafend to join the XXIst Corps; also the 534th Siege Battery of the 97th R.G.A. Brigade, and the 9th Mounted Artillery Brigade moved by the lateral road to Abbud and the XXIst Corps front. On the same night the XXth Corps extended its front to Rafat (exclusive) the 10th Division taking over the line from Tin Hat to Rafat.

Meanwhile Staff Officers from G.H.Q. went round Jerusalem with orderlies and paint pots, defacing the doors of houses with departmental names, and turning the inhabitants out so as to spread the news that G.H.Q. was to be quartered there.

And down in the heat of the Jordan Valley a curious fatigue was carried on by West Indies troops. Every day they were marched north and east along the dusty tracks, and every night brought back to their starting point by lorry, to commence again the next day.

Considerable works, Decauville railways, bridges, etc., were built for no other purpose than to deceive the Turks; and rows upon rows of dummy horses were erected to bamboozle enemy aeroplanes.

But " the chief factor in the secrecy maintained must be attributed, however, to the supremacy in the air which had been obtained by the Royal Air Force. The process of wearing down the enemy aircraft had been going on all through the summer. During one week in June, 100 hostile aeroplanes had crossed our lines. During the last week in August, this number had decreased to eighteen. In the next few days, a number were shot down, with the result that only four ventured to cross our lines during the period of concentration."—(Allenby.)

CONCENTRATION FOR ATTACK

The date and time for the main advance of the XXth Corps depended on the progress of the operations of the XXIst Corps and the Desert Mounted Corps on the 19th September. At first, General Chetwode had been ordered to be ready to commence his main advance by the evening of Z + 1 day (20th September), but on the 16th, it was decided that the 10th Division should be prepared to advance on the evening of the 19th.

The centre of the Corps front had been taken over by Watson's Force, and on the morning of the 18th the position of the Corps was as follows:

The 53rd Division, with the 39th Indian Mounted Battery attached, was concentrated in the approximate area Nejmeh-Rock Park-Kh. Abu Felah-Mezrah esh Sherkiyeh-Dar Jerir. Also a troop of the Corps Cavalry was placed at the disposal of General Mott for use on his right flank towards the Jordan Valley.

The 10th Division, less one battery 18 pdrs., but with the Hong Kong and Singapore Mountain Battery attached, were holding the line from Arura (inclusive) to Rafat (exclusive) with the remainder of the Division concentrated in Neby Saleh-Kefr Ain-Berukin-el Kefr area.

Watson's Force held from Highgate Ridge (inclusive) to Arura (exclusive)—about 15,000 yards—as follows :—

Corps Cavalry from Highgate Ridge (inclusive) to the Nablus road (exclusive).

2/155th Pioneers from the Nablus Road to J.31.c.

1/155th Pioneers held the K.12 defences.

" A " Group of Corps Reinforcements K.31.c to Abwein (inclusive).

" B " Group of Corps Reinforcements from Abwein to Arura.

Each group of the Corps Reinforcements Detachments was 350 strong.

The Corps Heavy Artillery, one heavy battery and four siege batteries, together with certain captured guns, were distributed as follows :—

FOR SUPPORT OF THE 53RD DIVISION.

103rd Brigade R.G.A.—R. Section 10th Heavy Batty. L. 3.c.
      L.   ,,   ,,   ,,   ,, N. 4.d.
      205th Siege Battery ..   .. L.14.c.
      387th   ,,   ,, (less 1 gun) L.26.a.
      392nd   ,,   ,, ... Q.32.a.

FOR THE SUPPORT OF THE 10TH DIVISION.

421st Siege Battery   D.15.a ⎫
1 gun 387th Siege Battery   A.27.b ⎪
2 captured   15 c.m. Howrs. K. 2.c. ⎬ Under command of O.C. 97th Bde. R.G.A.
2 ,,   105 c.m. ,,   H.31.c. ⎪
3 ,,   75 m.m. guns   H.31.c ⎭

After supporting the preliminary operations of the 53rd Division the 387th Siege Battery was to move across and support the 10th Division.

Two medium Trench Mortar Batteries were allotted to the 53rd Division, and one to the 10th.

Corps Operation Orders were issued on the 13th September. (*See* Appendix.)

As already stated the preliminary operation undertaken by the 53rd Division was to cross the Samieh to the general line Valley View-el Mugheir-Hindhead-Nairn Ridge. Once on this line they would have a clear advance along the watershed with no serious topographical obstacle before them. A second and no less important object would also be gained; the question of water was always a vital one throughout the campaign, and one becomes familiar with the tag to many orders " and secure the water supply." In this battle the country they were to win was exceptionally "dry"; but the Samieh yielded an unlimited quantity.

GENERAL MOTT'S PLAN

The main enemy defences consisted of a series of works on the line R. 19-Valley View-South of el Mugheir, with outposts at Keen's Knoll and Table Hill, covering the heads of the wadis Wye, Samieh, Cheshire and Katuniyeh; and a further series, swinging to the west on the line Kew Hill-Deir Abu Sekub-Kh. Abu Malul, with Bidston Hill and Forfar Hill held as outposts. In rear of the main positions, Square Hill, Hindhead, and Sh. Muhammed were prepared for defence. A strong position and very difficult of approach as the spurs on the north of the Basin were exceedingly steep.

The plan adopted by General Mott is an interesting one. He decided to attack with two brigades and work round what would be termed the rim of the Basin, each Brigade going an opposite way, and meeting on the other side. The formation of the ground and the enemy dispositions made it advisable to give the 160th Brigade, on the right, about two-thirds of the rim to deal with, while the 159th Brigade, on the left, would be responsible for the remaining third.

The plan for the 160th Brigade was that battalions should follow one another in succession to a starting point, Q.34.d; from here they would move at intervals across the Wadi Samieh, and it must be noted that their task was made the more formidable by having to cross at the deepest point Q.35 central, and move up the spur in Q.36.a. The left of this movement was to be covered by two companies of the 5/6th Royal Welch Fusiliers, attached from the 158th Brigade.

After crossing the Samieh, the leading battalion was to assault the first position, R.19.a and R.13.d (Wye Hill), and from thenceforth protect the right flank of the brigade. The succeeding battalions were then to "leapfrog" through, the second battalion protecting the right flank of the third and fourth as they, in turn, advanced.

It was not an easy manœuvre, as the Brigade would have a night march of some miles over difficult country, followed by a steep climb on a narrow front on the far side of the Basin, and then would have to fan out to attack a fortified position covering a considerable extent of ground. The rear battalion would have at least seven miles to march before reaching its final objective. But the plan had the great advantage of taking the Turkish positions in rear.

The plan for the 159th Brigade, on the other hand, consisted of an unavoidable series of frontal attacks. They were to move down from Round Hill, one battalion securing Bidston Hill and one Forfar Hill; the two would then advance on Sekub and Kh. Abu Malul, while a third battalion pushed through to Kew Hill and Pt. 2401. Provided that the 160th Brigade, in the course of their advance, was successful in securing Boulder's Boil and the positions south-west of El Mugheir, the 159th Brigade was to push forward troops and secure Hindhead, which dominated the whole country.

The correct timing of infantry movements and artillery operations was of the greatest importance. Zero hour was to be given by the 160th Brigade when the leading battalion arrived in a position to assault Wye Hill (R.19); all available artillery was to be concentrated on those works, lifting with the infantry assault to R.14, and Valley View. But the advance of the 159th Brigade from their position of assembly was not to take place until after the bombardment of Valley View; the reason being that the whole of the artillery should support the 160th Brigade as far as the Valley View positions, when part would be switched over to support the 159th Brigade.

The concentration for attack took place on the night 16/17th September. Tents were left standing in the old camps, and none was allowed to be erected in the concentration area; but there were, fortunately, plenty of fig and olive groves which afforded ample cover for the infantry during the day. The principle danger of discovery came from watering the horses in that sunbaked and dust-covered country. One enemy aeroplane did fly over the line on the 18th and, presumably, saw nothing. Unsuspicious? No; the Turkish Intelligence Service issued a warning that the British would attack on the 18th, but imagined that it would be on the eastern flank.

The regrouping of Sir E. Allenby's Army was not detected by agents on land or scouts in the sky. On the 15th, a scout noticed one small thing, and reported: " Some regrouping of cavalry units apparently in progress behind the enemy's left flank otherwise nothing unusual to report." On the 17th, the Turkish Intelligence issued a map showing the dispositions of the British Army, with the 53rd Division in reserve to the Australian Mounted Division on the right; the 60th Division in line on the right of the Nablus road; the 10th, the French Contingent (put down as Italian), 75th, 3rd Indian, 7th Indian all in their normal positions; the 4th Cavalry Division, Anzac Division, and Desert Corps all grouped on the right of the line, and only the 5th Cavalry Division on the left!

THE BATTLE

At 4.30 p.m., on the 18th, two British fighting aeroplanes commenced to patrol the 53rd Division front, and the 160th Brigade were able to abandon all aeroplane precautions. Battalions fell in and marched in column of route to the position of assembly in rear of a hill between El Munatir and Rock Park, and waited for the light to fade.

There was no such thing as darkness, merely a change from the glare of the sun to a soft light. "We could distinguish," says Colonel Garsia, "the outline of the Mountains of Moab forty miles away, and every feature on the opposite side of the basin stood out vividly."

At 7.15 p.m., the artillery opened slow fire on Keen's Knoll to drown the noise of the infantry approach and the leading battalion marched over the crest of the hill and commenced to scramble down the precipitous and slippery descent of the Samieh—a long column, still more or less in fours, showing clearly against the pale, yellow escarpment. But they were unobserved until they reached a plateau about three-quarters of the way down, when a few snipers beyond the Wadi opened fire and sent up some signal lights. For some time no artillery fire followed, and then it was very scattered; later, as the troops advanced a wild shoot was started.

There was no serious resistance and the 17th Infantry were in position to assault at 10 o'clock. By that time, no less than six telephone wires had been run out by specially trained parties, and the guns were waiting for Brigadier-General Pearson to give the Zero hour. At the word the bombardment started with a crash, and lasted for twenty minutes, lifting when the 17th went in with the bayonet.

The assault, coming from an unexpected direction, found little opposition. But Colonel B. J. Fagan was wounded.

The battle was now definitely launched, for this was Zero hour for the 159th Brigade. General Mott was not satisfied that the rate of artillery fire on Cheshire, Katuniyeh, and Merj wadis was sufficient to ensure that the enemy's retreat was blocked, and ordered it to be increased.

With the enemy swept away, the other battalions of the 160th Brigade, led by the Cape Corps and guided by the glow of special smoke shells fired at intervals by the Gunners on selected points at fixed times, marched through the gap and followed the rim of the basin for a couple of miles, but moved in rear of the Valley View positions. As they advanced the Cape Corps posted picquets overlooking the Jordan Valley, and took up a defensive position, facing north, about Square Hill and Kh. Jibeit;

they could not occupy Square Hill, which they found commanded from an un-named hill strongly held by the Turks.

Square Hill and Kh. Jibeit are beyond the rim of the basin, and when the Cape Corps turned from the rim, the 7th Royal Welch Fusiliers, who followed them, took up the advance, coming up on their left about End Hill. Two Turkish guns were firing on the right just below the Cape Corps, who sent out a patrol to capture them.

After leaving End Hill the 7th Royal Welch Fusiliers strayed a bit to the north. They had expected to find a road, but it was only a faint track which, in spite of the visibility at night, could not be seen because of the scrub. As they passed round and behind Valley View, a diversion was caused by alarmed and bewildered Turks breaking away from the Punjabis—who had turned left, inside the Fusiliers, and were attacking the Valley View positions in reverse—only to fall into the hands of the Welshmen.

The battalion split into two columns, each with a leading and a support company, when Colonel Harker suddenly realised that he was on the southwest slopes of Square Hill. He promptly ordered the leading company of his left column to take Sheikh Azeir, and the support company to push straight on and take Pt. 2362. Similarly, he directed the two companies of his right column on Mugheir and Boulder's Boil.

By 3 a.m. the positions were captured and a red parachute light was fired from Pt. 2362.

Sheikh Azeir, Pt. 2362, and Boulder's Boil were found manned and ready to receive an attack from the south and south-west. The defences were all constructed in a horse-shoe shape, and were rushed as fast as the men could go by two platoons of each company, one of them at either end of the horse-shoe. Only three shots were fired by the Turks, who were completely surprised, and put up their hands at once. At Boulder's Boil there was a standing bivouac camp; at Mugheir a battalion Headquarters, including the commanding officer, was captured. Altogether, 20 officers, 192 other ranks, two 4.2 howitzers, and 15 machine guns were taken.

The 160th Brigade suffered about 30 casualties in this first operation, and captured 37 officers, 410 other ranks, 28 machine guns and the two howitzers with their limbers. The Royal Welch Fusiliers had only two men wounded.

THE 159TH BRIGADE

The 159th Brigade had in the meantime completed its allotted third of the circle, having started half an hour after the Zero hour of the 160th

Brigade, and was waiting for the red signal light fired by the 7th Royal Welch Fusiliers.

This Brigade had no alternative but to attack the various Turkish positions frontally, and some stiff fighting occurred. The first objectives, Pt. 2362 (Bidston) and Forfar Hill, were taken by the 153rd Infantry (Colonel Withers) and the 3/152nd Infantry (Colonel Doveton)* at 11 p.m. The 153rd then went on and captured Pt. 2430. Pressing on against Sekub and Kew Hill they encountered heavy rifle and machine gun fire, and five officers were hit. The battalion was somewhat shaken, but were rallied by two British officers who led them forward, and eventually Sekub was taken. Six machine guns and a number of prisoners were captured.

But the battalion was not now strong enough to tackle Kew Hill. As they had advanced on Sekub their right flank had been protected by the 4/5th Welch Regiment who had used the bayonet to break up two wild Turkish attacks on that flank. The Welch Regiment was now ordered to assist the 153rd against Kew Hill, and the hill was captured by the two battalions at 12.45 a.m.

One company of the Welch Regiment then went forward to Hill 2401, killed several Turks and captured two machine guns.

Meanwhile, one company of the 2/153rd Infantry (Colonel James) which had followed the 153rd (Colonel Withers) up Bidston Hill had turned to the right and cleared the southern end of it. The rest of the battalion had moved up at Zero hour by way of the Wadi Abbad, and leaving the detached company to hold Cone Hill, continued their march north and came into reserve to the Welch Regiment.

After the capture of Forfar Hill, Colonel Doveton launched his battalion against Malul, and was engaged in the severest fighting of the day. The artillery bombardment of this strong position was not effective in as much as the Turks did not occupy the trenches, but either sought shelter or were accustomed to sleep in caves in rear and on the flanks. Consequently as the attacking troops rose at the moment fixed for the assault, when the artillery lifted, they were met by the fire of the untouched Turkish machine guns and broken up. They made a gallant effort; parties managed to get about 150 yards from the crest, and hung on.

The severity of the Turkish fire was such that Colonel Doveton could not get a call for artillery support through. The telephone wire to the

---

* These battalions appear in official documents under the names of their Commanding Officers, and were very generally referred to in that manner.

Brigade headquarters was cut, and visual signalling, the station being on top of a hill, was impossible; several runners tried to reach it and were killed. Finally, a runner did succeed in getting to Sekub where a message was sent through to Brigade, and a bombardment was ordered.

But there had been a lengthy delay, and Colonel Doveton had, meantime, organised two attacks on the hill, both of which had reached the trenches but had been driven out by showers of bombs. For the moment it seemed an impossible task, and the battalion was withdrawn to Forfar Hill. The bombardment did not take place.

The Turks were strong and prepared on this front. One company of Colonel Kidd's battalion, the 3/153rd Infantry (attached from the 158th Brigade) attempted to take Fife Knoll, but were beaten off; and a fighting patrol from this battalion found Amurieh strongly held. But it was still possible to surprise the enemy, and at 3 a.m., when the light signal was sent up by the 7th Royal Welch Fusiliers from Hill 2362, two companies of the 4/5th Welch Regiment advanced with such rapidity and boldness on Hindhead that this key position was captured before the main Turkish garrison had occupied their battle positions; they were found marching forward in column, and were dispersed by Lewis gun fire.

Simultaneously with the advance of the 159th Brigade two companies of the 4/11th Gurkha Rifles, 158th Brigade, "demonstrated" against Turmus Aya and cut off a post on the west of the village, killing all but one, whom they brought back prisoner. But they were met with heavy machine gun fire from the works about Abu el Auf, and having created the necessary impression they retired.

DAWN ON THE 19TH SEPTEMBER

At the break of dawn on the 19th, the programme of the 53rd Division was complete, except that Malul remained, in spite of the gallant efforts of Colonel Doveton's battalion, in the hands of the Turks.

Part of the task of the 53rd Division was to push forward the construction of roads behind the advance so that the artillery could move up, and two battalions of the 158th Brigade were waiting to carry on with this work, but it depended on the success of the attackers—Malul, unfortunately, commanded the whole of the Wadi along which the road was planned to run. The temptation was to attack the place again. General Mott, however, decided not to attempt anything further that day, as the men were tired and, moreover, the Division was much strung out and not well placed to resist a counter-attack if one should be made. But he ordered the 5/6th Royal Welch Fusiliers to relieve the 4/5th Welch Regiment before or after dark, when the 4/5th Welch and 2/153rd Infantry would form " Hohler's Force " and would capture Mount Mahommed and Ruin Hill, continue the advance south-west and secure Nairn Ridge and Malul. The 5/6th Royal Welch Fusiliers would meanwhile advance to the general line Kulason-Plateau. All troops engaged in this operation were to be under the command of Colonel Borthwick, who was to arrange for artillery support with Colonel Walker, 265th Field Artillery Brigade, and for machine gun support with Colonel Partridge.

But the remaining hours of daylight of the 19th were quiet on the 53rd Division front. The only event of importance had occurred about one o'clock in the afternoon, when a hundred or so of the enemy were discovered in their bivouac area behind Malul, calmly eating their lunch. Five batteries of artillery and eight machine guns were turned on them simultaneously. Apparently few escaped, and, no doubt this disaster to the Turks contributed to the easy advance of the Welch Regiment and 2/153rd in the evening. The attack was carried out at 7 p.m. with complete success and insignificant opposition.

XXIst CORPS FRONT

On the extreme left of the British line anything but quiet reigned. The 19th was a day of lament for the Turks.

In the early hours of the morning, the Royal Air Force set about bombing and destroying the Turkish signal communications by attacking the Headquarters of the VIIth and VIIIth Armies at Nablus and Tulkeram, and also el Afule. At 4.30 a.m., the massed artillery in the Coastal Plain opened an intense bombardment lasting 15 minutes; then the 75th and 60th Divisions assaulted the Turkish line. The result, and the speed of it, surpassed the most sanguine hopes; the line was smashed, and the roll up of the enemy commenced. At 7.30 a.m., the 5th Cavalry Division was crossing the Nahr Falik, and by mid-day was on the far side of the Nahr Iskanderuneh. The 5th and 4th Cavalry Divisions, the Australian Mounted Division, and the Desert Mounted Corps rode through and behind the Turkish army.

The success of Sir E. Allenby's ambitious scheme was assured. Soon after mid-day he ordered the XXth Corps to advance during the night 19/20th. General Chetwode, however, left General Mott to decide whether the 53rd Division would advance during the night or in the early morning; but both divisions of the XXth Corps were ordered to press the enemy relentlessly if any signs of general retreat were observed. This modification of Army Orders was necessary as the 53rd Artillery was already firing at the limit of range, and before they could move, Malul would have to be captured: an advance without artillery would mean a long delay if it was held up by enemy strong points. General Mott, therefore, issued orders for an advance at dawn. (*See* Appendix.)

As stated, the attack on Malul took place after sunset, and was successful.

10TH DIVISION FRONT

On the left of Watson's Force the Turkish defences on Furkhah Ridge, and further west on Kh er Ras and Mogg Ridge, were strong, but sited to meet a direct attack from the south. The 10th Division plan of attack involved three phases. First, the 29th Brigade was to attack Furkhah Ridge from the west, up the spurs north and south of the Wadi Rashid; second, the 29th would continue its advance to Selfit, while the 31st Brigade crossing the Wadi Mutwy was to put out a defensive flank to the north, and then roll up the Turks on Mogg Ridge from the east, taking them in flank and rear; third, an advance by the whole Division to the north-east, towards Iskaka and Jemmain.

The first two phases were successfully carried out by midnight; the third was ordered to commence at 6.30 a.m. on the 20th September.

THE BATTLE RESUMED ON THE 20TH.

Colonel Garsia says that the decision "to push on with the least possible delay, instead of leaving us for 48 hours on our new positions, as had been originally intended," and "the fact of our road construction having been retarded, made this somewhat disconcerting." But the 4/11th Gurkha Rifles and the 3/153rd Infantry were put on the work of making the Wadi Forth road immediately Malul had fallen, and batteries were pushed forward as soon as possible; the road, however, was not finished until dawn, so the batteries were later than had been expected.

General Mott's orders were that, as soon as the Wadi Forth road was completed, the 158th Brigade would concentrate about Hindhead, returning to the command of Brigadier-General Vernon, and would then occupy Pt. 2906-Kh Bkt el Kusr. The 159th Brigade would move, echeloned on the left of the 158th, to Ras el Tawil. The 160th Brigade would picquet the right flank, until the progress of Chaytor's Force in the Jordan Valley relieved it of that duty, and keep all unemployed troops ready to move at short notice.

160TH BRIGADE

It so happened that the attack on the 20th was opened by the 160th Brigade. The line held was Z Hill (17th), Crest Hill to Dhib Hill (21st Punjabis), Square Hill (Cape Corps), Knib Knoll to Boulder's Boil (7th R.W.F.). It was desired to throw the flank forward and, after a ten minutes' bombardment, the Cape Corps advanced and captured Gallows Hill and Kh Jibeit: Outpost Hill was not attacked, but was reported strongly held.

All battalions of the 160th Brigade were then ordered to concentrate about El Mugheir at 7.30 a.m., to take part in the general advance along the watershed to El Domeh. But, at 7.30 severe fighting broke out on Kh Jibeit.

After severe shelling of the Cape Corps and the Brigade concentration area, the Turks counter-attacked. The Cape Corps had two companies forward holding the captured hills; all the officers of these companies became casualties, and it was impossible to find out what was happening. It soon became clear, however, that they were being driven back by the Turks, and one of the support companies was sent to the right to relieve the pressure. The latter company assaulted and succeeded in reaching the crest of Outpost Hill, but was speedily driven back again.

The 21st Punjabis, and later the 17th Infantry, were sent up in support. Meanwhile the Cape Corps were hard pressed, in close fighting with bombs, and fell back slowly. There was no response from the artillery which, at that time, was actually moving forward. Between 9 and 10 a.m., the Commanding Officer, Colonel Morris, was hit a second time, and Major Hay took over command. No less than 13 officers had been hit, of whom six were killed, and Major Hay decided to withdraw to Square Hill. The battalion had been reduced to 350.

The Turks appeared very active, and reinforcements were seen approaching from the north of Gallows Hill. But now the 267th Field Artillery Brigade came into action, and the heavy batteries commenced to shell Kh Jibeit. The 17th Infantry were ordered to leave one company to hold End and Dhib Hills and attack at once with the other three.

The Field Artillery started a half-hour bombardment of Gallows Hill, Kh. Jibeit, and Crest Hill at 12.25 p.m., and at 12.50 this was supplemented by the 160th machine gun company giving overhead support fire from Square Hill. The 17th Infantry started to advance. The Turks were seen to be utterly demoralised by the bombardment, and to be running about without arms. The positions were reoccupied without trouble;

about 150 prisoners being taken, including a battalion commander. By 1.45 p.m. the 160th Brigade line ran, End Hill-Dhib Hill-Square Hill-Outpost Hill-Kh. Jibeit-Gallows Hill-Knib Knoll. Large bodies of Turks were seen to be retiring north, and the 265th Field Artillery Brigade came into action against them.

The counter attack on the Cape Corps had been made by the 109th Turkish Regiment, recently arrived from the Caucasus, and not previously identified.

158TH BRIGADE

While all this was going on on the right, Brigadier-General Vernon was trying to operate in the centre. The 5/6th Royal Welch Fusiliers had taken up a position on the Plateau, and came under their own Brigadier when he arrived there at 1 a.m. (They had been attached 159th Brigade.)

The 4/11th Gurkha Rifles and 3/153rd Infantry had been working all night on the Wadi Forth road, and at dawn were ordered to concentrate near Hindhead.

The 3/154th were in Merj Wadi, " where," says Brigadier-General Vernon, " I had no communication except by orderly over a very bad country."

The Gurkha Rifles and 3/153rd arrived at the foot of Hindhead at 4 a.m., 20th instant, " I opened my Headquarters at 1 a.m., and sent a mounted officer to order the 3/154th to concentrate there as soon as possible. An Officer whom I had sent the previous afternoon had not returned, and I subsequently discovered he failed to deliver my message. This battalion did not reach Hindhead until 11.30 a.m. The 5/6th Royal Welch Fusiliers were holding the Plateau and came under my orders when I arrived there. My orders were to advance at dawn, but I was unable to comply as I had no troops to do it with."

The Gurkhas and 3/153rd found the slopes of Hindhead so steep that they only arrived behind the line held by the Royal Welch Fusiliers at 8.30 a.m. The Gurkhas, as advance guard, marched through, and were directed on the line Pt. 2906-Kh Bkt el Kusr. By that time the Turkish counter attack on the 160th Brigade was going strong.

The objective given the 158th Brigade was a line of hills stretched across the main plateau, and containing many underfeatures. It was an admirable bit of country for fighting a rearguard action, and the Turks had a plentiful supply of machine guns. Brigadier-General Vernon found that his troops were meeting with increasing oppositions; they were finally checked about mid-day on the line O.16 and 17.

The 3/153rd Infantry, who were still at Pt. 2788, were ordered up, and artillery support called for. But Colonel Garsia had to reply that none could be given, as all available guns were in action against the enemy attack on the right flank. And when the position there had been restored the switching over of guns necessitated laying out more telephone wires so that there was a long delay.

General Mott became anxious. Unless the Turks were pressed a number would escape by way of the Jordan Valley. Brigadier-General Vernon was therefore told " that it was imperative that I should get on, and as no cable had arrived for the Forward Observing Officer I was ordered to carry on without one. The artillery gave me what assistance they could, but the ridge had been strongly reinforced and the Turks meant to hold it until nightfall. A proper artillery bombardment was necessary to enable me to capture it and this was not available. At 4.40 p.m., the attack having made little progress, I decided at the G.O.C.'s suggestion, to postpone the attack until after dark."

The decision was forced on General Mott. If the attack was pressed and failed, it would result in disorganisation and interfere with an effective night march, but if, as was practically certain, the Turks moved back at sundown, the advance could continue with greater rapidity. Also the men were tired and a rest would help them.

159TH BRIGADE

On the extreme left of the Division front, the 159th Brigade had concentrated at 4 a.m. in the neighbourhood of Ruin Hill. The 153rd Infantry, supported by the 4/5th Welch, were ordered to co-operate with the advance of the 158th Brigade, and capture Ras el Tawil. These battalions started to move, but at 12.30 p.m. Brigadier-General Money was informed by Division Headquarters that, owing to the Turkish counter attack, the ground over which the two battalions would have to advance was exposed, and that they had been ordered to return. The Brigadier was also informed that he could act independently, and so ordered the 2/153rd to attack Ras el Tawil from the south-west.

At 3.10 p.m., Colonel James reported the occupation of the hill, and also of hills at O.15 and 14.

10TH DIVISION FRONT

During the day, Watson's Force ceased to exit, and the Corps Cavalry reconnoitred down the Nablus road until fired on. But on their left the 10th Division had met with a similar experience to that of the 53rd. The third phase of their attack, towards Iskaka and Merda, had been timed for 6.30 a.m. The 29th Brigade was able to start at 6.45 and make a little progress, but was held up before reaching its objectives by artillery and machine gun fire. No support could be obtained from the 10th Division Artillery because of road difficulties, and the guns were only brought up during the afternoon. The 31st Brigade did not move until 8.45 a.m. again owing to road troubles. The 2/42nd Deolis made nine attempts to take one hill, without success. The attack was resumed by both Brigades in the afternoon, and the line pushed forward to include Kefr Harris and Harris.

Everywhere on the XXth Corps front some progress had been made, but the difficult nature of the country for wheels enabled the infantry to get beyond the range of the artillery, and they were unable to break the resistance of machine guns and artillery served by a resolute Turkish rearguard.

GENERAL ADVANCE ORDERED

General Mott had the news that Beisan had been occupied by the Desert Mounted Corps, but in the 25 miles that lay between him and that place there were several roads down into the Jordan Valley. The nearest and principal road, from Nablus, ran through Mejdel Bene Fadl to the Damieh Bridge, over the Jordan, and was only some four miles away. There was a second road beyond, through Beit Furik, and a third, through Beit Dejan, both running close together and joining below the terrible Ghor country. These were about ten miles away, and were little more than mountain tracks, impassable for wheels. It was, therefore, of paramount importance to cut the road to the Damieh Bridge.

The Corps Commander ordered a general advance " absolutely regardless of fatigue of men or animals."

The 158th Brigade was ordered to be on the line Pt. 2906-O.10.d by 1 a.m. on the 21st September, and advancing with all speed to occupy the cross roads at F.17 (the Damieh Bridge road) by dawn; they would then march straight on Akrabeh. The 159th was to advance on the left. The 160th would protect the right flank of the Division against any enterprise by the Turks still in the Jordan Valley, and guard the Samieh water supply: it was reported that the 14th and remnants of the 53rd Turkish Divisions were on the right, in the Valley.

158TH BRIGADE

At 11 p.m., 20th September, when the 158th Brigade moved forward, it was found, as had been anticipated that the Turks had retired. The 5/6th Royal Welch Fusiliers formed the advance guard, and passed over the hill in O.10.d, followed by the 3/154th and 3/153rd Infantry; The Gurkha Rifles remained at Pt. 2906 until 5.30 a.m.

There was no opposition, and at 5 a.m. the road crossing at F.17 was secured and the enemy telephone wires cut.

The main road was blocked! Brigadier-General Vernon now ordered a halt for breakfast. The artillery closed up, and hearing that there was water in the village of Kusrah the forward batteries took the opportunity of watering their horses.

The country in front was open, with Akrabeh Hill about two and a half miles away, and with a low intermediate ridge on which the Turkish rearguard had taken up a position. Behind Akrabeh, the main road, on which the Brigade was sitting, emerged from a gorge before it turned south. The next road leading down to the Jordan, through Beit Furik, was about three and a half miles north of the turn, and between it and the main road was the lofty ridge of El Tuwanik, the highest point east of Nablus. From the crest of El Tuwanik both the Beit Furik and Beit Dejan roads could be denied to the enemy, but El Tuwanik was about nine miles from the Brigade.

As the 158th Brigade were resting and eating their breakfasts, the whole panorama lying clear and sharp before them, there emerged from the gorge behind Akrabeh, a large body of the enemy marching down the main road to the Damieh Bridge; but, instead of following the road they turned off it, to their left, and proceeded to climb the roadless ridge of El Tuwanik.

The artillery was in position, but Tuwanik was beyond the range of the guns, and the horses were watering at Kusrah. It is, however, doubtful whether they could have done much had the teams been there, as there were elements of Turkish rearguards before Akrabeh; but it was mortifying to watch several hundred Turks march calmly over the crest of the ridge and escape down the Beit Furik Valley beyond.

The roads were very bad. Major R. Wyman wrote: "A/265th had led the column yesterday so to-day we were in the rear. The R.E. had been trying to make some sort of road out of Merj Sia, but when we moved off at 8 a.m. the going was very bad, and it was a job getting along. There was considerable delay owing to guns and vehicles getting stuck—it was up hill, of course. We advanced about nine miles to-day. Treharne's Battery came into action once on the road, and " Johnnie " sent a few shells back, but it was only for a very short time. I was a long way ahead of the Battery, and at one point General Walker, Colonel Walker, Treharne, and I saw a large column of Turks winding up the slope of El Tuwanik—a magnificent target but the batteries were a long way back. Treharne and I both got back as quickly as we could, but it was too late. I got rather indefinite orders to 'Push on,' which I did."

The advance was resumed at 8.30 a.m., the 5/6th Royal Welch Fusiliers picquetting the hills as they moved forward. During this operation one Lewis gun team, acting on its own initiative, captured twelve officers and 143 other ranks, and 5 machine guns.

At 12.15 p.m. the 3/154th Infantry secured Kh. el Kerum, after a sharp encounter with a rearguard party, in which it was well supported by a section of machine guns under Captain Franklin. This proved to be the last encounter of the campaign. At 3 p.m. the 3/153rd Infantry passed over El Tuwanik and marched on to Beit Dejan. All the roads were then blocked.

During the advance of the 158th Brigade, the 159th had for a short time moved in rear of them, and then swerved off to the left. The leading battalion, the 4/5th Welch Regiment, entered Kusrah at 4 a.m. Turkish camp fires were seen in the vicinity of Jurieh, but though the Welshmen pushed on with all speed the enemy were alarmed and bolted, leaving stores, wagons, and some of them their arms; only a few were captured.

At 8.30 a.m. the Brigade was ordered to concentrate at Jurish; they moved to Akrabeh during the afternoon.

At 11 p.m., the Corps ordered the Division to halt, and at 6.30 a.m. on the 22nd, General Chetwode telegraphed the news that the Turkish Army west of the Jordan had ceased to exist.

CAPTURE OF TURKISH ARMIES

The 60th, 7th, and 3rd Divisions had no fighting on the 21st. All the cavalry were through the enemy lines; every centre had been occupied by them; the 13th Cavalry Brigade rode straight across the Plain and just missed capturing Liman von Sanders at Nazareth; the Turkish army, streaming from the hills, fell into their hands and were herded together and marched off like sheep.

The Turks were crushed. Hammered by the Infantry in the hills, they were mercilessly harried by the Air Force as they retired. The action of the Air Force is instructive. The pursuit by this new arm was in many respects more terrifying than pursuit by cavalry, for in effect it was pursuit by a superior form of artillery, the shell, or bomb, being controlled to the last moment.

A few miles north of Nablus where the road enters a gorge, at the head of the Wadi Farah, it runs for several miles on a ledge. A long Turkish column was attacked from the air as it passed through the defile; the leading teams were bombed, the teams in rear plunged forward, more bombs fell, and in a few minutes the whole defile was blocked. A similar attack from the air was carried out a few miles to the west.

"The whole war edifice," says Colonel Garcia, "collapsed like a house of cards. No outposts were put out, and from the depths of war we passed in the twinkling of an eye into the depths of peace."

The captures by the Division, throughout the final operations, were 1,195 prisoners, 9 guns (including the notorious 15 c.m. gun that had shelled Jaffa, Ram Allah, and Jericho), and about 50 machine guns.

On the 23rd the battlefield was cleared, and the next day the brigades worked on the Nablus road.

On the 26th the Division moved back to the Tell Asur—et Tell area, the artillery to Beitunia.

On the 8th October they started to move to the Latron-Ludd area, and on the 26th commenced to arrive at Side Bishr.

Demobilisation started on 20th December.

The Armistice with the Turks did not come into force until 31st October. Although the XXIst Corps marched north along the coast, the final stages of the campaign fell to the cavalry.

On the 26th September the 4th Cavalry Division started from Beisan for Damascus, followed by the Australian Mounted Division, and, from the direction of Nazareth, the 5th Cavalry Division. On the 30th the Australian Mounted Division had closed the exits from the town to the north, while the 5th Cavalry Division had reached the southern outskirts of the town.

On 1st October the Desert Mounted Corps and the Arab Army entered Damascus together.

ROYAL FIELD ARTILLERY, 53RD DIVISION.
INSPECTION AT ALEXANDRIA.

The pursuit continued. On the night of the 26th October, the rearguards of the broken Turkish armies were near Deir el Jenel, twenty miles north-west of Aleppo, and the 5th Cavalry Division was astride the roads leading from Aleppo to Killis and Katma, but too weak to continue the advance until the arrival of the Australian Mounted Division, which was approaching. Before the Australians could arrive and descend on Alexandretta the Armistice was signed.

Between the 19th September and the 26th October, 75,000 prisoners had been taken, and about 360 guns.

With so many units as go to make a Division one cannot record all the intimate and personal details which live in the memory of individuals who served with the Division. The 53rd Division was a "happy family"; intercourse between infantry and artillery, engineers, train and medical services was free, and friendships were wide. The effort of the campaign, the hardships of resisting extremes of heat and cold, the discomfort, even the misery, all were recompensed by the joviality and good cheer of fraternal meetings where troubles took flight. Simple pleasures noted in diaries—the arrival of bottles of beer, songs, the acquisition of some gastronomic rarity to mark a change in the daily diet—simple, but so sincere that regret can be expressed for the passing of those "good times." On leaving Gallipoli, Captain Ashton wrote, "in some ways I am sorry to go." So it is with the comradeship of war, an inexplicable, elusive, unreasonable regret when it is all over, but none the less strong.

And the Division took part in a successful campaign; Allenby's advance will serve as a model for all time. Two incidents only stand out when the soul of the Division was made bitter by disappointment—Gallipoli and the First Battle of Gaza. The Gallipoli controversy can never be settled so long as the Military Staff work on one side, and the Government adoption of half measures on the other require defence. But the quality of the troops should not be brought into the argument. Regulars, territorials, and new army troops all suffered alike from the evil fate that brooded over the Peninsula. The facts speak for themselves.

A division hurled piecemeal into a battle directed by nobody in particular has a right to feel itself aggrieved. But the failure of the enterprise does not so much concern the 53rd Division as the behaviour of the troops, whose gallantry and devotion were beyond praise.

If any bitterness survives the First Battle of Gaza it is hoped that this record, embodying many previously hidden facts, may cause interest to take its place. It is a most interesting battle. The infantry and cavalry did their jobs well, beyond criticism, but we have here, for sober study, the difficulties of command.

The scorch of summer, the bitter, cutting wind of winter, the beauty and grimness of this strange country, the smells and flies, the dignified Bedouin, Polyglot Jerusalem, the astounding Valley of the Jordan; these are ineffaceable memories. Unceasing effort was demanded; toil, sweat, blood; there were hours of depression and hours, too, of strange content, for the whole philosophy of life is found in war, where fate is crude and moves with swifter steps than usual, but men live to regret the good times and happy fellowships. At home, some weep.

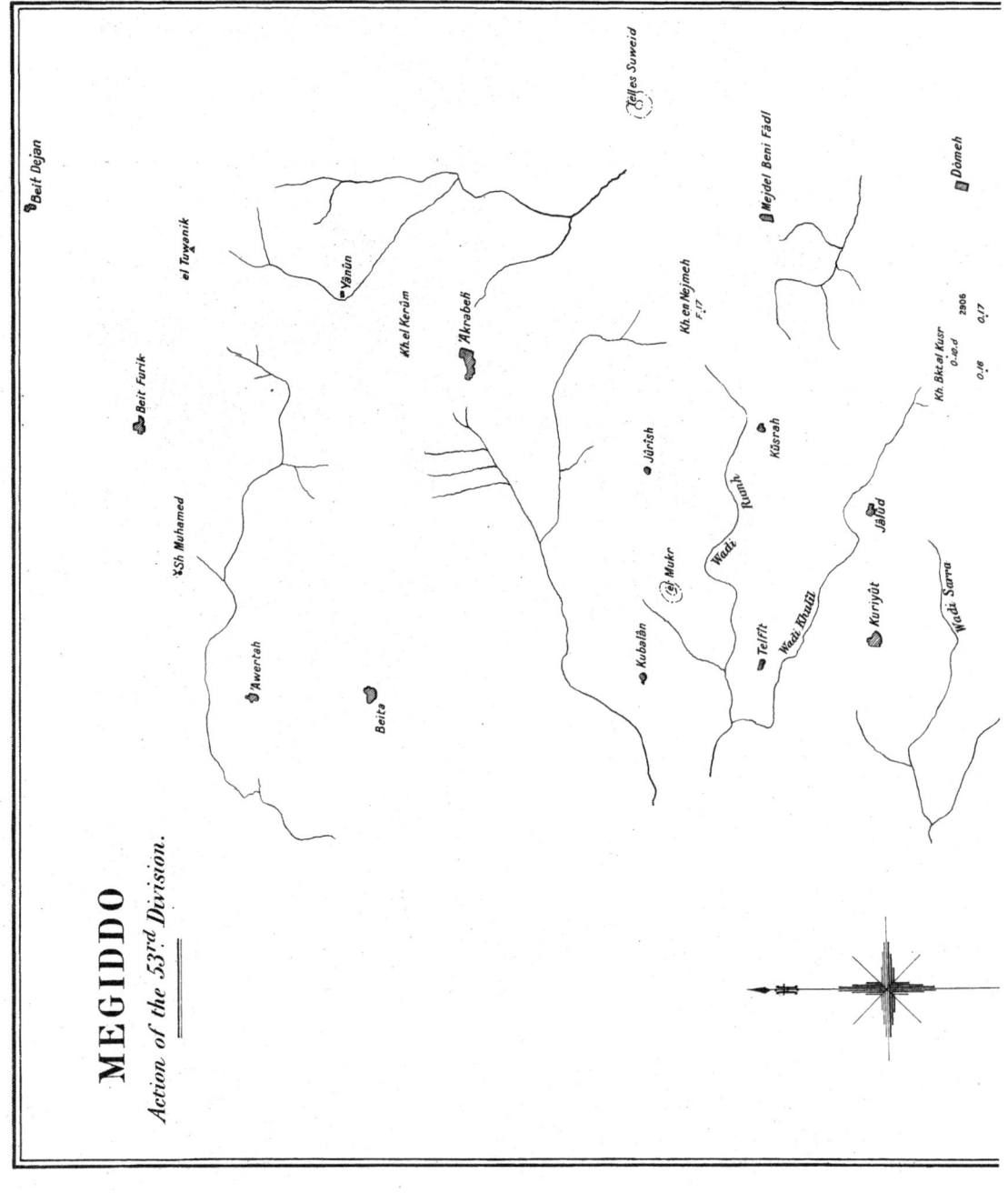

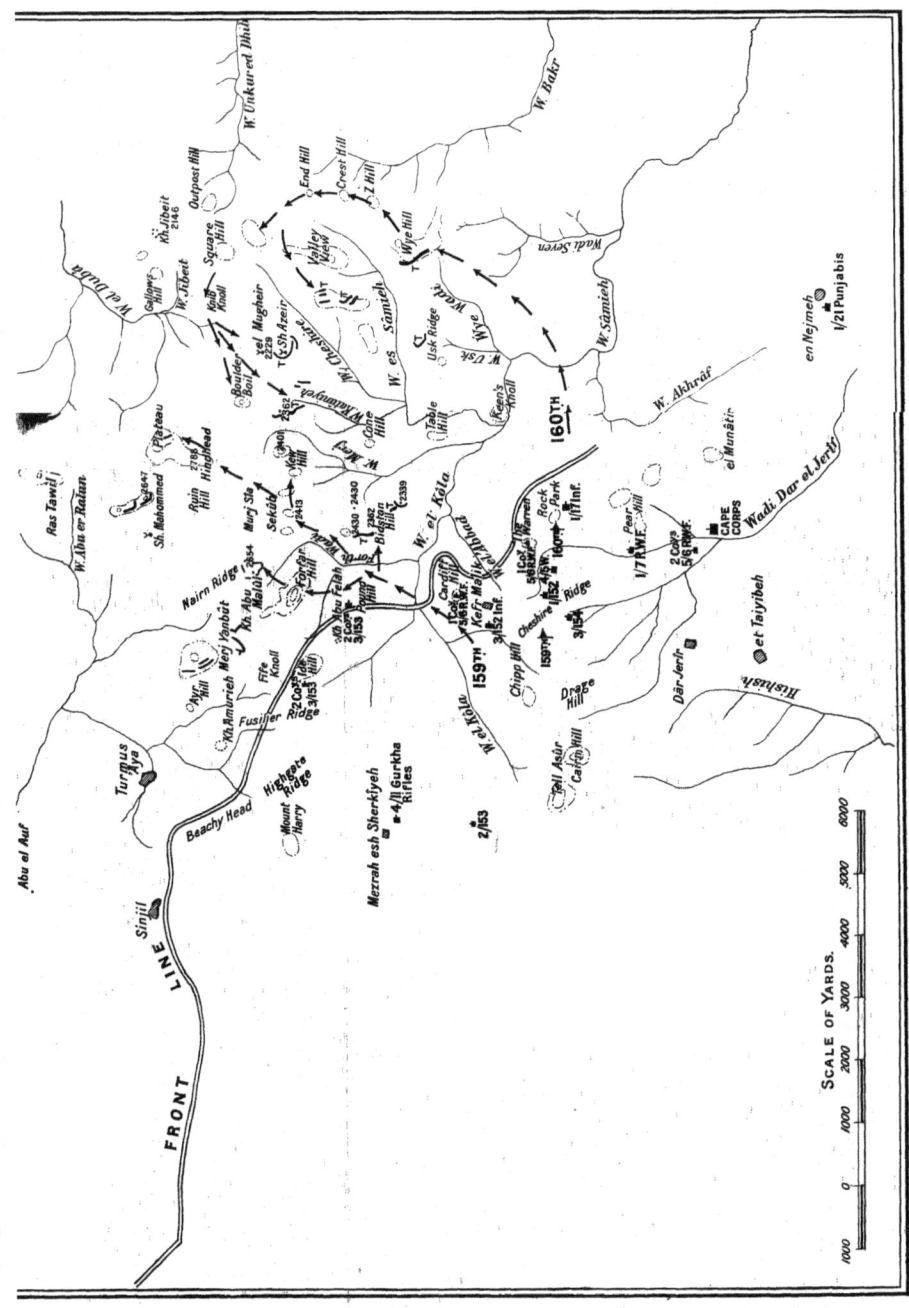

COMMANDING OFFICERS

5TH ROYAL WELCH FUSILIERS.

	Lt.-Col. B. S. Phillips.
13/ 8/15	Capt. F. H. Borthwick.
9/10/15	Lt.-Col. C. S. Rome.
28/ 1/16	Lt.-Col F. H. Borthwick.
23/ 9/16	Major W. Beswick.
7/11/16	Lt.-Col. F. H. Borthwick.
26/ 4/18	Major T. H. Parry (act. while C.O. Cmdg. Bde.)
1/ 8/18	Lt.-Col. F. H. Borthwick.

6TH ROYAL WELCH FUSILIERS.

	Lt.-Col. T. W. James.
9/10/15	Lt.-Col. C. S. Rome.
	Amalgamated.
17/ 7/16	Capt. F. Mills.
10/ 9/16	Lt.-Col. C. S. Rome.
5/ 4/17	Lt.-Col. F. Mills.
19/ 3/18	Lt.-Col. E. H. Evans.
	Amalgamated.

7TH ROYAL WELCH FUSILIERS.

	Lt.-Col. A. E. J. Reveley.
28/12/15	Capt. J. O. W. Williams.
8/ 3/15	Major T. H. Harker.
26/ 8/16	Major Owen Owen.
2/10/16	Lt.-Col. T. H. Harker.
24/ 6/17	Major Owen Owen.
7/ 8/17	Lt.-Col. T. H. Harker.

1ST HEREFORDS.

	Lt.-Col. G. Drage.
20/ 8/15	Lt.-Col. C. S. Rome.
29/ 8/15	Lt.-Col G. Drage.
29/ 6/16	Major A. L. B. Green.
14/ 9/16	Lt.-Col. G. Drage.
15/10/16	Major A. L. B. Green.
3/12/16	Lt.-Col. G. Drage.
26/ 3/18	Lt.-Col. E. M. Lawrence.
7/ 9/18	Major W. F. Chipp.
10/ 9/18	Lt.-Col. E. B. Powell.
15/ 9/18	Major W. F. Chipp.
25/ 9/18	Lt.-Col. Lyons.
29/ 9/18	Major W. F. Chipp.
17/10/18	Lt.-Col. Meldon.
27/10/18	Lt.-Col. E. H. Evans.

COMMANDING OFFICERS

4TH CHESHIRES.

	Lt.-Col. G. H. Swindells.
10/ 8/15	Major J. A. Pemberton.
/10/15	Lt.-Col. G. H. Swindells.
24/ 1/17	Major J. A. Pemberton.
2/ 2/17	Lt.-Col. G. H. Swindells.
9/ 5/17	Major E. W. Morris (while C.O. cmdg. Bde)
9/ 6/17	Lt.-Col. G. H. Swindells.
8/ 8/18	Major E. W. Morris.
27/ 8/18	Lt.-Col. F. de W. Harman.
4/ 9/18	Capt. Danson.
5/ 9/18	Major O. E. W. Morris.
28/ 9/18	Lt.-Col. G. Drage.

7TH CHESHIRES.

	Lt.-Col. H. Backhouse.
14/ 8/15	Major W. P. Reade (while C.O. cmdg. Bde.)
24/ 8/15	Lt.-Col. H. Backhouse.
20/11/15	Major W. P. Reade.
27/ 8/16	Major H. L. Moir.
14/10/16	Lt.-Col. H. M. Lawrence.
26/ 3/18	Lt.-Col. H. L. Moir.
6/10/18	Capt. C. D. Flunder.
6/11/18	Lt.-Col. H. L. Moir.

4TH WELCH REGIMENT.

	Lt-Col. W. Bramwell Jones
14/ 8/15	Maj. T. V. C. Thistlethwaite
8/10/15	Maj. H. H. W. Southey.
1/ 1/16	Capt. F. H. Linton.
13/ 2/16	Lt.-Col. H. H. W. Southey.
15/ 2/16	Lt.-Col. G. P. Pridham.
27/ 2/16	Capt. F. H. Linton.
18/10/16	Lt.-Col. H. J. Kinsman.
21/ 4/17	Major J. A. Pemberton.
27/ 6/17	Lt.-Col. H. J. Kinsman.
25/ 8/17	Major R. W. P. Evans.
29/ 8/17	Lt.-Col. J. M. Hulton.
4/11/17	Major J. A. Pemberton.
/12/17	Lt.-Col. J. M. Hulton.
21/ 1/18	Major R. W. P. Evans.
4/ 3/18	Major J. A. Pemberton.
7/ 4/18	Lt.-Col. J. M. Hulton.
26/ 6/18	Major J. W. Downes.
1/ 8/18	Lt.-Col. A. P. Hohler.

5TH WELCH REGIMENT.

	Lt.-Col. M. Morgan.
11/8/15	Maj. W. Dowdeswell.

} Amalgamated.

	Lt.-Col. G. P. Pridham.
24/12/16	Lt.-Col. H. L. Stephenson.
14/ 2/17	Major H. H. W. Southey.
12/ 3/17	Lt.-Col. H. R. Bowen.
29/ 3/17	Major J. A. Pemberton.
20/ 4/17	Lt.-Col. H. R. Bowen.

} Amalgamated.

COMMANDING OFFICERS

4TH SUSSEX.

	Lt.-Col. W. R. Compion.
5/10/15	Major S. W. Beale.
26/10/15	Major R. J. Few.
23/12/15	Lt.-Col. H. S. Ashworth.
23/ 6/17	Major S. W. Beale
14/ 4/17	Lt.-Col. T. M. Bridges.
5/ 6/18	Major G. S. Constable.
29/ 7/18	Capt. R. C. G. Middleton.
4/ 8/18	Lt.-Col. G. S. Constable.
14/ 8/18	Lt.-Col. W. R. Campion.

2/4TH QUEENS.

	Lt.-Col. F. D. Watney.
26/ 9/15	Capt. L. S. B. Hull.
4/10/15	Capt. J. G. McNaught.
21/10/15	Major S. W. Beale Amalgamated.
28/12/15	Lt.-Col. F. D. Watney.
5/ 2/16	Major R. J. Few.
1/ 3/16	Lt.-Col. F. D. Watney.
4/ 7/16	Major R. J. Few.
21/ 8/16	Lt.-Col. H. W. M. Watson.
3/12/16	Major R. J. Few.
23/ 1/17	Lt.-Col. H. St. C. Wilkins.
29/ 4/17	Major R. J. Few.
10/ 5/17	Lt.-Col. H. St. C. Wilkins.
3/11/17	Lt.-Col. S. D. Roper.
14/ 5/18	Maj. H. E. Stanley-Murray
19/ 5/18	Major P. Jude.
25/ 5/18	Lt.-Col. W. J. M. Hill.

2/4TH ROYAL WEST KENTS.

	Lt.-Col. A. T. Simpson.
16/ 8/15	Major H. Smithers.
8/10/15	Capt. F. Johnson.
20/10/15	Major. E. J. F. Vaughan.
21/12/15	Lt.-Col. A. T. Simpson.
5/ 3/16	Lt.-Col. A. E. Norton.
25/ 6/16	Capt. E. W. Dillon.
28/ 7/16	Lt.-Col. N. E. Money.
19/ 4/17	Major A. P. Hohler.
1/ 5/17	Lt.-Col. N. E. Money.
10/ 8/17	Capt. C. Hodgson.
3/ 9/17	Lt.-Col. N. E. Money.
28/10/17	Major P. Jude.
20/11/17	Lt.-Col. W. Beswick.

2/10TH MIDDLESEX.

	Lt.-Col. C. Pank.
24/ 7/16	Lt.-Col. V. L. N. Pearson.
3/ 5/17	Lt.-Col. A. P. Hohler.
12/17	Major W. A. Odling.
1/ 5/18	Lt.-Col. A. P. Hohler.

APPENDICES

APPENDIX I

Embarkation at Devonport.

		PERSONNEL		TRANSPORT		
		OFF.	O.R.	H.	4W.	2W.
14th July. *S.S. Caledonia*						
H.Q. 158th Inf. Bde		5	30	—	4	—
Section Signals						
5th R.W. Fusiliers		29	969	—	15	4
6th R.W. Fusiliers		29	969	—	15	4
Supply Details		8	38	—	4	—
Transport Details		4	20	—	—	—
Staff Officer (Divn.)		1	1	—	—	—
Officer Interpreters		4	—	—	—	—
		81	2,027	—	38	8
15th July. *S.S. City of Edinburgh*.						
Supply Details		—	5	8	—	—
K.K. Cable Section		1	35	30	4	—
7th R.W. Fusiliers		10	535	—	15	4
Clearing Station		—	5	9	—	—
		11	580	47	19	4
14th July. *S.S. Wiltshire*.						
Transport Divn. H.Q.		2	49	67	1	1
Divn. Sigs. (H.Q. & 1 Sect.)		3	124	83	12	1
„ Cyclist Coy.		8	195	2	1	—
S.A.A. Column		4	95	34	40	1
1/1st Welsh Field Amb.		6	13	10	—	—
H.Q. Divn. R.E.		3	11	9	1	1
158th Inf. Bde.*		1	37	55	—	—
159th Inf. Bde.*		1	37	55	10	—
160th Inf. Bde.*		1	37	55	—	—
3rd Welsh Fld. Amb.		10	197	10	17	7
Cheshire Fld. Coy. R.E.		—	3	4	—	—
Welsh Fld. Coy. R.E.		—	3	4	—	—
2nd Welsh Fld. Amb.		—	7	10	—	—
		39	808	398	82	11

* Bde. Transport and Bn. Pack Animals.

APPENDICES

		PERSONNEL		TRANSPORT		
		OFF.	O.R.	H.	4W.	2W.
16th July.	*S.S. Euripides.*					
	H.Q. Adv. Base	⎫				1
	H.Q. Intermediate	⎬ 33	74	—	—	motor
	H.Q. 2nd Adv. Base	⎭				
	1/1st Hereford Regt.	29	969	—	15	4
	1/4th Cheshire Regt.	29	969	—	15	4
	1st Welsh Fld. Amb.	3	183	—	17	7
		95	2,195	—	48	15
17th July.	*S.S. Huntsend (Lutzow).*					
	Divn. H.Q.	12	29	—	—	—
	H.Q. 159th Inf. Bde.	⎫ 5	30	—	2	—
	Signal Section	⎭				
	7th Cheshire Regt.	29	969	—	11	4
	4th Welch Regt.	29	969	—	11	4
	7th R.W. Fusiliers	13	200	—	—	—
		89	2,197	—	24	8
17th July.	*S.S. Ulysses.*					
	7th R.W. Fusiliers	6	234	—	—	—
	4th Royal Sussex	29	969	—	3	4
	2/4th R. West Surrey	29	969	—	3	4
	H.Q. 160th Inf. Bde. (Signal Section)	5	30	—	4	—
	Rev. S. H. Campion	1	—	—	—	
		70	2,202	—	10	8
18th July.	*S.S. Huntsgreen.*					
	5th Welch Regt.	29	969	—	15	4
	2/10th Middlesex	29	969	—	15	4
	2/1st Cheshire Fld. Coy.	6	173	—	9	8
	C.C.S.	8	73	—	—	—
	Divn. Sanitary Sect.	1	25	—	1	—
	Inf. Base Depot	3	9	1	—	—
	Nurses, No. 3 Australian General Hospital	50	—	—	—	—
		126	2,218	1	40	17

		PERSONNEL		TRANSPORT		
		OFF.	O.R.	H.	4W.	2W.
19th July. *S.S. Northland.*						
2/4th R. West Kents	..	29	969	—	3	4
1st Welsh Fld. Amb.	..	6	173	—	3	9
2nd Welsh Fld. Amb.	..	10	190	—	17	7
		45	1,332	—	29	20

APPENDIX II

BRECKNOCK BATTALION SOUTH WALES BORDERERS

Went to India with the 43rd Division in October, 1914, arriving the 3rd December. They were then sent back to Aden, arriving on the 12th December, 1914. They left Aden again for India on the 5th August, 1915, and were attached to the 5th Indian (Mhow) Division.

6TH BATTALION CHESHIRE REGIMENT

Went to France in November, 1914, and were posted to the 15th Brigade, 5th Division on 17th December, 1914. They became G.H.Q. troops on the 1st March, 1915. Joined the 20th Brigade, 7th Division, on the 9th January, 1916. They were transferred to the 118th Brigade, 39th Division, in March, 1916. Transferred to the 75th Brigade, 25th Division, on the 28th May, 1918, and absorbed the 11th battalion on the 14th June! Transferred in a composite brigade to the 50th Division on the 22nd June, 1918. Transferred to the 21st Brigade, 30th Division on the 7th July, 1918.

2ND BATTALION MONMOUTHSHIRE REGIMENT

Went to France in November, 1914. They were posted to the 12th Brigade, 4th Division, on the 20th November, 1914. They were amalgamated with the 1st and 3rd Battalions in the 84th Brigade, 28th Division, on the 27th May, 1915. They resumed independent formation and rejoined the 12th Brigade, 4th Division, on the 25th July, 1915. Transferred, with the Brigade, to the 36th Division on the 2nd November, 1915. The battalion was transferred to the Lines of communication on the 31st January, 1916, and to the 29th Division as Pioneers on the 1st May, 1916.

4TH ROYAL WELCH FUSILIERS

Went to France in December, 1914, and were posted to the 3rd Brigade, 1st Division, on the 7th December, 1914. Transferred to the 47th Division as Pioneers on the 1st September, 1915.

6th Welch Regiment

To France in December, 1914. On lines of communication till 5th July, 1915, then posted to 84th Brigade, 28th Division. Transferred to 3rd Brigade, 1st Division, 22nd October, 1915. Became Pioneers, in the same Division, on 15th May, 1916.

4th Battalion Shropshire Light Infantry

Went to India, December, 1914, with the 44th Division. Moved to Singapore (two companies to Hong Kong) in March, 1915. Brought back in June, 1917, arrived in France on 29th July, 1917. Joined 190th Brigade 63rd Division, 18th August, 1917. Transferred to 56th Brigade, 19th Division 3rd February, 1918.

5th Battalion Cheshire Regiment

Went to France in February, 1915. Posted to 14th Brigade, 5th Division, 19th February, 1915. Became a Pioneer battalion, 27th November, 1915. Transferred to 56th Division (1st London) 12th February, 1916, as Pioneer Battalion.

1st Battalion Monmouthshire Regiment

Went to France in February, 1915. Joined the V Corps 18th February, 1915. Posted to 84th Brigade, then with the 5th Division, 28th February, 1915. Transferred, with Brigade, to the 28th Division, 6th April, 1915. Amalgamated with the 2nd and 3rd Battalions 27th May, 1915, in same Brigade. Resumed separate formation 11th August, 1915. Transferred to 46th Division as Pioneers, 3rd September, 1915.

3rd Battalion Monmouthshire Regiment

Went to France in February, 1915, and joined V Corps, 18th February, 1915. Posted to 83rd Brigade, 5th Division, 28th February, 1915. Transferred, with Brigade, to 28th Division, 6th April, 1915. Amalgamated with 1st and 2nd Battalions, 27th March. 1915. Resumed independent formation 11th August, 1915, and rejoined 83rd Brigade. Transferred to 49th Division, as Pioneers, 2nd September, 1915. To G.H.Q. 9th August, 1916, to be drafted out.

APPENDIX III

Corps Order for the Capture of Jerusalem

XXth Corps Order No. 17

Advanced Headquarters, XXth Corps,
5th December, 1917.

Reference 1in. Map.

1. The XXth Corps pivotting on the NEBY SAMWIL and BEIT IZZA defences will attack the enemy south and west of Jerusalem and the Corps Commander intends :—

   (a) To secure the general line Point 2670 Kh. el TAWIL (Z.7)—NEBY SAMWIL.

   (b) To block the approaches to Jerusalem from Jericho.

2. The 53rd Division, less one Brigade group, with the Corps Cavalry Regiment attached will advance on December 6th from the Dilbeh area to the Bethlehem-Beit Jala area which must be reached on December 7th.

3. (i.) The attack of the XXth Corps will be carried out on December 8th by the 53rd Division, less one group, 60th Division and 74th Division (less one Brigade group) in the order named from right to left.

   (ii.) The 53rd Division will protect the right flank of the Corps operating under special instructions attached to this order.

   (iii.) The dividing line between the 60th and 74th Divisions will be the Enab-Jerusalem road as far as Lifta (village and road inclusive to the 60th Division) and thence the Wadi Beit Hannina as far as Y.15.d.6.6.

4. (i.) The attack will be divided into four stages and the tasks and objectives of the 60th and 74th Divisions in each stage are as follows :—

1st Stage.

The 60th Division will capture the enemy works between the railway in B.36 and the Enab-Jerusalem road in Y.25.

74th Division will capture the enemy works covering Beit Iksa between the Enab-Jerusalem road in Y.25 and the Wadi el Abbeideh (T.12d.).

The commencement of the advance of the 74th Division will be timed by that of the 60th Division, G.O.C. 60th Division to report to Corps Headquarters by 0800 on December 6th the hour at which his advance will begin.

2nd Stage.

The 60th Division will advance to the line of the Jerusalem-Lifta road on the approximate front H.11.c.4.5.-Lifta (inclusive).

3rd Stage.

The 60th Division will advance to the general line of the track which leaves the Jerusalem-Nablus road at H.5.d.9.6., and runs through Y.28 to Kh. Mekikah.

The 74th Division will advance to the spur which runs south-east from Neby Samwil and on which is marked the word " TOMBS " in Square Y.8.c. and Kh. Ras el Bad in Square Y.14b.

4th Stage.

The 60th Division will advance to a line astride the Jerusalem-Nablus road about Shafat and push forward thence to secure the high ground about Kh. Ras el Tawil.

The 74th Division will link up with the 60th Division occupying Beit Hannina if the ground is suitable for this purpose.

The G.O.'s C. 53rd Division and 60th Division will arrange to send out patrols to establish communication, and will arrange for co-operation between the 53rd group east of Jerusalem (vide instructions to G.O.C. 53rd Division) and the right flank of the 60th Division north of Jerusalem.

5. The 96th Heavy Artillery Group (less one 6in. Battery at Beit Likia) will be placed from 0900 on December the 7th under the command of the 60th Division, who will be responsible for its employment in consultation with the G.O.C. Royal Artillery, XXth Corps, who will be at 60th Division headquaretrs.

6. Orders for movements of trains and convoys will be issued by D.A. and Q.M.G. XXth Corps.

7. Reports to Advanced XXth Corps at LATRUN.

8. Acknowledge.

Issued at 10 a.m. to 53rd Division.

W. H. BARTHOLOMEW,
Brig.-General,
General Staff XXth Corps.

APPENDIX IV

Corps Orders for Advance from Jerusalem.

XXth Corps Order, No. 19. 20th December, 1917.

1. The Corps Commander intends to secure the general line : Burkah-Beitin-el Balua-Kh el Burj (U15.a)-Kh el Tireh-Pt. 2435 Abu el Ainein (P 16.c)-Deir Ibzia-Suffa.

This line will probably be advanced further at a subsequent date.

2. The 60th Division, reinforced if necessary by one infantry brigade of the 53rd Division, will form the " Right Attack," and will advance northwards along the Jerusalem-Nablus road with the object of seizing ground to secure the possession of Bireh and Ram Allah, while the " Left Attack " (10th and 74th Divisions, less two Infantry Brigades), under the command of G.O.C. 10th Division will advance in an easterly direction from the front Tireh-Suffa.

One Infantry Brigade 74th Division will hold the line from Beit Izza, inclusive, to Beit Ur et Tahta, exclusive.

One Infantry Brigade 74th Division will be in Corps Reserve.

53rd Division will form the right flank guard of the Corps.

3. The date of the advance of the " Left Attack " will be notified later, and will be known as Z day.

4. (i.) The 53rd Division with the Corps Cavalry Regiment attached will cover Jerusalem, and will protect the right flank of the Corps, by occupying suitable positions on the general line Anata-Hismeh-Jeba-Burkah, as the 60th Division advances.

The G.O.C. 60th Division will be responsible for the clearing of the Jerusalem-Nablus road for the passage of the 53rd Division troops detailed to occupy positions east of the road.

From 1400 hours on Z day, G.O.C. 60th Division may call on G.O.C. 53rd Division to place one infantry brigade at his disposal if required.

(ii.) The 60th Division will advance on the night Z-2/Z-1 to the line W.24 central-Kh Erayah-Pt. 2480 (W.27.d)-el Jib (inclusive) to cover the advance of the Divisional Artillery and batteries of the 96th Heavy Artillery group to positions from which fire can be brought to bear on the objectives of the " Left Attack." Artillery to be in position by dawn on Z day.

(iii.) On Z day the 10th Division and 74th Division, less two infantry brigades (Left Attack), under the command of Major-General Longley, C.B., commanding 10th Division, will attack Kh Bir esh Shafa-Sh. Abu es Zeitan ridge and the enemy between the Wadi es Sunt and the Wadi Sad.

First Objective. Eastern end of Bir es Shafa-Sh. Abu es Zeitan ridge, overlooking Beitania, and thence through P.33, central to P.13.

Second Objective.—The General line P.39 central el Muntar (P.29)—high ground near Khurbet Rubin.

In the event of the progress of the Left Attack being sufficiently rapid to afford a reasonable prospect of the whole operation being completed on one day, the 60th Division will be called upon to resume its advance at the shortest notice, but, in order to ensure co-operation, no advance by the Left Attack to its second objective will be made without Corps orders.

(iv) The G.O.C. 74th Division will place two battalions from his brigade holding the line Beit Izza (inclusive)—Beit Ur et Tahta (exclusive) at the disposal G.O.C. Left Attack, at an hour on Z day to be arranged direct between G.Os.C.

The remaining brigade of the 74th Division which will be in Corps Reserve will assemble in the Beit Izza-Kubeibeh area by dawn on Z day, and will be prepared, on receipt of orders from Headquarters, to operate northwards towards Kh et Tireh should it be necessary.

5. ARTILLERY.—The 96th Heavy Artillery Group (less one section 60 pdrs.,) attached 53rd Division, will be distributed by dawn on Z day as follows :—

Two 6in. Howitzer Batteries, and one 60 pdr. Battery on the Jerusalem-Nablus road.

One 60 pdr. Battery Kh. el Burj.

One 6in. Battery near Beit Ur et Tahta.

The Group will be employed primarily in neutralising the enemy artillery, but may be called upon by G.Os.C. divisions to provide direct support to the infantry, when guns can be spared for this task.

Etc., etc. (Supply).

REFERENCE XXTH CORPS ORDER NO. 19.

1. (i) In order to broaden the front of the attack, the brigade of the 74th Division hitherto earmarked as Corps Reserve is placed at the disposal

of G.O.C. 74th Division, who will advance his line to the general line Pt. 2462 (R24.c)—R.22.d at the same time as the 60th Division advances to the line W24 central—Kh. Erayah-Pt. 2480 (W27.d)—el Jib (inclusive) via para. 4 (ii) of XXth Corps Order No. 19.

G.O.C. 60th Division will determine the hour at which this advance is to take place, and will inform G.O.C. 74th Division, repeating the message to XXth Corps headquarters.

(ii) When the advance northwards is resumed by the 60th Division from the line W24 central—Kh Erayah—Pt. 2480 (W27.d)—el Jib, G.O.C. 74th Division will co-operate with the object of filling the gap between the left of the 60th Division and the right of the Left Attack.

Dividing line between the 60th Division and 74th Division el Jib—Rafat—Ram Allah, all inclusive to the 60th Division.

(iii) The Brigade 74th Division holding the line Beit Izza (inclusive)—Beit Ur et Tahta (exclusive), less two battalions placed at the disposal G.O.C. Left Attack, will form the Corps Reserve as soon as they can be safely withdrawn from the line, and will concentrate near Beit Izza.

2. In the event of the enemy attacking the 60th Division before its preliminary advance is made, vida para. 4 (ii) of XXth Corps Order No. 19 as appears possible, the advance planned for Z day by the Left Attack will take place at the earliest possible moment that can be arranged by the G.O.C. Left Attack, with the object of securing his objectives while the enemy is occupied with the attack on the 60th Division.

In this case G.O.C. Left Attack will give Corps Headquarters as early notice as possible of the time he will be ready to attack.

W. H. BARTHOLOMEW, Brig.-Gen.,
General Staff XXth Corps.

Headquarters, XXth Corps.
24th December, 1917.

APPENDIX V

Division Order for Advance on Jericho.

18th February, 1918.

53RD DIVISION OPERATION ORDER No. 17.

1. INFORMATION.—(a) The Corps Commander intends to drive the enemy from his position covering Jericho from the west, to occupy the town

temporarily, and clear the valley west of the Jordan of the enemy as far as the Wadi el Aujah.

The attack will be made by the Anzac Mounted Division (less artillery and one brigade), 60th Division, reinforced by one brigade of the 74th Division, and the 53rd Division.

The attack will be divided into two stages, of which the first will take place on the 19th February. The tasks and objectives are as below:—

First Stage—(b) On the 19th February the 60th Division, to which will be attached temporarily one regiment of the Anzac Mounted Division, will occupy the line el Muntar-Ras Umm Deisis-Arak Ibrahim-Ras el Tawil-high ground in C.2.d.

The 53rd Division line will be extended eastwards to include the high ground in V.6 and the Kh.W. el Asas-Kh. el Murabar ridge, half a mile west of Rummum.

El Muntar must be occupied before 0600 on the 19th February by the 60th Division, the remaining objectives being occupied as early as possible in the day by the 60th Division.

Second Stage—(c) i. As early as possible on the 20th February. The 60th Division will continue its advance in three columns from the line el Muntar-Ras Umm Deisis-Ras el Tawil.

Right column from el Muntar, objective Jebel Ekteif.

Centre column astride the Jerusalem-Jericho road, objective Talat ed Dumm.

Left Column from Ras el Tawil.

All three columns will advance further eastwards, beyond the objectives allotted, towards the Jordan Valley as soon as the G.O.C. 60th Division considers they are in a position to do so, so that they can co-operate with the Mounted Brigade which will advance from the south on Jericho to drive the enemy east of the Jordan, or northwards along the Jericho-Beisan road.

The infantry advance will not be continued further east than the general line Rijm Esk Shemaliyeh-Kh. Kakum, unless it is necessary to enable the Anzac Mounted Brigade to complete its task, and then only with the sanction of the G.O.C. XXth Corps.

II. The 53rd Division will swing forward its right flank in a northerly direction, to positions from which the use of the road and track leading from Taiyibeh towards Jericho can be denied to the enemy. Advance to begin as early as possible before 0600 hours. No advance east to the

Wadi el Asa will be made without the sanction of the Corps Headquarters.

III. The troops of the Anzac Mounted Division, operating under special instructions, will advance before daylight from the el Muntar area by tracks east of the line el Muntar-Jebel Ekteif into the Jordan Valley to threaten the enemy's retreat, afterwards occupying the general line bridge at El Ghoraniyeh-crossing over the Wadi el Aujah on the Beisan road angle on the Roman road (113 B.10.d.).

The 53rd Division will carry out the rôle allotted to it in para. 1 as follows :—

First Stage—(*a*) the 181st Brigade, 60th Division, will be advancing so as to occupy Splash Hill (C.2 central) by dawn on the 19th February. From this position their attack will be carried out on Ras el Tawil under cover of a bombardment which will commence at dawn.

The 160th Infantry Brigade will advance their outpost line during the night 18/19th February, so as to secure the northern approaches to the high ground V.5 and 6, and Rummon village, before dawn (special attention being paid to the Wadi at A.19 central), and will occupy the high ground V.5 and 6 and Rummon Village before dawn (as or soon after as possible) on the 19th February in accordance with the scheme of the 160th Brigade Commander, already approved. The 160th Brigade Commander will arrange with the G.O.C. 159th Brigade for machine gun co-operation from Kh. el Alla. As much information as possible as regards crossings in the Wadi Asa will be obtained during this operation.

(*b*) ARTILLERY SUPPORT.—The 160th Artillery Group, under Lieut.-Colonel T. H. Walker, will support the 160th Brigade during these operations. This group will consist of the following : A/265, C/265, C/266. Support from the Heavy Artillery can be obtained from the Heavy Artillery Liaison Officer attached to the 160th Brigade headquarters.

(*c*) ROYAL ENGINEERS.—Three Sections 436 Field Company R.E. are placed at the disposal 160th Brigade Commander.

3. Para. 1 of these Operation Orders is not to be communicated in writing.

4. Information as regards the enemy is attached as an appendix.

5. Orders for the second stage will be issued at a later date.

6. Aeroplane flares will be carried, and ground sheets put out at Advanced Divisional Headquarters and all Brigade Headquarters.

7. Advanced Divisional Headquarters will be at Grey Hill, immediately west of et Tell.

8. Acknowledge.

APPENDIX VI

Division Order for Tell Asur.

53RD DIVISION OPERATION ORDER No. 22.

8th March, 1918.

1. It is the intention of the Corps Commander that the XXth Corps will advance to the line Mugheir-Sinjil-Jiljilia-Abwein road.

The advance will commence on the 9th March, and the following objectives are allotted to Divisions on the first day :—

181st Brigade, 60th Division	Kh. el Beiyudat-Ab Tellul.
53rd Division (with 1st A.L.H. Brigade attached).	Kh. Abu Felah-Mezrah esh Sherkiyeh (exclusive).
74th Division	Mezrah esh Sherkiyeh (inclusive). High ground in K.12.
10th Division	Neby Saleh-high ground in D.7 and 8.

2. The first objectives of the 53rd Division will be S.16.a-S.
3. c-L.30.c and Tell Asur.

Every endeavour will be made to reach these objectives by dawn.

3. (*a*) The 159th Brigade will direct the two battalions, now in the vicinity of Nejmeh and Lilia, to seize the high ground in S.16.a. and S.8.c, and one battalion, now in Taiyibeh area, to advance simultaneously with the 158th Brigade to clear Dar Jerir, cross the wadi and work up the spur in a north-west direction, and gain the high ground in L.36.c, retaining the remaining battalion in Brigade Reserve.

(*b*) The 158th Brigade will advance on to the high ground in L.30.c and L.35.c on a two battalion front, keeping west of the Wadi Dar Jerir and east of a north and south line through the Cairn in L.35.c. Tell Asur will be occupied by the 158th Brigade as soon as possible after the arrival on this line, and communication established with the right brigade of the 74th Division.

The 159th Brigade will arrange to co-ordinate their advance with that of the 158th Brigade.

(*c*) One battalion 160th Brigade, at present holding the line between the left of the 158th Brigade and the right of the 74th Division, will conform to the advance of the 158th Brigade as far as the track running east and west through N. 2, 3 and 4, the remainder of the Brigade will be in Divisional Reserve, and will be employed in making a road from Beitin to Tell Asur as soon as the situation permits.

4. ARTILLERY.

(a) *Divisional Artillery.*—The 265th Brigade R.F.A. and the 10th Mountain Battery will support the advance of the 159th Brigade.

The 266th, 267th, and 301st Brigades R.F.A. will support the advance of the 158th Brigade.

Whilst being in direct support of respective infantry Brigades, all artillery brigades will remain under control of C.R.A., so that the fire of all batteries can be brought to bear, as far as possible, on the front of either brigade.

(b) *Heavy Artillery.*—383rd Siege Battery R.G.A. (M.30.c, 8.3) and 1 Section 91st Heavy Battery R.G.A. (V.14.d. 6.9) will be in support of the 53rd Division. These batteries will each have a F.O.O., who will push forward with the attack as fast and as far as his communications with his guns permit. These F.O.O.'s will keep the Infantry constantly informed of the position of their O.P.'s, so that local Infantry Commanders can apply direct to a Heavy Artillery F.O.O. for the fire of the battery under his control.

5. As soon as the first objective is gained, the 158th and 159th Brigades will push forward Advance Guards towards the line Kh. Abu Felah-Mezrah Esh Sherkiyeh, dividing line between Brigades L.30 central to Kh. Abu Felah, inclusive, to the 158th Brigade. The dividing line between the 158th Brigade and the 74th Division will be a line drawn from N. 14 central to Mezrah esh Sherkiyeh, inclusive, to the 74th Division.

6. MOUNTED TROOPS.—The 1st A.L.H. Brigade, less one regiment, will remain in bivouac at Beitin until such time as the situation permits of its marching north towards Tell Asur.

One Regiment of this Brigade will march from Beitania on the 8th instant, so as to arrive at Rummon before dark, where it will bivouac for the night.

This Regiment will be ready at dawn on the 9th instant, to proceed via the Dar Jerir crossing over the Wadi Dar Jerir and relieve the Infantry garrison at Nejmeh. It will also follow up the advance of the 159th Brigade, paying particular attention to the protection of the right flank of this Brigade, and will in addition send out patrols to gain contact with the mounted troops of the 60th Division operating on the Aujah, and secure the water in the Wadi Aujah in the neighbourhood of Nejmeh.

7. ROYAL ENGINEERS.—Two sections 437th Field Company R.E. are placed under the orders of the B.G.C. 159th Brigade.

Lieut. John for roads.

Lieut. Walters for water.

Two Sections 439th Field Company R.E. are placed under the orders of the B.G.C. 159th Brigade.

Lieut. Davies for roads.

2/Lieut. Sutton for water.

Four Sections R.E. will be held in reserve under C.R.E. for special road work, and to assist the 160th Brigade.

8. AEROPLANES.—Contact aeroplanes will fly over the battle area at 0900 on the 9th March; after that hour only when asked for by Divisions.

Troops will carry flares, to be lit by the foremost unit when called for.

The signal for calling for flares will be a series of A's on the Klaxon horn, or white Very Lights. Troops will answer either or both signals.

9. Watches will be synchronised at 0600 daily until further orders.

10. Orders as regards medical arrangements, roads, water, and supply will be issued separately.

11. P. OF W. COLLECTING STATION.—

(a) For first objective A.P.M. will open an advanced station at Taiyibeh, brigades providing guards as needed.

(b) Advanced station for second objective will be notified later.

(c) Main collecting station will remain at Divisional Headquarters (U.12.a).

12. Divisional Battle Headquarters will open on Rummon Hill (V.5.b) at 1800 on the 8th instant.

13. Acknowledge.

Issued at 0600.

APPENDIX VII

Instructions for April Offensive XXIst Corps.

1. The 159th Infantry Brigade Group is co-operating in the forthcoming operations of the XXIst Corps.

2. The XXIst Corps final objective is the line : Kh. el Fakhakhir-Bidieh-Azzun-Jiyus-Kh. Ibreikih-Miskeh-mouth of the Nahr el Falik.

A preliminary objective is the capture of as many enemy and guns as possible in the main Turkish defensive system of Tabsor, which lies west of the Turkish railway.

3. The advance of the XXIst Corps is being made by the 75th Division, on the right, the 54th Division in the centre, and the 7th Division on the left, assisted by a Cavalry Division whose rôle is to cut off the retreat of the enemy from the Tabsor system, or in the event of their having retired early, to carry out an energetic pursuit as far as the Tul Keram line.

4. The 159th Brigade Group will assist in these operations by protecting the right flank of the Corps. The Brigade Group will be working in close co-operation with the 75th Division and with the Brigades of that Division, but will be working directly under XXIst Corps.

5. That part of the operation undertaken by the 75th Division in which the Brigade is chiefly concerned is to be carried out in three stages :—

(a) The advance of their line to Berukin-Kh. Fakhakhir-Sheikh Subi and Arara.

(b) The advance of the line to Bidieh-M.5 central.

(c) The final advance of the line to Azzun-Kh. el Khareijeh.

The first stage of these operations takes place on the 9th April. The 10th Division are co-operating—the 29th Infantry Brigade advancing their left to the hill in A.16d.

The dates on which the stages (b) and (c) will take place will be communicated later.

6. On the night 10/11th April, the 159th Brigade Group takes over that part of the line held by the 232nd Infantry Brigade, viz., Berukin-Kh. Fakhakhir-Wadi Lehham in approximately S.25.b.

It is the intention of the G.O.C. to hold this line with two battalions—the 4th Welch Regiment on the right, and the 5th Welch Regiment on the left, supported by approximately two sections M.G.'s and the 265th Brigade R.F.A.

Orders for the relief of the 232nd Brigade on the night 10/11th will follow, but the O's.C. 4th and 5th Welch Regiments, and the 159th Coy., M.G.C. should take the earliest opportunity of going forward and econnoitring the line of the 232nd Infantry Brigade.

The 159th L.T.M. Battery will be prepared to take up positions in the line as required. There will be no T.M. Battery with the 232nd Brigade.

Brigade Headquarters will, at this stage, move to the neighbourhood of El Kefr.

7. Until the first objective of the 75th Division has been taken, it is, of course, impossible definitely to lay down the subsequent action of the Brigade Group.

It is hoped that the 10th Division will take over Berukin.

If this is done, the 4th Welch will come into reserve about Sheikh Subi, and the 5th Welch Regiment will then become responsible for the right rear of the Brigade Group.

After the 75th Division have secured the Bidieh line, which will include the taking of the important height of Sheikh Abdulla, both these places will be taken over by the 159th Brigade Group. The 4th Cheshire Regiment will probably become responsible for the defence of both these places, with the 7th Cheshire Regiment in support of them, while Brigade headquarters will move to Mesha.

8. The action for the 159th Brigade Group for the third stage can even less definitely be laid down.

The northern boundary extends as far as Kefr Thilth inclusive, and the G.O.C. intends that the 7th Cheshire Regiment should follow up the right flank of the 75th Division, while the 4th Welch Regiment move up further north to the neighbourhood of Mesha, in order to be in reserve to the Brigade Group and somewhere about the centre of the Brigade Group line.

The 5th Welch Regiment's left will probably be extended to include Sheikh Abdulla, the 4th Cheshire's left to include Kh. es Sumrah or Senurieh inclusive, with the 7th Cheshire Regiment continuing the line to Kh. Kefr. Thilth inclusive.

9. The above proposals for the second and third stages are only tentative but will give a general idea of the intentions of the G.O.C.

When the final line of the Brigade Group has been firmly established, the G.O.C. will, if it is possible, withdraw one battalion, holding the front line lightly, with the two reserve battalions, continuing the defence in depth supported by M.G.'s.

10. The 265th Brigade R.F.A. will be prepared to occupy positions to cover the front of the Brigade Group in all stages. The O.C. 265th Brigade R.F.A. will work in the closest conjunction with the C.R.A., 75th Division, and will help that Division where possible.

In the third stage, viz.: when the final line has been secured, the artillery of the 75th Division is assisting the 159th Brigade Group as far as the Kefr Thilth flank is concerned.

11. The contents of this letter are to be treated as strictly confidential, and are issued purely for the information of Unit Commanders.

Acknowledge.

Issue—

4th Cheshire Regt.	265th Bde. R.F.A.
7th Cheshire Regt.	Sec., 437th Coy. R.E.
4th Welch Regt.	2nd Welsh Field Amb.
5th Welch Regt.	Staff Captain.
159th Coy. M.G.C.	O. i/c. Bde. Signals.
159th L.T.M. Batty.	

APPENDIX VIII

Orders for the Battles of Megiddo.

XXth Corps Operation Order No. 42.

13th September, 1918.

Ref. 1/40,000—1/63,360 Maps.

1. On Z day, the date of which will be notified later, the Army will take the offensive. The object is to inflict a decisive defeat on the enemy, and to advance to the general line of the high ground Mesharik Nablus-Yasid (098.L.9)-Sh. Beiazid (098.K.9)-Attara-Jebel Bir Asur (098.B.25)-Belah (098.A.22)-Yemma (083.N.26).

2. (*a*) The main attack will be made by the XXIst Corps with five divisions against the enemy's right, between the foothills east of the railway and the sea. This attack will commence on Z day at an hour that will be known as "XXIst Corps Zero hour."

(b) As soon as the crossings over the Nahr Falik are cleared of the enemy by the advance of the XXIst Corps, the Desert Mounted Corps, passing round the left of the XXIst Corps, will be directed on El Afule and Beisan with the object of cutting the enemy's railway communications and blocking his retreat in a north and north-easterly direction.

(c) As soon as the XXIst Corps has gained the general line Three Bushes Hill (C.4/N.25)-high ground (C.3/K.14)-Foothills east of Kalkilieh-North-eastern edge of Et Tireh (D.3/Y.13)-North bank of the Nahr Falik, it will move north-eastwards and advance to seize the high ground east of the railway between Deir Sheraf and Attara.

One Division and a Cavalry Brigade will advance via Tul Keram on Attara; while two other divisions will advance up the El Funduk road on Deir Sheraf, and by Felamieh-Beit Lid on Messudieh, respectively.

The right division of the XXIst Corps (54th Division) will not advance further east than an approximate north and south line through Bidieh, unless required to assist the XXth Corps.

(d) "Chaytor's Force" will hold the present front in the Jordan Valley, and may be required later to advance as far as Jisr ed Damie.

3. The XXth Corps will attack astride the Nablus road to gain possession of a line south of Nablus, from which it will be in a position to co-operate with the XXIst Corps, and to advance to the high ground north and north-east of Nablus.

The date and hour of the advance of the XXth Corps will depend upon the progress of the main attack and the action of the enemy. The Corps will be prepared to advance by 1800 hours on Z-1 day.

4. The advance of the XXth Corps will take the form of a converging attack from the two outer flanks directed on the general line Akrabeh-Jemmain-Kefr Harris. The centre of the enemy's line from Norfolk Hill to the Wadi er Rumh, will not be attacked at all.

From the Akrabeh-Jemmain-Kefr Harris line the advance will be continued, so as to reach as early as possible the line Akrabeh-Awertah-Sh. Selman el Farsi, and any other positions which it is found desirable to seize prior to an advance against the high ground about Nablus.

5. The 10th and 53rd Divisions will, therefore, be concentrated as under, the centre of the present Corps front being taken over by a mixed force under the command of Lieut.-Colonel S. Watson, 1/155th Pioneers, to be known as "Watson's Force."

53rd Division.—To be concentrated east of the Nablus road in the approximate area Nejmeh-Kh Abu Felah-Mezrah esh Sherikiyeh-Dar Jerir before dawn on Z-1 day.

10th Division.—To be concentrated in the approximate area Neby Saleh-Kefr Ain-Berukin-el Kefr (less detachments left temporarily between Arura and Kefr Ain, and between el Kefr and Rafat) before dawn on Z-1 day.

6. On the night Z-1/Z the 53rd Division will bring up its right flank, and seize the general line Square Hill (P.31.c)-Hindhead-Nairn Ridge preparatory to a general advance.

7. When the order for the general advance is given, " Watson's Force " will remain in position, while the 10th and 53rd Divisions advance to the following objectives :

53rd Division—

1st Objective—The line Domeh-Pt. 2908 (O.17.b)-Ras et Tawil, the left being extended to secure the works in O.13 and J.18 if found necessary.

2nd Objective—Mejdel Beni Fadl-Kusrah-Sh. Hatim.

3rd Objective—The high ground south of Akrabeh-Kubalan.

4th Objective—The high ground north of Akrabeh-Awertah.

The 53rd Division will be prepared to picquet the roads leading from the valley into its right flank, between el Mughheir and Mejdel Beni Fadl; and, if necessary, to push detachments, with artillery, eastwards down these roads, to assist the forward movement of a portion of " Chaytor's Force," should this latter receive order to advance.

10th Division—

1st Objective—The general line of the Furkhah defences in B.6.c-Kh. esh Shellal-high ground in T.13.

2nd Objective—The high ground Sh Abu Zarad-Merda-Kefr Harris-Harris.

3rd Objective—High ground south of Kusah-et Tarud-Mazar Abd el Hakk-Alim el Hada.

4th Objective—The Sh. Selman el Farsi ridge, throwing out a defensive flank to the north-west as may be found necessary.

The 10th Division will establish touch with the division of the XXIst Corps advancing up the El Funduk road on its left as early as possible.

8. It is of great importance that the actions of both divisions should secure the road junction in Z.14 early in the advance, and thus shorten their lines of supply.

9. The 53rd and 10th Divisions will establish Battle Headquarters at, or near, Jalus and Selfit respectively as soon as the situation permits.

10. Paragraphs 1, 2 and 3 of these orders are not to appear in any written orders; and only such portions of them will be communicated verbally to Brigade Commanders as is essential for the performance of their tasks. Brigade and Regimental Orders will define only their own objectives and those of the units in immediate touch with them, and will give no indication of the general Corps Plan.

No written orders of any description are to be taken into action; officers will mark immediate objectives only on their maps, inconspicuously.

11. The Artillery Plan, Administrative Instructions, and Instructions on Signals, Co-operation with R.A.F., and for " Watson's Force " are being issued separately.

12. Advance Corps Battle Headquarters will be established at Ram Allah on Z day.

13. Acknowledge.

Issued at 12.30.

A. P. WAVELL, Brigadier-General,
General Staff, XXth Corps.

53RD DIVISION OPERATION ORDER No. 40.

15th September, 1918.

Ref. 1/40,000 Map.

1. The Division will concentrate on the nights 15/16th, 16/17th, 17/18th, in accordance with march table attached.

2. All moves will take place between the hours of 1845 and 0400.

3. It is of the utmost importance to conceal this concentration, and the following precautions will be strictly observed.

(a) All marches will be made at night, after 1845 hours, and troops must reach bivouacs by 0400 hours.

(b) No tents will be erected, and bivouacs must be hidden. Troops must be concealed from hostile aircraft, and will be confined to their bivouac areas throughout the day.

(c) Orders for daily moves will be issued at the last possible moment.

(d) Arrangements and orders connected with moves are not to be mentioned in telegrams, and all correspondence on the subject, which should be reduced to a minimum, will be conducted by D.R.L.S.

4. On completion of relief in No. 2 Sector, of troops of 159th Infantry Brigade, the command of No. 2 Sector will pass to Lieut.-Colonel Dundas, 4/11th Gurkha Rifles.

No. 4 Sub-sector will pass from his command to that of Lieut.-Colonel Watson after the completion of reliefs by " Watson's Force " on 16/17th instant.

5. On completion of reliefs in No. 1 Sector, by troops of the 158th Infantry Brigade, the command of this Sector (Rock Park, etc.) will pass to B.G.C. 159th Infantry Brigade. The B.G.C. 160th Infantry Brigade will retain command of Rock Park, and the Nejmeh garrison will pass under his orders at 0800, 17th inst.

6. On the 17/18th the C.R.A. will arrange to control the traffic on the Strand road from 1900 onwards. D/A.P.M. 53rd Division will give him the necessary assistance.

7. On the 18/19th the B.G.C. 159th Infantry Brigade will arrange to control the traffic on the Strand road. The D/A.P.M. will give him the necessary assistance.

8. Completion of reliefs will be reported to this office.

9. Acknowledge.

53RD DIVISION ORDER No. 41.

16th September, 1918.

Ref. 1/40,000 Maps.

Jerusalem 2nd edition.

Damieh 2nd edition.

Telfit 4th edition.

NOTE.—The features in Q.4, c.3.0 and Q.9.b.6.6 will be known as Hill 2401 and Kew Hill respectively.

1. Information concerning the disposition of the enemy's forces in front of us has been issued separately to all concerned.

2. On a night to be known as Z-1/Z night, the right of the 53rd Division will be advanced to the general line Square Hill (P.31.c)-Hindhead-Nairn Ridge.

3. As soon as it is dusk, the 160th Infantry Brigade (with one company of the 158th Bde. attached) will advance from the line Nejmeh-Rock Park to the general line Watershed separating the sources of the Wadis Bakr and Es Samieh-Square Hill-Boulder's Boil-Hill 2362.

4. The Wadi Samieh will be crossed about Q.35 central. The first objective will be the works in R.19.a. The assault on these works will be preceded by an Artillery bombardment. The hour for it to commence will be notified by the O.C. leading battalion, 160th Infantry Brigade, to the C.R.A. and will be known as Zero hour.

If all other means of communication fail, a light signal, consisting of Rifle Grenade No. 32 (green), will be fired. This will mean " Zero hour will be in ten minutes from now." The advance will be continued via the head of the Wadi Samieh and El Mugheir with the object of taking the enemy's main positions in reverse, after the first of them has been broken through.

Special arrangements will be made for picketting the right flank on the high ground overlooking the Wadi Bakr and Unkur el Dhib. Square Hill and the high ground in R.8 Central will be solidly held.

5. The Company 158th Brigade, attached to 160th Brigade will be employed in protecting the left flank of the advance as far as the point of crossing the Wadi Samieh (Q.35 Central). Its mission will be to seize Keen's Knoll, but only if the garrison of that work interferes with the operations in hand.

6. At an hour to be notified on the night Z-1/Z to the B.G.C. 159th Brigade by Divisional Headquarters (which will not be before Zero hour, or before 2130) the 159th Brigade will advance from about Round Hill to the general line Bidston Hill-Hill 2401 (Q.4.c)-Deir Abu Sekub-Kh Abu Malul-Nairn Ridge. Arrangements will also be made to mop up the Merj Wadi from Q.15, b.5.0 to Q.10 a.6.0.

7. In conjunction with the advance of the 159th Brigade, the battalion 158th Brigade holding No. 2 Sub-sector will seize Fife Knoll.

This operation will be conducted under the orders of Lieut.-Colonel Borthwick, D.S.O., who will relieve the B.G.C. 159th Brigade of direct responsibility for the command of No. 1 Sector on the 18th instant, at an hour to be fixed by the latter and reported to this office.

8. At the same time as the advance of the 159th Brigade commences, a detachment of the 158th Brigade, consisting of not more than three companies, will seize Turmus Aya. The opening of the bombardment in support of this operation will be synchronised with that on Bidston Hill.

A suitable position in the neighbourhood of Turmus Aya will be retained if practicable, with the object of inflicting loss on any Turks who should attempt, after dawn, to make their escape across Plumton Plain from the wooded country about Aya Hill and Turmus Top.

9. As soon as the 159th Brigade reaches the line Hill 2401-Deir Sekub, the battalion 158th Brigade (less two companies) holding the Warren and Cardiff Hill, will move to about Table Hill, where it will be in Divisional Reserve and available to support the 160th Brigade if necessary.

In the meanwhile it will mop up the Samieh Basin (exclusive)-Merj Wadi about Q.15.b.5.0.

It will be joined at Table Hill by the company protecting the left flank 160th Brigade, with whom it must get in touch.

10. As soon as Hill 2362 has been captured by the 160th Brigade, a light signal, consisting of Rifle Grenade No. 32 (red) will be fired from that hill.

Provided this signal is made before 0330 the 159th Brigade will thereupon advance its right and seize Hindhead, pushing forward detachments to the Plateau. Should the signal be made after 0330 the matter will be referred to Divisional Headquarters for decision whether the attack is to take place at once or not.

11. When the advance against Hindhead by the 159th Brigade commences, the 160th Brigade will co-operate by pushing forward detachments to the general line Kh. Jibeit-Hill in O.30.d.9.1-Hill in O.36.c.9.3.

The boundary between the two brigades will be a line joining Boulder's Boil (inclusive to 160th) and O.29 Central.

12. The artillery available to support the operations will be organised

in two groups under the orders of the C.R.A. and will consist of—

Right Group—18 pdrs.	..	18	*Left Group*—18 pdrs.	..	18
4.5 Howrs.		4	4.5 Howrs.		8
6in.	..	4	6in.	..	7
60 pdrs.	..	2	M.T.M.'s	.	10
2.7 Mount		4			

13. Both groups will support the 160th Brigade until Zero-60, when the guns of the left group will switch to support the advance of the 159th Brigade. The time required for the switch will be 25 minutes.

14. Artillery programmes have been worked out on time tables, which are continuous from their respective Zero hours until the completion of the operation (except the attack on Hindhead). They are divided into phases, corresponding with the infantry objectives. The intervals between phases, as at present arranged, can be varied on receipt of a signal message, provided time is allowed for communication to batteries; but no alteration can be made in any time table of any one phase, once it has commenced.

15. In order to guide the Infantry, single guns will fire at short and regular intervals on points which the B.G.C. 160th Brigade will notify the C.R.A. For this purpose smoke shell will be used on account of its distinct burst.

16. On completion of the task allotted to it in its present emplacement (*vide* para. 17 (*d*))—the 39th Mountain Battery will move forward. It will come under the orders of B.G.C. 160th Brigade, and will reach Valley View in time to get into position in that neighbourhood by daylight.

17. During the night Z-1/Z the following subsidiary objectives will be shelled :—

(*a*) Norfolk Hill—Abu Auf and El Burj systems by selected batteries Left Group : 2,000-2,100; Object to distract the Turks' attention from our right.

(*a*) Wadi bed near Keens Knoll; to drown sound of movement of the 160th Brigade, hour to be notified the C.R.A. by B.G.C. 160th Brigade.

(*c*) Selected points on Cheshire, Katunia and Merj Wadis; to cut off the retreat of Turks garrisoning positions at bottom of Samieh Basin.

(*d*) Selected points in R.25 to block the Wadi Severn.

(*e*) About R.14.b (Wadi Bakr) and Domeh crossing (P.19.a); to impede the movement of reinforcements.

The objectives mentioned in (*c*), (*d*) and (*e*) will not be shelled until after Zero hour.

18. *Machine Guns*—(a) The 160th M.G. Coy. will be attached to the 160th Brigade; (b) the 159th M.G. Coy. will be attached to the 159th Brigade; (c) the 158th M.G. Coy. will be disposed as follows :—

(1.) For supporting the 159th Brigade.
- 1 Section on Cardiff Hill.
- 1 Section on Round Hill.
- 1 Section on Ide Hill.

(2.) For supporting the 158th Brigade.
- 1 Section on Beachy Head;

and (d) the Cape Corps M.G. Coy. (two Sections) will be in Divisional Reserve.

19. On the night Z-1/Z, as soon as circumstances permit, the following works on roads will commence. All troops employed will work under the orders of the C.R.E.

(a) Morris Hill—Wadi Samieh; thence up the Wadi es Zawieh and Es Samieh.

Labour available—158th Pioneer Coy.
       159th   ,,   ,,
       160th   ,,   ,,
      1 Company Inf. 158th Brigade
       (attached 160th Brigade).

(b) Wadi Kola—Forth Wadi and Merj Sia.—

Labour available—72nd Coy. S. & M.
       53rd Cyclist Coy.
       1 Batt. 158th Brigade.

Both the above roads will be made fit for wheels and will be linked up with the Turkish system.

(c) Merj Wadi : fit for camels. To be commenced on Z day.

Labour available—Detachments from troops mentioned in (a), also working parties from Infantry battalion mentioned in Para. 9, if it is not required tactically.

20. It is important that the work on the Forth Wadi road should not be interfered with by the enemy. Should he do so from the direction of Merj el Yambut, the 159th Brigade will at once seize the works in L.6.b/ Q.1.a. The necessary dispositions with this object in view will be made provisionally beforehand.

21. The means of communication to be employed between Infantry brigades and H.Q. Divisional Artillery will be as follows, in the order of priority as stated :—

    (*a*) Telephone ;
    (*b*) Lamp ;
    (*c*) Light signals, to be used only as stated in paragraphs 4 and 10.

22. All ranks will be warned that the bayonet only is to be used, and that, whenever resistance is met with, the enemy must be rushed without hesitation.

23. Compass bearings of all objectives will be taken before hand, and the operation will be carried through according to programme in spite of mist or fog.

24. The line of furthest objective will be consolidated, all positions held in depth.

25. Advanced Division Headquarters will be established at L.35.d at 1800 on the night 17/18th September.

26. Brigade and regimental orders will define only their own objectives, and those of units immediately in touch with them.

27. No written orders of any description are to be taken into action ; officers will mark immediate objectives only on their maps, inconspicuously.

28. The Artillery plan is being issued by the C.R.A. direct to all concerned. Administrative instructions, and instructions for the disposal of prisoners, co-operation with the R.A.F. inter-communication, and miscellaneous subjects, are being issued separately.

29. Acknowledge.

53RD DIVISION ORDER NO. 42.   19th September, 1918.
    Ref. 1/40,000 Maps. Telfit 4th edition,
          Sidieh.

1. In view of the rapid successes already obtained by the XXIst Corps and Desert Mounted Corps, the advance of the 10th Division will be made to-night from about Furkah, with the object of reaching a line High ground south of Kusrah-Et Tarud-Mazar-Abd el Hakk-Alim el Hada.

2. The 53rd Division will advance early to-morrow morning to the line Domeh—Pt. 2906-Kh. Ekt el Kusr—Ras el Tawil, the left wing extended to secure the work in O.13 and J.18, if found necessary.

3. The advance will be continued during the day towards the line Mejdel-Beni Fadl-Kusrah-Sh Hatim, with the special object of blocking the Mejdel Beni Fadl U.13 road, which must be done, even if the whole of the second objective cannot be reached.

4. The advance will be continued beyond the above objectives to the general line High ground south of Akrabeh-Kubalan if the situation permits.

5. Indications already point to the probability of the enemy commencing a general retreat on our front. Once this begins, the Corps Commander relies on all commanders to press the advance relentlessly, regardless of man or horse. Troops should patrol boldly to-night to get early indications of any movement by the enemy, which will be reported priority.

6. During the early hours of the night the Turkish position of Mount Mahommed (O.27.c) and Kh. Malul will be captured by the two battalions of the 159th, which will then take up an outpost line facing west and north-west, covering the position won. The remainder of the 159th Brigade will concentrate during the night west of Ruin Hill.

7. At dusk the 5/6th Royal Welch Fusiliers, 158th Brigade, advanced to the general line Kulason-Plateau (both inclusive). The remainder of the 158th Brigade will concentrate in the neighbourhood of Hindhead, as soon as the Forth Wadi road is completed.

8. On arrival at Hindhead Brigadier-General Vernon will resume command of the whole of his Brigade.

9. On completion of the Wadi es Zawieh road (a) the company of the 5/6th Royal Welch Fusiliers employed on it will rejoin its own Brigade. (b) The 53rd Division Cyclist Company will come under the orders of the B.G.C. 160th Brigade. (c) Brigade Pioneer Companies will remain under the orders of the C.R.E., except the 160th Brigade Company, which reverts to its own Brigade.

10. The 39th Mountain Battery and the No. 4 Troop, C Squadron Queens Own Worcestershire Hussars will remain under the orders of the B.G.C. 160th Brigade.

11. Early in the morning of the 20th, at an hour to be notified to these Headquarters, the 158th Brigade will push out advance guards, with a view to occupying the line 2906-Kh. Bkt el Kusr.

12. The 159th Brigade will move echeloned behind on the left of the 158th Brigade to Ras el Tawil.

13. The 160th Brigade will leave picquets on the watershed of the Samieh Basin, blocking roads leading up from the Jordan Valley, until definite information is received that owing to the progress of Chaytor's Force they are no longer required. The remainder of the Brigade will be ready to move at short notice.

14. During the night 19/20th, the C.R.A. will move forward selected

batteries to support the Infantry advance. These will be attached to respective Infantry Brigades which will then become Brigade Groups.

15. The 53rd Machine Gun Battalion will be disposed in accordance with arrangements to be notified direct to Infantry Brigades by O.C. Machine Gun Battalion.

16. It will be the mission of the 159th Brigade to picquet the left of the advance of the Division by occupying in succession the line of Bluffs Sh Matim, El Mukr, Kubalan. It is of great importance that the action of both the 53rd and 10th Divisions should secure the road junction in Z.14 early in the advance, and thus shorten the lines of supply. The B.G.C. 160th Brigade will keep this object in view.

17. It may also be necessary to occupy Gebel Rakhwat, so as to obtain control of the Kuryut water supply.

18. The C.R.E. will carry out any work necessary to provide a wheeled track for the Division in the line of advance of the 158th Brigade.

19. Administrative and Medical instructions separately.

20. The O.C. Signals will open a Divisional Report Centre at Hindhead at 0800, and be prepared to move it forward as the advance progresses. Brigades will be linked up to the Advance Report Centre at night only.

21. Acknowledge.

APPENDIX IX

The Five Battalions in France.

The tremendous German onslaughts in France were being continued. At the end of April and early in May, 1918, they were hammering on the Aisne, and by the end of May had gained the north bank of the Marne, from Dormans to Chateau Thierry, and were advancing astride the Aisne to the outskirts of the Villers Cotterets Forest, and across the high ground north-east of Attichy. British Forces took part in this battle under the command of the French Fifth Army.

On the 7th June a fresh battle broke out on the French front, between Noyon and Montdidier.

At the beginning of July the belief was held at French headquarters that the Germans were about to attack in strength east and west of Rheims, and that the attack would probably spread to the Argonne and threaten a wide sector of the French position.

" Marshal Foch accordingly withdrew the whole of the French forces, some eight divisions, from Flanders, and transferred them southward to the French front. In addition he asked that four British divisions might be moved, two of them to areas south of the Somme and two to positions astride that river, so as to ensure the connection between the French and British Armies about Amiens, and to enable him to move four French Divisions farther east to his right flank. After carefully weighing the situation, I agreed to his proposal, and immediately orders were given for the movement.

"On the 13th July a further request was received from Marshal Foch that these four British Divisions might be placed unreservedly at his disposal, and that four other divisions might be dispatched to take their places behind the junction of the Allied Armies. This request was also agreed to, and the 15th, 34th, 51st, and 62nd British Divisions, constituting the XXIInd Corps, under the command of Lieut.-General Sir A. Godley, were accordingly sent down to the French front.

"Meanwhile, on the 15th July, the enemy had launched his expected attack east and southwest of Rheims, and, after making some progress at first and effecting the passage of the Marne, was held up by the French, American and Italian Forces on those fronts. On the 18th July, Marshal Foch launched the great counter-offensive which he had long been preparing on the front between Chateau Thierry and Soissons, supporting this successful stroke by vigorous attacks also on other parts of the German salient. In this fighting, the XXIInd Corps became involved." (Haig—Despatches.)

And with the XXIInd Corps our five battalions.

. . . . .

The five battalions arrived at the end of June in the neighbourhood of Proven. The 34th Division, reduced to a cadre and employed in training American troops, was to be reconstituted; the battalions were posted to this Division.

The Officer-Commanding was Major General C. L. Nicholson, and he formed the 101st Infantry Brigade, under Brigadier-General W. J. Woodcock, of the 2/4th Queens, 4th Royal Sussex, and the 2nd Loyal North Lancashire battalions; the 102nd Infantry Brigade under Brigadier-General E. Hilliam, of the 4th Cheshires, the 7th Cheshires, and the 1st Herefords; the 103rd Infantry Brigade, under Brigadier-General J. G. Chaplin, of the 5th Kings Own Scottish Borderers, the 8th Scottish Rifles, and the 5th Argyll and Sutherland Highlanders.

There was a short period of training, while the Division was held in XIth Corps reserve in the Proven-St. Jan ter Biesan area, and then, on the 15th, orders were received to entrain and proceed south the next day.

Trains ran via Pontoise to Chantilly and the stations south of it as far as Louvres. Detrainment commenced on the 18th, and the Division assembled round Senlis. Thence by bus to Largny, west of Villers Cotterets, and a night march, 20/21st, to Vivieres, north of the Foret Domaniale de Retz.

Actually the Division was in the XXth Corps (French) area, but General Nicholson was placed under the orders of the XXXth French Corps and ordered to relieve the 38th French Division, about Parcy-Tigny, on the night of the 22/23rd.

The 101st Infantry Brigade, then at Puiseaux, marched at 4 a.m. on the 22nd, and arrived at Villers-Helon at 6.30 a.m. The other two brigades marched about 9 a.m., and took up positions of readiness in the valley and wood north of Villers-Helon.

Relief was complete and the Divisional Artillery in position by 3 a.m. on the 23rd. Divisional headquarters were in a cave, close to the Ferme du Chavigny.

The 34th Division was now the left of the XXXth French Corps, with the 58th Division of the XXth French Corps on its left, and the 19th French Division on its right.

The situation in front of the two Corps was that the enemy held a line Buzancy-Villemontoire-Tigny-Coutremain-West edge of the Bois du Plessier-le Plessier-Huleu.

The plan was that the XXth Corps, by the capture of Tigny-Villemontoire and Taux, should turn the wood north of Hartennes en Taux. At the same time the right of the XXXth Corps would advance on the Orme du Grand Rozoy, and turn the Bois du Plessier and Bois de St. Jean.

The rôle of the 34th Division, and the French units on its immediate right and left, was to connect these two movements, one from the north and one from the south, and to advance due eastwards, to the high ground east of the Soissons-Chateau Thierry road, in the general direction of Launoy.

In addition to its own 152nd and 160th Field Artillery Brigades, the Division was covered by the 32nd and 41st Regiments of French Artillery and a heavy group of twelve 155 m.m. howitzers.

There was a special instruction which laid down how the actual order for attack was to be given: (a) by telephone, (b) by wireless, or power buzzer, (c) by rockets. Red rockets were to be sent up from the high ground near Villers Helon and at Blanzy, and if the rockets were sent off at 6.30 the hour of attack would be 6.30 plus 20 minutes, *i.e.*, 6.50.

Brigades, battalions, and companies were ordered to post sentries to watch for the rockets, and commanders observing rockets would immediately communicate the time when they were fired to the nearest artillery group or battery.

The two major attacks, north and south, were launched, and at 6.30 a.m. reports were recieved by General Nicholson from the 58th Division, on the left, that the northern attack of the XXth Corps was progressing favourably, and a warning message was telephoned to the 101st and 102nd Infantry Brigades to be ready to move at short notice.

At 7.15 a.m. a telephone message was received from the Corps Commander ordering the 34th Division to attack. Messages were despatched to units and rockets sent up. This made Zero hour 7.50 a.m. But the message to the rocket station took some time to get through, owing to indifferent communication, and the rocket signal was not seen by brigades. The 102nd Brigade received the telephone message and got it through to battalions, but the 101st Brigade wires were down. The result was that the assaulting battalions of the 102nd Brigade started under the barrage, and those of the 101st did not start until some five minutes or so after.

The 34th Division attacked with the 101st Brigade on the right, the 102nd on the left, and the 103rd in reserve. Following the advance from the right, the 2nd Loyal North Lancs, leading the assault, advanced a short distance, and was then held up by machine gun fire from the Bois de Chanois, and from Coutremain. The 19th French Division, on their right, were, for the same reason, unable to advance at all. So about 10.30 a.m. the Loyal North Lancs were ordered to fall back on their original line. The Queens and Sussex did not move at all.

The 102nd Brigade advanced on a two-battalion front—7th Cheshires on the right, Herefords on the left—and following close to the barrage arrived to about 300 yards of the west edge of the Bois de Reugny, a total of about 1,200 yards. Here they were held up by machine gun fire from the wood in front of them, from Tigny, on the left, and from the Bois de Chanois on the right. The French, on the left of the 102nd Brigade, did not advance against Tigny at all. The Brigade was ordered to consolidate the line it was on and form a flank, facing Tigny, to gain touch with the 58th French Division to the west of the village.

Nothing more was done. The two brigades remained as they were until relieved on the 28th July, when they went back to the Bois de Nadon-Bois de Boeuf area.

But the Division was immediately ordered to move again, during the night 28/29th, to the Bois de la Baillette, with the object of launching an attack in the direction of Beugneux and Grand Rozoy.

The Division was now on the right of the 25th French Division, and the left of the XIth French Corps. The rôle allotted to it was to capture the high ground north of the Grand Rozoy-Beugneux-Cramaille Road, with the object of forcing the enemy to withdraw from his positions along the Chateau Thierry-Soissons Road.

The 103rd Brigade went in on the right with the 8th Scottish Rifles and 5th K.O.S.B. in line, and the Argyll and Sutherland Highlanders in reserve; the 101st Brigade on the left, with the Sussex and Queens in line and the 2nd Loyal North Lancs in reserve.

The Divisional Artillery, with three Regiments of French Artillery and three groups of French 155 m.m. howitzers, covered the Division front.

Zero hour was 4.10 a.m.

Preceded by a heavy rolling barrage, both Brigades advanced without difficulty to the line of a small brook—the Green line—where, according to plan, a halt was made until 6 a.m. The next objective was the Brown line. But here, after some progress, the 103rd Brigade was brought to a standstill by machine gun fire from Beugneux. On the left, the 101st Brigade was also unable to move. The 102nd Brigade was ordered up, but before fresh impetus could be given to the advance, the enemy counter-attacked and drove all troops back to their original line. All three Brigades were mixed up, and the reorganisation took some time. They were finally disposed, 103rd, 102nd, 101st.

Shortly after dark the French were driven out of le Grand Rozoy, which necessitated a defensive flank being formed by the 101st Brigade. The village was recaptured in the early morning, and the following day passed without incident.

A second attempt was arranged for on the 1st August. During the night 31st July/1st August, the 102nd Brigade, leaving the 7th Cheshires to hold an outpost line, slipped out, and the 103rd and 101st Brigades extended their inner flanks. The 103rd Brigade had the 5th K.O.S.B. and 5th Argyll and Sutherland with three companies, and the 8th Scottish Rifles with two companies in the front line; the 101st Brigade attacked on a two battalion front, the Sussex and Queens each having three companies in the front line.

One hundred and eight field guns, and thirty-two howitzers covered the Division. The attack was preceded by harassing fire which gradually developed into a heavy bombardment, lasting from 4 to 4.45 a.m. At

4.49 a.m. a rolling barrage was put down in front of the infantry and the assault began.

On the right the 103rd Brigade stormed Hill 158, and the village of Beigneaux was turned north and south. On the left the 101st Brigade met with considerable opposition in the woods north of the Grand Rozoy-Beugneux road. Pressing on with Stokes mortars, the enemy machine guns were silenced, and many taken in the wood. By 6 a.m., the Brown line was reached by the whole of the attacking troops of the Division.

Following in rear of the assaulting Brigades were two battalions of the 102nd Brigade, the Herefords and 4th Cheshires. When the Brown line was reached these two battalions passed over it, with the object of covering the advance of the 127th French Division by securing the high ground about Pt. 104. The Herefords were given Bucy le Bras Ferme, on the right, but were unable to make any progress. They were eventually withdrawn.

But, on the left, with le Mont Jour as their objective, the 4th Cheshires were led by the gallant Colonel Swindells, in face of intense machine gun fire, to capture and hold the position until relieved by the 27th Division. Colonel Swindells was mortally wounded. His body was recovered after the action.

The line remained stationary until the later afternoon, when it became evident that the valleys on either side of the hill must be taken, as hostile action east of it was causing the 68th French Division, in the village of Servenay, considerable trouble. At 7 p.m., a joint advance of the whole of the 34th Division and the left of the 68th French Division, was made under a creeping barrage, and the line carried forward to the required position.

During the night the 102nd Brigade (less 7th Cheshires) were withdrawn, and early the next morning the 25th French Division passed through the 34th and following the retiring enemy. The Division then concentrated in the Grand Rozoy-Beugneux-Bois de Baillette area. Between the 4th and 7th August, the Division entrained at Nanteuil, Armoy Villers, le Plessis Belleville, and Dainmartin, and left the French zone.

Marshal Foch's great counter offensive, of which this was a part, was a success, and completely changed the whole situation. Hindenburg and Ludendorf had planned their supreme effort to victory, and had failed. At this stage of the war the final reserves of the German nation were not only in sight but had been actually launched into battle, and their man power was receding. On the other hand, although brigades in the British

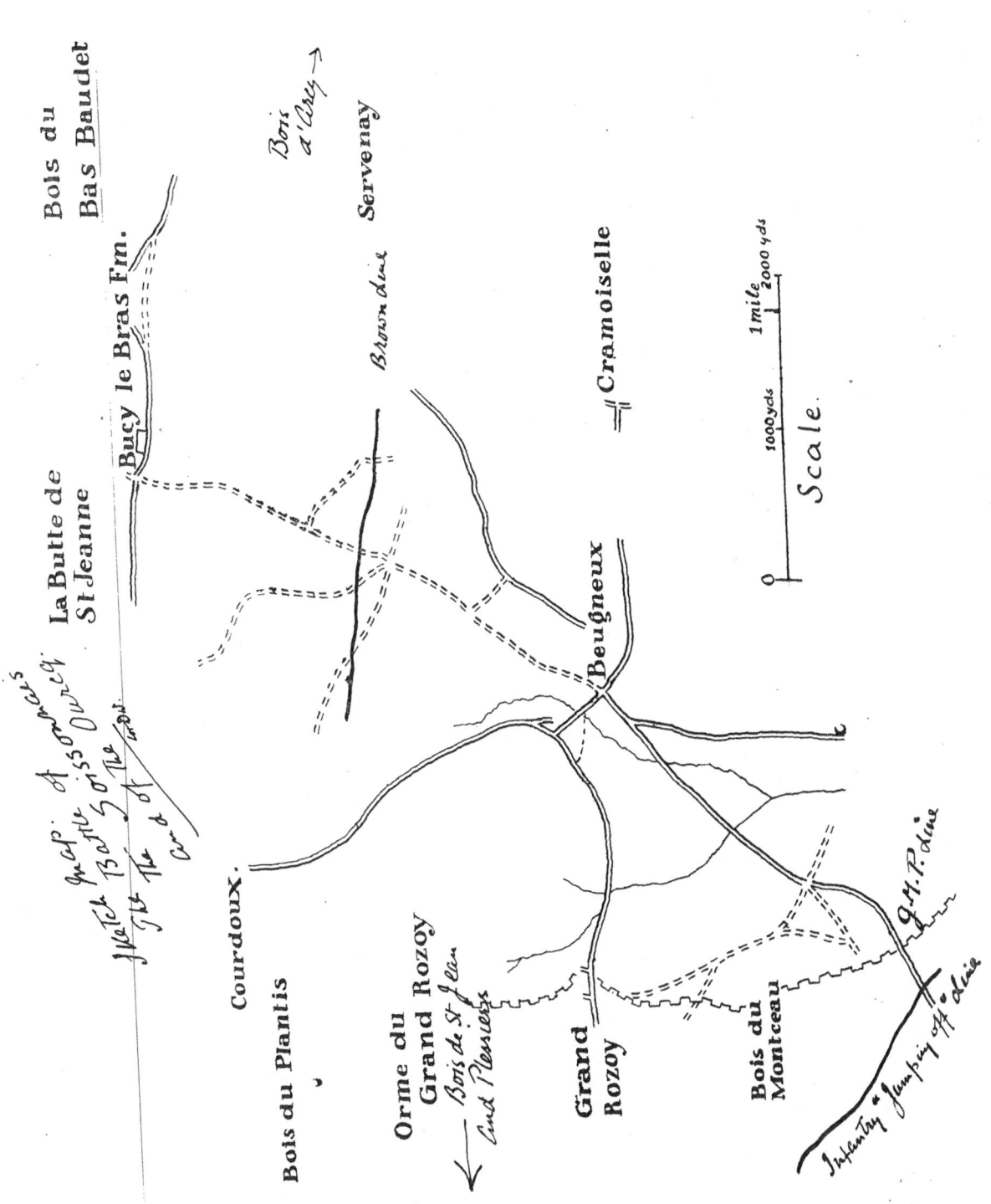

army had been reduced to three battalions, and various similar reductions had been made in the French army, the American army was ready to function in mass. Marshal Foch therefore ordered the Allied Commanders in Chief to prepare plans for local offensives with the object of freeing certain railways. In the British zone this took the form of an attack on the Albert-Montdidier front to disengage Amiens and free the Amiens-Paris railway. The French First army (General Debeney) was placed under the orders of Sir Douglas Haig, and attacked with the British Fourth army (General Rawlinson) on the 8th August. The result was a crushing blow to the Germans.

The Battle of Amiens, which lasted five days, was followed by the Battle of Bapaume, from the 21st August to the 1st September, in which the Third and Fourth British Armies drove the Germans from one side of the old Somme battlefield to the other.

But after the first counter-stroke delivered by Marshal Foch, the enemy had seen the necessity of shortening his line. The obvious place was the Lys Salient. Towards the end of July he was actively employed in removing the ammunition, which he had accumulated there for a further offensive, and by the 5th August had commenced to withdraw on the southern flanks of the Salient.

The 34th Division arrived in the Second Army area during the 5/7th August and came into G.H.Q. Reserve. From the 8th to the 16th August they were engaged in training and refitting. From the 21st to the 29th August they held the Ypres sector of the IInd Corps. On the 30th August, the Scherpenberg sector of the XIXth Corps was taken over.

By this time the withdrawal of the enemy had moved north and on the 31st August he commenced to retire opposite the 34th Division. The relief was not yet complete, the dispositions on the sector being 124th Brigade, 101st Brigade and 103rd Brigade in reserve. The 124th Brigade on the right were able to advance with no opposition, but the 101st Brigade, and the 27th American Division on their left, found a certain amount of resistance; by 6.30 p.m. the Queens and the Loyal North Lancs. were in the Vierstraat Switch. That night the 103rd Brigade relieved the 124th.

On the 1st September the advance commenced at 9 a.m., and the Queens and Sussex reached Petit Bois, which was the final objective given for the day, only to find themselves in the air; they had to withdraw some distance to get in touch with the 103rd Brigade who had met with opposition. They remained in the position won until relieved by the 102nd Brigade on the 3rd September.

The 102nd Brigade took over the whole line and found themselves up against a strong rearguard. The 7th Cheshires and Herefords attacked under a creeping barrage, but were only able to make slight progress. The Lys Salient, however, had disappeared; Kemmel Hill was once more in British hands and the general line ran—Givenchy, Neuve Chapelle, Nieppe, Ploegstreet, Voormezeele.

On other parts of the British front German attempts to stand were broken. On the 2nd September the Drocourt-Queant line was pierced, and the Hindenburg system stormed. From the 12th to the 18th September the Battle of Havrincourt and Epehy was fought, further south. From the 27th September to the 5th October the Battle of Cambrai drove the Germans still nearer the Fatherland. And meanwhile preparations were being made for the IInd Army to attack in conjunction with the Belgian army.

The front held by the 34th Division had been extended on the 22nd, and the Vierstraat sector taken over from the 41st Division. The attack was launched on the 28th September, and the Division occupied the Wytscheate-Messines Ridge, and advanced to the Ypres-Comines Canal.

The 101st Brigade did the initial attack, and the state of the enemy was such that the Sussex, who were to send out a strong patrol and capture a crater called Spanbroekmolen on the 28th had already done so with a patrol under Lieut. R. B. Mason on the 25th; the Queens with the Loyal North Lancs. on their left, captured the next crater, Warsaw, early in the morning, killing 37 of the enemy, and capturing seven.

Resting on this first objective, called the Blue line, all day, the Brigade was ordered to push on at 7 p.m. The night was pitch dark and the "going" bad, but by midnight patrols of the Queens and Loyal North Lancs. were in Wytscheate village. Thence to the Canal there was no opposition.

The attack surpassed all expectations that day. To the north of the 34th Division, which with the 30th and 31st Divisions was undertaking a minor operation, the rest of the British and Belgian troops had advanced beyond the limits of the Third Battle of Ypres. And by the evening of the 1st October, the left bank of the Lys was cleared from Comines southwards, while north of the town troops were up to Wervicq, Gheluwe, and Ledeghem.

On the 3rd October, the 34th Division took over the front facing the village of Gheluwe and started preparations to attack the outskirts of Menin.

On the 12th October, two platoons of the Sussex, under Captain Lewis and Lieut. Read, carried out a successful raid south of the village, and captured a prisoner of the 39th German Division, without casualties; a most important identification.

Two days later, at 5.35 a.m., the attack on Menin opened, with the 102nd Brigade on the right and the 103rd on the left. The 102nd had the 7th Cheshires on the right, the 4th Cheshires on the left—the junction being the south-west corner of Gheluwe—and the Herefords in support. Each battalion advanced on a two-company front, with one in support and one in reserve; two Stokes mortars and a section of machine guns accompanied each battalion. The enemy had opened a counter preparation at 4.30 a.m., but their bombardment caused few casualties and the troops advanced behind a barrage which lifted 100 yards a minute. There was a little opposition from a few strong points and farms that had been missed by the barrage, but the two assaulting battalions passed quickly to the first objective, being greatly assisted by smoke shells from the Light Trench Mortars.

Reorganisation was carried out during the 14 minutes pause on the first objective, and at 6.18 the advance was resumed. Again the opposition was slight, and the enemy more disposed to surrender than to fight. The final objectives were reached to time and a quick exploitation of the success enabled patrols from the right to push to the east of the village of Coucou; while, on the left, patrols went along the Menin road and occupied Job Farm.

The thick mist and smoke of the barrage made it difficult to get information. The line had been considerably extended to the left, in efforts to get in touch with units on that flank, and the 4th Cheshires had lost heavily in officers; Captains L. L. B. Angus, E. Briscoe, and B. A. R. Jones, Lieuts. C. Oakes, F. A. Southam, S. Hough, F. Wilson, C. E. Findlay, and C. J. Parr were all wounded in this engagement; and about 7.30 p.m. a counter attack drove back the left of the line, but not far. One company of Herefords digging near Gheluwe was then sent up to reinforce the 4th Cheshires.

There was no serious complication. During the night the 4th re-occupied the line they had temporarily abandoned, and early in the morning of the 15th, the 4th and 7th Cheshires were ordered to push forward and establish themselves on the Menin road if this could be done without casualties. Troops passed through Menin and occupied Brulee Farm and the Cycle Track by 9 a.m.

At dusk the Herefords took over the front line, and succeeded in the early morning in crossing the Lys near Marathon Bridge, putting an enemy post to flight and capturing a machine gun.

At mid-day, a bombardment by field guns was organised to cover a crossing of the river Lys opposite Rascal's Retreat. A raft was constructed by the Pioneers of the 4th Cheshires, and at 12.55 the first party of Herefords, led by 2/Lt. Jenkins of the 4th Cheshires, crossed under cover of the artillery and Lewis guns. This was an excellent piece of work, as the raft only held two or three men, but it was a lengthy business, and it was 4 o'clock in the afternoon before a company was transported to the other side. The position was held and handed over to the 90th Brigade on relief, in spite of a violent bombardment from the enemy.

At 11 p.m. that night the whole Brigade was relieved and rested in an area north of Gheluwe.

In this engagement 4 officers and 44 other ranks were killed; 10 officers and 196 other ranks wounded; and 47 were missing.

Meanwhile, on the 15th, the 101st Brigade had relieved the 124th from the left of the 103rd to the outskirts of Wevelghem which was cleared by patrols of the Sussex and Loyal North Lancs. But the crossing of the Lys was not completed until 2 p.m. on the 17th.

The advance was continued on the 18th by the 101st Brigade, with the 103rd in support and the 102nd in reserve, until it was held up on the 19th in front of Belleghem. The next day the 30th Division passed through and the 34th came into Corps Reserve.

The whole of this northern attack, which started on the 14th, had been made under the command of the King of the Belgians, and, on the coast, swept right up to Ostend, which fell on the 17th. Three days later the northern flank of the Allied force rested on the Dutch frontier. There was, then, a large body of troops east of Lille, on the northern side of the town, while successful engagements on the le Cateau front had turned the Lille defences on the south; the German forces between the Sensee and the Lys were once more compelled to withdraw, closely followed by British troops.

On the 23rd October the 102nd Brigade took over a small length of front east of Courtrai-Bossuyt Canal in order to attack in conjunction with the 41st Division on the left. The line taken over ran from the Canal tunnel (held by the enemy) to Achterhoek-Baveghenknok-Paehderish, and was held by the Herefords on the left and the 7th Cheshires on the right. The 4th Cheshires were in reserve.

The 123rd Brigade, on the left, were to attack on the east of the Canal, and the Herefords, who were within 300 yards of the tunnel, through which the canal runs, were to cross over it and follow the right battalion of the 123rd Brigade (23rd Middlesex) as it attacked south-east, and fill the gap between them and the Canal. The 4th Cheshires were to take over the line left by the Herefords.

Zero hour was 2.15 a.m. on the 24th October, but an hour later the Herefords reported considerable machine gun fire across the tunnel, and it was evident that no progress had been made by the 123rd Brigade. The Herefords remained in readiness to move all day.

The plan was somewhat changed for the next day's operation. The 4th Cheshires were moved during the night to the east of the Canal, via Knokke Bridge on the left, and took up a position between the bridge and the right of the 123rd Brigade.

The attack opened on the 25th at 3 a.m. with an attempt, gallantly made by the 7th Cheshires, to cross the Canal by Locks 3, 4, and 7. They suffered some 40 casualties and did not succeed.

But the main attack started at 9.2 a.m., and as the barrage crept forward, and the 123rd Brigade advanced, the 4th Cheshires moved up on the right of the 23rd Middlesex, extending as they went to keep in touch with the bank of the Canal. By 9.30 the right of the 4th Cheshires began to move clear of the Canal, and the Herefords then crossed the Tunnel and followed in rear.

The advance was rapid, with slight opposition. At 2.15 p.m. two companies of the 4th Cheshires were east of Moen. Colonel Drage* found himself out of touch with the 123rd Brigade, on his left, but reorganised his battalion, and with praiseworthy initiative recommenced the advance with the Herefords on his left forming a defensive flank. The 7th Cheshires had managed, by this time, to cross the Canal at Lock 5 and gain touch with the right of the 4th.

At 4 p.m. the Brigade had advanced to Autryve.

During the night the line was reorganised with the 7th Cheshires on the right, in touch with the 30th Division, and the 4th Cheshires on the left to Autryve; and so remained until relieved by the 21st Brigade of the 30th Division on the night 26/27th, when they moved to the St. Anne area.

Meanwhile, farther south, the Battle of the Selle River had been fought (17th to 25th October).

On the 27th, while the other two brigades were resting, the 101st Brigade took over the line occupied by the 108th and 109th Brigade, and advanced during the night some 1,000 yards. The enemy positions were on the Anseghem-Beegstraat road, and preparations were afoot for a general attack in conjunction with the 31st Division, on the right, and

---

* Godfrey Drage, brother to Gilbert Drage who commanded the Herefords in Palestine.

troops of the French Army on the left. It was decided that the attack should be made by the 103rd Brigade with one battalion of the 101st attached. So the 103rd relieved the 101st, the Queens being attached for the operation. The idea was that the Queens should fill any gap that might occur between the 103rd and the right of the French, and a Liaison Company was formed—half British, half French, and the whole under the command of Captain R. W. Nuttall—to go forward with the attacking troops. But it so happened that little was demanded of them.

The barrage opened at 5.35 a.m. Operating with the 103rd Brigade were 30 French tanks, and rapid progress was made on the right. But on the left—the French front—the enemy was very active and the ground marshy and unsuitable for tanks. The infantry could not advance, and the Liaison Company did not move beyond Winterken.

German rearguards, posted on the ridge running north-west and south-east through Boschkaut, held up all further advance, but moved off during the night.

The pursuit was continued the next day until 1 o'clock (1st November) when the 31st Division, on the right, and the 41st French Division, on the left, squeezed the 34th Division out and joined hands. The 34th Division then became Corps Reserve and concentrated in the triangle formed by Courtrai-River Lys to Menin-Keselberg-Moorseele-Schoonwater-Road to railway crossing ¾-mile southeast of Heule.

On the 9th November the enemy was in general retreat on the whole British front. The Second Army crossed the Scheldt and reached the outskirts of Renaix. In the early morning of the 11th, the 3rd Canadian Division entered Mons, the whole of the German defending force being killed or taken prisoners.

But on the 11th, the 34th Division received the fateful wire :—

"Hostilities will cease at 1100 hours on November 11th. Troops will stand fast on the line reached at that hour, which will be reported by wire to G.H.Q. Defensive precautions will be maintained. There will be no intercourse of any description with the enemy until receipt of instructions from G.H.Q. Further instructions follow."

The Division commenced to march forward on the 14th November, and on the 19th were halted at Papignies, Flobecq, Ogy, Lahamaide Lessines owing to supply difficulties.

The sector allotted to the British Forces in the occupation of the Rhine Provinces was too narrow to permit the employment of more than one Army Command. The occupation was carried out by General Plumer's Second Army, but, in the readjustment, the 34th Division was not included.